Algorithms For Interviews

A Problem Solving Approach

Adnan Aziz
Amit Prakash

algorithmsforinterviews.com

Adnan Aziz is a professor at the Department of Electrical and Computer Engineering at The University of Texas at Austin, where he conducts research and teaches classes in applied algorithms. He received his PhD from The University of California at Berkeley; his undergraduate degree is from IIT Kanpur. He has worked at Google, Qualcomm, IBM, and several software startups. When not designing algorithms, he plays with his children, Laila, Imran, and Omar.

Amit Prakash is a Member of the Technical Staff at Google, where he works primarily on machine learning problems that arise in the context of online advertising. Prior to that he worked at Microsoft in the web search team. He received his PhD from The University of Texas at Austin; his undergraduate degree is from IIT Kanpur. When he is not improving the quality of ads, he indulges in his passions for puzzles, movies, travel, and adventures with his wife.

This book was typeset by the authors using Lesley Lamport's LATEXdocument preparation system and Peter Wilson's Memoir class. The cover design was done using Inkscape. MacOSaiX was used to create the front cover image; it approximates Shela Nye's portrait of Alan Turing using a collection of public domain images of famous computer scientists and mathematicians. The graphic on the back cover was created by Nidhi Rohatgi.

The companion website for the book includes a list of known errors for each version of the book. If you come across a technical error, please write to us and we will cheerfully send you $0.42. Please refer to the website for details.

Version 1.0.0 (September 1, 2010)

Website: http://algorithmsforinterviews.com

ISBN: 1453792996
EAN-13: 9781453792995

Table of Contents

III Solutions   **109**

Prologue

Let's begin with the picture on the front cover. You may have observed that the portrait of Alan Turing is constructed from a number of pictures ("tiles") of great computer scientists and mathematicians.

Suppose you were asked in an interview to design a program that takes an image and a collection of $s \times s$-sized tiles and produce a mosaic from the tiles that resembles the image. A good way to begin may be to partition the image into $s \times s$-sized squares, compute the average color of each such image square, and then find the tile that is closest to it in the color space. Here distance in color space can be $L2$-norm over Red-Green-Blue (RGB) intensities for the color. As you look more carefully at the problem, you might conclude that it would be better to match each tile with an image square that has a similar structure. One way could be to perform a coarse pixelization (2×2 or 3×3) of each image square and finding the tile that is "closest" to the image square under a distance

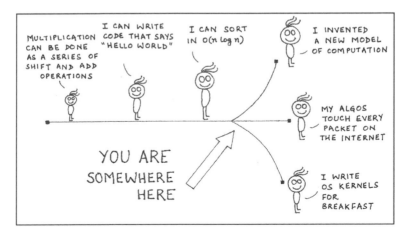

Figure 1. Evolution of a computer scientist

function defined over all pixel colors (for example, $L2$-norm over RGB values for each pixel). Depending on how you represent the tiles, you end up with the problem of finding the closest point from a set of points in a k-dimensional space.

If there are m tiles and the image is partitioned into n squares, then a brute-force approach would have $O(m \cdot n)$ time complexity. You could improve on this by first indexing the tiles using an appropriate search tree. A more detailed discussion on this approach is presented in Problem 8.1 and its solution.

If in a 45-60 minute interview, you can work through the above ideas, write some pseudocode for your algorithm, and analyze its complexity, you would have had a fairly successful interview. In particular, you would have demonstrated to your interviewer that you possess several key skills:

- The ability to rigorously formulate real-world problems.
- The skills to solve problems and design algorithms.
- The tools to go from an algorithm to a working program.
- The analytical techniques required to determine the computational complexity of your solution.

Book Overview

Algorithms for Interviews (AFI) aims to help engineers interviewing for software development positions. The primary focus of AFI is algorithm design. The entire book is presented through problems interspersed with discussions. The problems cover key concepts and are well-motivated, challenging, and fun to solve.

We do not emphasize platforms and programming languages since they differ across jobs, and can be acquired fairly easily. Interviews at most large software companies focus more on algorithms, problem solving, and design skills than on specific domain knowledge. Also, platforms and programming languages can change quickly as requirements change but the qualities mentioned above will always be fundamental to any successful software endeavor.

The questions we present should all be solvable within a one hour interview and in many cases, take substantially less time. A question may take more or less time to complete, depending on the amount of coding that is asked for.

Our solutions vary in terms of detail—for some problems we present detailed implementations in Java/C++/Python; for others, we simply sketch solutions. Some use fairly technical machinery, e.g., max-flow, randomized analysis, etc. You will encounter such problems only if you claim specialized knowledge, e.g., graph algorithms, complexity theory, etc.

Interviewing is about more than being able to design algorithms quickly. You also need to know how to present yourself, how to ask for help when you are stuck, how to come across as being excited about the company, and knowing what you can do for them. We discuss the non-technical aspects of interviewing in Chapter 12. You can practice with friends or by yourself; in either case, be sure to time yourself. Interview at as many places as you can without it taking away from your job or classes. The experience will help you and you may discover you like companies that you did not know much about.

Although an interviewer may occasionally ask a question directly from AFI, you should not base your preparation on memorizing solutions from AFI. We sincerely hope that reading this book will be enjoyable and improve your algorithm design skills. The end goal is to make you a better engineer as well as better prepared for software interviews.

Level and Prerequisites

Most of AFI requires its readers to have basic familiarity with algorithms taught in a typical undergraduate-level algorithms class. The chapters on meta-algorithms, graphs, and intractability use more advanced machinery and may require additional review.

Each chapter begins with a review of key concepts. This review is not meant to be comprehensive and if you are not familiar with the material, you should first study the corresponding chapter in an algorithms textbook. There are dozens of such texts and our preference is to master one or two good books rather than superficially sample many. We like *Algorithms* by Dasgupta, Papadimitriou, and Vazirani because it is succinct and beautifully written; *Introduction to Algorithms* by Cormen, Leiserson, Rivest, and Stein is more detailed and serves as a good reference.

Since our focus is on problems that can be solved in an interview relatively completely, there are many elegant algorithm design problems which we do not include. Similarly, we do not have any straightforward review-type problems; you may want to brush up on these using introductory programming and data-structures texts.

The field of algorithms is vast and there are many specialized topics, such as computational geometry, numerical analysis, logic algorithms, etc. Unless you claim knowledge of such topics, it is highly unlikely that you will be asked a question which requires esoteric knowledge. While an interview problem may seem specialized at first glance, it is invariably the case that the basic algorithms described in this book are sufficient to solve it.

4

Acknowledgments

The problems in this book come from diverse sources—our own experiences, colleagues, friends, papers, books, Internet bulletin boards, etc. To paraphrase Paul Halmos from his wonderful book *Problems for Mathematicians, Young and Old*: "I do not give credits—who discovered what? Who was first? Whose solution is the best? It would not be fair to give credit in some cases and not in others. No one knows who discovered the theorem that bears Pythagoras' name and it does not matter. The beauty of the subject speaks for itself and so be it."

One person whose help and support has improved the quality of this book and made it fun to read is our cartoonist, editor, and proofreader, Nidhi Rohatgi. Several of our friends and students gave feedback on this book—we would especially like to thank Ian Varley, who wrote solutions to several problems, and Senthil Chellappan, Gayatri Ramachandran, and Alper Sen for proofreading several chapters.

We both want to thank all the people who have been a source of enlightenment and inspiration to us through the years.

I, Adnan Aziz, would like to thank teachers, friends, and students from IIT Kanpur, UC Berkeley, and UT Austin. I would especially like to thank my friends Vineet Gupta and Vigyan Singhal, and my teachers Robert Solovay, Robert Brayton, Richard Karp, Raimund Seidel, and Somenath Biswas for introducing me to the joys of algorithms. My co-author, Amit Prakash, has been a wonderful collaborator—this book is a testament to his intellect, creativity, and enthusiasm.

I, Amit Prakash, have my co-author and mentor, Adnan Aziz, to thank the most for this book. To a great extent, my problem solving skills have been shaped by Adnan. There have been occasions in life when I would not have made through without his help. He is also the best possible collaborator I can think of for any intellectual endeavor.

Over the years, I have been fortunate to have great teachers at IIT Kanpur and UT Austin. I would especially like to thank Professors Scott Nettles, Vijaya Ramachandran, and Gustavo de Veciana. I would also like to thank my friends and colleagues at Google, Microsoft, and UT Austin for all the stimulating conversations and problem solving sessions. Lastly and most importantly, I want to thank my family who have been a constant source of support, excitement, and joy for all my life and especially during the process of writing this book.

ADNAN AZIZ
adnan@algorithmsforinterviews.com

AMIT PRAKASH
amit@algorithmsforinterviews.com

Problem Solving Techniques

> It's not that I'm so smart, it's just
> that I stay with problems longer.
>
> ————————————————
>
> A. Einstein.

Developing problem solving skills is like learning to play a musical instrument—a book or a teacher can point you in the right direction, but only your hard work will take you where you want to go. Like a musician, you need to know underlying concepts but theory is no substitute for practice; for this reason, AFI consists primarily of problems.

Great problem solvers have skills that cannot be captured by a set of rules. Still, when faced with a challenging algorithm design problem it is helpful to have a small set of general principles that may be applicable. We enumerate a collection of such principles in Table 1. Often, you may have to use more than one of these techniques.

We will now look at some concrete examples of how these techniques can be applied.

DIVIDE-AND-CONQUER AND GENERALIZATION

A triomino is formed by joining three unit-sized squares in an L-shape. A mutilated chessboard (henceforth 8×8 Mboard) is made up of 64 unit-sized squares arranged in an 8×8 square, minus the top left square. Supposed you are asked to design an algorithm which computes a placement of 21 triominos that covers the 8×8 Mboard. (Since there are 63 squares in the 8×8 Mboard and we have 21 triominos, a valid placement cannot have overlapping triominos or triominos which extend out of the 8×8 Mboard.)

Divide-and-conquer is a good strategy to attack this problem. Instead of the 8×8 Mboard, let's consider an $n \times n$ Mboard. A 2×2 Mboard can be covered with 1 triomino since it is of the same exact shape. You may hypothesize that a triomino placement for an $n \times n$ Mboard with the top left square missing can be used to compute a placement for an $n+1 \times n+1$

5

Technique	Description
Divide-and-conquer	Can you divide the problem into two or more smaller independent subproblems and solve the original problem using solutions to the subproblems?
Recursion, dynamic programming	If you have access to solutions for smaller instances of a given problem, can you easily construct a solution to the problem?
Case analysis	Can you split the input/execution into a number of cases and solve each case in isolation?
Generalization	Is there a problem that subsumes your problem and is easier to solve?
Data-structures	Is there a data-structure that directly maps to the given problem?
Iterative refinement	Most problems can be solved using a brute-force approach. Can you formalize such a solution and improve upon it?
Small examples	Can you find a solution to small concrete instances of the problem and then build a solution that can be generalized to arbitrary instances?
Reduction	Can you use a problem with a known solution as a subroutine?
Graph modeling	Can you describe your problem using a graph and solve it using an existing algorithm?
Write an equation	Can you express relationships in your problem in the form of equations (or inequalities)?
Auxiliary elements	Can you add some new element to your problem to get closer to a solution?
Variation	Can you solve a slightly different problem and map its solution to your problem?
Parallelism	Can you decompose your problem into subproblems that can be solved independently on different machines?
Caching	Can you store some of your computation and look it up later to save work?
Symmetry	Is there symmetry in the input space or solution space that can be exploited?

Table 1. Common problem solving techniques.

Mboard. However you will quickly see that this line of reasoning does not lead you anywhere.

Another hypothesis is that if a placement exists for an $n \times n$ Mboard, then one also exists for a $2n \times 2n$ Mboard. This does work: take 4 $n \times n$ Mboards and arrange them to form a $2n \times 2n$ square in such a way that three of the Mboards have their missing square set towards the center and one Mboard has its missing square outward to coincide with the missing corner of a $2n \times 2n$ Mboard. The gap in the center can be covered with a triomino and, by hypothesis, we can cover the 4 $n \times n$ Mboards with triominos as well. Hence a placement exists for any n that is a power of 2. In particular, a placement exists for the $2^3 \times 2^3$ Mboard; the recursion used in the proof can be directly coded to find the actual coverings as well. Observe that this problem demonstrates divide-and-conquer as well as generalization (from 8×8 to $2^n \times 2^n$).

RECURSION AND DYNAMIC PROGRAMMING

Suppose you were to design an algorithm that takes an unparenthesized expression containing addition and multiplication operators, and returns the parenthesization that maximizes the value of the expression. For example, the expression $5 - 3 \cdot 4 + 6$ yields any of the following values:

$$
\begin{aligned}
-25 &= 5 - \big(3 \cdot (4 + 6)\big) \\
-13 &= 5 - \big((3 \cdot 4) + 6\big) \\
20 &= (5 - 3) \cdot (4 + 6) \\
-1 &= \big(5 - (3 \cdot 4)\big) + 6 \\
14 &= \big((5 - 3) \cdot 4\big) + 6
\end{aligned}
$$

If we recursively compute the parenthesization for each subexpression that maximizes its value, it is easy to identify the optimum top level parenthesization—parenthesize on each side of the operators and determine which operator maximizes the value of the total expression.

Recursive computation of the maximizing parenthesization for subexpressions leads to repeated calls with identical arguments. Dynamic programming avoids these repeated computations; refer to Problem 3.11 for a detailed exposition.

CASE ANALYSIS

You are given a set S of 25 distinct integers and a CPU that has a special instruction, SORT5, that can sort 5 integers in one cycle. Your task is to identify the 3 largest integers in S using SORT5 to compare and sort subsets of S; furthermore, you must minimize the number of calls to SORT5.

If all we had to compute was the largest integer in the set, the optimum approach would be to form 5 disjoint subsets $S_1, \ldots, S_5$ of S, sort each subset, and then sort $\{\max S_1, \ldots, \max S_5\}$. This takes 6 calls to SORT5 but leaves ambiguity about the second and third largest integers.

It may seem like many calls to SORT5 are still needed. However if you do a careful case analysis and eliminate all $x \in S$ for which there are at least 3 integers in S larger than x, only 5 integers remain and hence just one more call to SORT5 is needed to compute the result. Details are given in the solution to Problem 2.5.

FIND A GOOD DATA STRUCTURE

Suppose you are given a set of files, each containing stock quote information. Each line contains starts with a timestamp. The files are individually sorted by this value. You are to design an algorithm that combines these quotes into a single file R containing these quotes, sorted by the timestamps.

This problem can be solved by a multistage merge process, but there is a trivial solution using a min-heap data structure, where quotes are ordered by timestamp. First build the min-heap with the first quote from each file; then iteratively extract the minimum entry e from the min-heap, write it to R, and add in the next entry in the file corresponding to e. Details are given in Problem 2.10.

ITERATIVE REFINEMENT OF BRUTE-FORCE SOLUTION

Consider the problem of string search (*cf.* Problem 5.1): given two strings s (search string) and T (text), find all occurrences of s in T. Since s can occur at any offset in T, the brute-force solution is to test for a match at every offset. This algorithm is perfectly correct; its time complexity is $O(n \cdot m)$, where n and m are the lengths of s and T.

After trying some examples, you may see that there are several ways in which to improve the time complexity of the brute-force algorithm. For example, if the character $T[i]$ is not present in s you can suitably advance the matching. Furthermore, this skipping works better if we match the search string from its end and work backwards. These refinements will make the algorithm very fast (linear-time) on random text and search strings; however, the worst case complexity remains $O(n \cdot m)$.

You can make the additional observation that a partial match of s which does not result in a full match implies other offsets which cannot lead to full matches. For example, if $s = abdabcabc$ and if, starting backwards, we have a partial match up to $abcabc$ that does not result in a full match, we know that the next possible matching offset has to be at least 3 positions ahead (where we can match the second abc from the partial match).

By putting together these refinements you will have arrived at the famous Boyer-Moore string search algorithm—its worst-case time complexity is $O(n+m)$ (which is the best possible from a theoretical perspective); it is also one of the fastest string search algorithms in practice.

SMALL EXAMPLES

Problems that seem difficult to solve in the abstract, can become much more tractable when you examine small concrete instances. For instance, consider the following problem: there are 500 closed doors along a corridor, numbered from 1 to 500. A person walks through the corridor and opens each door. Another person walks through the corridor and closes every alternate door. Continuing in this manner, the i-th person comes and toggles the position of every i-th door starting from door i. You are to determine exactly how many doors are open after the 500-th person has walked through the corridor.

It is very difficult to solve this problem using abstract variables. However if you try the problem for $1, 2, 3, 4, 10$, and 20 doors, it takes under a minute to see that the doors that remain open are $1, 4, 9, 16 \ldots$, regardless of the total number of doors. The pattern is obvious—the doors that remain open are those numbered by perfect squares. Once you make this connection, it is easy to prove it for the general case. Hence the total number of open doors is $\lfloor \sqrt{500} \rfloor = 22$. Refer to Problem 9.4 for a detailed solution.

REDUCTION

Consider the problem of finding if one string is a rotation of the other, e.g., "car" and "arc" are rotations of each other A natural approach may be to rotate the first string by every possible offset and then compare it with the second string. This algorithm would have quadratic time complexity.

You may notice that this problem is quite similar to string search which can be done in linear time, albeit using a somewhat complex algorithm. So it would be natural to try to reduce this problem to string search. Indeed, if we concatenate the second string with itself and search for the first string in the resulting string, we will find a match iff the two original strings are rotations of each other. This reduction yields a linear-time algorithm for our problem; details are given in Problem 5.4.

Usually you try to reduce your problem to an easier problem. But sometimes, you need to reduce a problem known to be difficult to your given problem to show that your problem is difficult. Such problems are described in Chapter 6.

GRAPH MODELING

Drawing pictures is a great way to brainstorm for a potential solution. If the relationships in a given problem can be represented using a graph, quite often the problem can be reduced to a well-known graph problem. For example, suppose you are given a set of barter rates between commodities and you are supposed to find out if an arbitrage exists, i.e., there is a way by which you can start with a units of some commodity C and perform a series of barters which results in having more than a units of C.

We can model the problem with a graph where commodities correspond to vertices, barters correspond to edges, and the edge weight is set to the logarithm of the barter rate. If we can find a cycle in the graph with a positive weight, we would have found such a series of exchanges. Such a cycle can be solved using the Bellman-Ford algorithm (*cf.* Problem 4.19).

WRITE AN EQUATION

Some problems can be solved by expressing them in the language of mathematics. For example, suppose you were asked to write an algorithm that computed binomial coefficients, $\binom{n}{k} = \frac{n!}{k!(n-k)!}$.

The problem with computing the binomial coefficient directly from the definition is that the factorial function grows very quickly and can overflow an integer variable. If we use floating point representations for numbers, we lose precision and the problem of overflow does not go away. These problems potentially exist even if the final value of $\binom{n}{k}$ is small. One can try to factor the numerator and denominator and try and cancel out common terms but factorization is itself a hard problem.

The binomial coefficients satisfy the *addition formula*:

$$\binom{n}{k} = \binom{n-1}{k} + \binom{n-1}{k-1}.$$

This identity leads to a straightforward recursion for computing $\binom{n}{k}$ which avoids the problems mentioned above. Dynamic programming has to be used to achieve good time complexity—details are in Problem 9.1.

AUXILIARY ELEMENTS

Consider an 8×8 square board in which two squares on diagonally opposite corners are removed. You are given a set of thirty-one 2×1 dominoes and are asked to cover the board with them.

After some (or a lot) of trial-and-error, you may begin to wonder if a such a configuration exists. Proving an impossibility result may seem hard. However if you think of the 8×8 square board as a chessboard, you will observe that the removed corners are of the same color. Hence the board consists of either 30 white squares and 32 black squares or vice versa. Since a domino will always cover two adjacent squares, any arrangement of dominoes must cover the same number of black and white squares. Hence no such configuration exists.

The original problem did not talk about the colors of the squares. Adding these colors to the squares makes it easy to prove impossibility, illustrating the strategy of adding auxiliary elements.

VARIATION

Suppose we were asked to design an algorithm which takes as input an undirected graph and produces as output a black or white coloring of the vertices such that for every vertex, at least half of its neighbors differ in color from it.

We could try to solve this problem by assigning arbitrary colors to vertices and then flipping colors wherever constraints are not met. However this approach does not converge on all examples.

It turns out we can define a slightly different problem whose solution will yield the coloring we are looking for. Define an edge to be *diverse* if its ends have different colors. It is easy to verify that a color assignment that maximizes the number of diverse edges also satisfies the constraint of the original problem. The number of diverse edges can be maximized greedily flipping the colors of vertices that would lead to a higher number of diverse edges; details are given in Problem 4.11.

PARALLELISM

In the context of interview questions, parallelism is useful when dealing with scale, i.e., when the problem is so large that it is impossible to solve it on a single machine or it would take a very long time. The key insight you need to display is how to decompose the problem such that (1.) each subproblem can be solved relatively independently and (2.) constructing the solution to the original problem from solutions to the subproblems is not expensive in terms of CPU time, main memory, and network usage.

Consider the problem of sorting a petascale integer array. If we know the distribution of the numbers, the best approach would be to define equal-sized ranges of integers and send one range to one machine for sorting. The sorted numbers would just need to be concatenated in the correct order. If the distribution is not known then we can send equal-sized arbitrary subsets to each machine and then merge the sorted results using a min-heap. For details on petascale sorting, please refer to Problem 2.2.

CACHING

Caching is a great tool whenever there is a possibility of repeating computations. For example, the central idea behind dynamic programming is caching results from intermediate computations. Caching becomes extremely useful in another setting where requests come to a service in an online fashion and a small number of requests take up a significant amount of compute power. Workloads on web services exhibit this property; Problem 7.1 describes one such problem.

SYMMETRY

While symmetry is a simple concept it can be used to solve very difficult problems, sometimes in less than intuitive ways. Consider a 2-player game in which players alternately take bites from a chocolate bar. The chocolate bar is an $n \times m$ rectangle; a bite must remove a square and all squares above and to the right in the chocolate bar. The first player to eat the lower leftmost square loses (think of it as being poisoned).

Suppose we are asked whether we would prefer to play first or second. One approach is to make the observation that the game is symmetrical for Player 1 and Player 2, except for their starting state. If we assume that there is no winning strategy for Player 1, then there must be a way for Player 2 to win if Player 1 bites the top right square in his first move. Whatever move Player 2 makes after that can always be made by Player 1 as his first move. Hence Player 1 can always win. For a detailed discussion, refer to the Problem 9.13.

CONCLUSION

In addition to developing intuition for which technique may apply to which problem, it is also important to know when your technique is not working and quickly move to your next best guess. In an interview setting, even if you do not end up solving the problem entirely, you will get credit for applying these techniques in a systematic way and clearly communicating your approach to the problem. We cover nontechnical aspects of problem solving in Chapter 12.

Part I

Problems

Chapter 1

Searching

> Searching is a basic tool that every programmer should keep in mind for use in a wide variety of situations.
>
> ---
>
> "The Art of Computer Programming, Volume 3 - Sorting and Searching," D. Knuth, 1973

Given an arbitrary collection of n keys, the only way to determine if a search key is present is by examining each element which yields $\Theta(n)$ complexity. If the collection is "organized", searching can be sped up dramatically. Of course, inserts and deletes have to preserve the organization; there are several ways of achieving this.

Binary Search

Binary search is at the heart of more interview questions than any other single algorithm. Fundamentally, binary search is a natural divide-and-conquer strategy for searching. The idea is to eliminate half the keys from consideration by keeping the keys in a sorted array. If the search key is not equal to the middle element of the array, one of the two sets of keys to the left and to the right of the middle element can be eliminated from further consideration.

Questions based on binary search are ideal from the interviewers perspective: it is a basic technique that every reasonable candidate is supposed to know and it can be implemented in a few lines of code. On the other hand, binary search is much trickier to implement correctly than it appears—you should implement it as well as write corner case tests to ensure you understand it properly.

Many published implementations are incorrect in subtle and not-so-subtle ways—a study reported that it is correctly implemented in only five out of twenty textbooks. Jon Bentley, in his book *Programming Pearls* reported that he assigned binary search in a course for professional programmers and found that 90% percent failed to code it correctly despite having ample time. (Bentley's students would have been gratified to know that his own published implementation of binary search, in a chapter titled "Writing Correct Programs", contained a bug that remained undetected for over twenty years.)

Binary search can be written in many ways—recursive, iterative, different idioms for conditionals, etc. Here is an iterative implementation adapted from Bentley's book, which includes his bug.

```
1   public class BinSearch {
2     static int search( int [] A, int K ) {
3       int l = 0;
4       int u = A.length −1;
5       int m;
6       while ( l <= u ) {
7         m = (l+u) /2;
8         if (A[m] < K) {
9           l = m + 1;
10        } else if (A[m] == K) {
11          return m;
12        } else {
13          u = m−1;
14        }
15      }
16      return −1;
17    }
18  }
```

The error is in the assignment `m = (l+u)/2`; it can lead to overflow and should be replaced by `m = l + (u-l)/2`.

The time complexity of binary search is given by $B(n) = c + B(n/2)$. This solves to $B(n) = O(\log n)$, which is far superior to the $O(n)$ approach needed when the keys are unsorted. A disadvantage of binary search is that it requires a sorted array and sorting an array takes $O(n \log n)$ time. However if there are many searches to perform, the time taken to sort is not an issue.

We begin with a problem that on the face of it has nothing to do with binary search.

1.1 COMPUTING SQUARE ROOTS

Square root computations can be implemented using sophisticated numerical techniques involving iterative methods and logarithms. However if you were asked to implement a square root function, you would not be expected to know these techniques.

Problem 1.1: Implement a fast integer square root function that takes in a 32-bit unsigned integer and returns another 32-bit unsigned integer that is the floor of the square root of the input.

There are many variants of searching a sorted array that require a little more thinking and create opportunities for missing corner cases. For the following problems, A is a sorted array of integers.

1.2   SEARCH A SORTED ARRAY FOR k

Write a method that takes a sorted array A of integers and a key k and returns the index of first occurrence of k in A. Return -1 if k does not appear in A. Write tests to verify your code.

1.3   SEARCH A SORTED ARRAY FOR THE FIRST ELEMENT LARGER THAN k

Design an efficient algorithm that finds the index of the first occurrence an element larger than a specified key k; return -1 if every element is less than or equal to k.

1.4   SEARCH A SORTED ARRAY FOR $A[i] = i$

Suppose that in addition to being sorted, the entries of A are distinct integers. Design an efficient algorithm for finding an index i such that $A[i] = i$ or indicating that no such index exists.

1.5   SEARCH AN ARRAY OF UNKNOWN LENGTH

Suppose you do not know the length of A in advance; accessing $A[i]$ for i beyond the end of the array throws an exception.

Problem 1.5: Find the index of the first occurrence in A of a specified key k; return -1 if k does not appear in A.

1.6   MISSING ELEMENT, LIMITED RESOURCES

The storage capacity of hard drives dwarfs that of RAM. This can lead to interesting time-space tradeoffs.

Problem 1.6: Given a file containing roughly 300 million social security numbers (9-digit numbers), find a 9-digit number that is not in the file. You have unlimited drive space but only 2 megabytes of RAM at your disposal.

1.7 INTERSECT TWO SORTED ARRAYS

A natural implementation for a search engine is to retrieve documents that match the set of words in a query by maintaining an inverted index. Each page is assigned an integer identifier, its *document-id*. An inverted index is a mapping that takes a word w and returns a sorted array of page-ids which contain w—the sort order could be, for example, the page rank in descending order. When a query contains multiple words, the search engine finds the sorted array for each word and then computes the intersection of these arrays—these are the pages containing all the words in the query. The most computationally intensive step of doing this is finding the intersection of the sorted arrays.

Problem 1.7: Given sorted arrays A and B of lengths n and m respectively, return an array C containing elements common to A and B. The array C should be free of duplicates. How would you perform this intersection if—(1.) $n \approx m$ and (2.) $n \ll m$?

Hashing

Hashing is another approach to searching. Hashing is qualitatively different from binary search—the idea of hashing is to store keys in an array of length m. Keys are stored in array locations based on the "hash code" of the key. The hash code is an integer computed from the key by a hash function. If the hash function is chosen well, the keys are distributed across the array locations uniformly randomly.

There is always the possibility of two keys mapping to the same location, in which case a "collision" is said to occur. The standard mechanism to deal with collisions is to maintain a linked list of keys at each location. Lookups, inserts, and deletes take $O(1 + n/m)$ complexity, where n is the number of keys. If the "load" n/m grows large, the table can be rehashed to one with a larger number of locations; the keys are moved to the new table. Rehashing is expensive ($\Theta(n + m)$ time) but if it is performed infrequently (for example, if performed every time the load increases by $2\times$), its amortized cost is low.

Compared to binary search trees (discussed on Page 20), inserting and deleting in a hash table is more efficient (assuming the load is constant). One disadvantage of hashing is the need for a good hash function but this is rarely an issue in practice. Similarly, rehashing is not a problem outside of realtime systems and even for such systems, a separate thread can perform the rehashing.

1.8   ANAGRAMS

Anagrams are popular word play puzzles, where by rearranging letters of one set of words, you get another set of words. For example, "eleven plus two" is an anagram for "twelve plus one". Crossword puzzle enthusiasts would like to be able to generate all possible anagrams for a given set of letters.

Problem 1.8: Given a dictionary of English words, return the set of all words grouped into subsets of words that are all anagrams of each other.

1.9   SEARCH FOR A PAIR WHICH SUMS TO S

Let A be a sorted array of integers and S a target integer.

Problem 1.9: Design an efficient algorithm for determining if there exist a pair of indices i, j (not necessarily distinct) such that $A[i] + A[j] = S$.

1.10   ANONYMOUS LETTER

A hash can be viewed as a dictionary. As a result, hashing commonly appears when processing with strings.

Problem 1.10: You are required to write a method that takes two text documents: an anonymous letter L and text from a magazine M. Your method is to return true if L can be written using M and false otherwise. (If a letter appears k times in L, it must appear at least k times in M.)

1.11   PAIRING USERS BY ATTRIBUTES

You are building a social networking site where each user specifies a set of attributes. You would like to pair each user with another unpaired user that specified exactly the same set of attributes.

Specifically, you are given a sequence of users where each user has a unique key, say a 32-bit integer and a set of attributes specified as a set of strings. As soon as you read a user, you should pair it with another previously read user with identical attributes who is currently unpaired, if such a user exists. If the user cannot be paired, you should keep him in the unpaired set.

Problem 1.11: How would you implement this matching process efficiently? How would you implement it if we allow an approximate match of attributes as well?

1.12   MISSING ELEMENT

Hashing can be used to find an element which is not present in a given set.

Problem 1.12: Given an array A of integers, find an integer k that is not present in A. Assume that the integers are 32-bit signed integers.

1.13 ROBOT BATTERY CAPACITY

A robot needs to travel along a path that includes several ascents and descents. When it goes up, it uses its battery as a source of energy and when it goes down, it recovers the potential energy back into the battery. The battery recharging process is ideal: on descending, every Joule of gravitational potential energy converts into a Joule of electrical energy that is stored in the battery. The battery has a limited capacity and once it reaches its storage capacity, the energy generated from the robot going down is lost.

Problem 1.13: Given a robot with the energy regeneration ability described above, the mass of the robot m and a sequence of three-dimensional co-ordinates that the robot needs to traverse, how would you determine the minimum battery capacity needed for the robot to complete the trajectory? (Assume the robot starts with a fully charged battery and the battery is used only for overcoming gravity.)

1.14 SEARCH FOR MAJORITY

There are several applications where you want to identify tokens in a given stream that have more than a certain fraction of the total number of occurrences in a relatively inexpensive manner. For example, we may want to identify the users using the largest fraction of the network bandwidth or IP addresses originating the most HTTP requests. Here we will try to solve a simplified version of this problem called "majority-find".

Problem 1.14: You are reading a sequence of words from a very long stream. You know *a priori* that more than half the words are repetitions of a single word W but the positions where W occurs are unknown. Design an efficient algorithm that reads this stream only once and uses only a constant amount of memory to identify W.

1.15 SEARCH FOR FREQUENT ITEMS

In practice, we may not be interested in just the majority token but all the tokens whose count exceeds say 1% of the total token count. It is easy to show that it is impossible to do this in a single pass when you have limited memory but if you are allowed to pass through the stream twice, it is possible to identify the common tokens.

Problem 1.15: You are reading a sequence of strings separated by white space from a very large stream. You are allowed to read the stream twice.

Devise an algorithm that uses only $O(k)$ memory to identify all the words that occur more than $\lceil \frac{n}{k} \rceil$ times in the stream, where n is the length of the stream.

Binary Search Trees

A problem with arrays is adding and deleting elements to an array is computationally expensive, particularly when the array needs to stay sorted. Binary Search Trees (BSTs) are similar to arrays in that the keys are in a sorted order but they are easier to perform insertions and deletions into. BSTs require more space than arrays since each node has to have a pointer to its children and its parent.

The key lookup, insert, and delete operations for BSTs take time proportional to the height of the tree, which can in worst-case be $\Theta(n)$, if inserts and deletes are naïvely implemented. However there are implementations of insert and delete which guarantee the tree has height $\Theta(\log n)$. These require storing and updating additional data at the tree nodes. Red-black trees are an example of such balanced BSTs and they are the workhorse of modern data-structure libraries—for example, they are used in the C++ STL library to implement sets.

Keep in mind that BSTs are, in certain respects, qualitatively different from the trees described in Chapter 5 (Algorithms on Graphs) and it is important to understand these differences. Specifically, in a BST, there is positionality as well as order associated with the children of nodes. Furthermore, the values stored at nodes have to respect the BST property— the key stored at a node is greater than or equal to the keys stored in the nodes of its left subchild and less than or equal to the values stored in the nodes of its right subchild.

1.16   SEARCH BST FOR A KEY

Searching for a key in a BST is very similar to searching in a sorted array. Recursion is more natural but for performance, a while-loop is preferred.

Problem 1.16:   Given a BST T, first write a recursive function that searches for key K, then write an iterative function.

1.17   SEARCH BST FOR $x > k$

BSTs offer more than the ability to search for a key—they can be used to find the min and max elements, look for the successor or predecessor of a given search key (which may or may not be present in the BST), and enumerate the elements in a sorted order.

Problem 1.17:   Given a BST T and a key K, write a method that searches for the first entry larger than K.

1.18   SEARCHING TWO SORTED ARRAYS

Given a sorted array A, if you want to find the k-th smallest element, you can simply return $A[k-1]$ which is an $O(1)$ operation. If you are given two sorted arrays of length n and m and you need to find the k-th smallest element in the union of the two arrays, you could potentially merge the two sorted arrays and then look for the answer but that would take $O(n+m)$ time. You can build the merged array only till the first k elements. This would be a $O(k)$ operation. Can you do better than this?

Problem 1.18: You are given two sorted arrays of lengths m and n. Give a $O(\log m + \log n)$ time algorithm for computing the k-th smallest element in the union of the two arrays. Keep in mind that the elements may be repeated.

1.19   INTERSECTING LINES

Suppose you are designing a rectangular printed circuit board (PCB) where you are supposed to connect a set of points from one edge to another set of points at the opposite edge. The metal lines connecting these points should not intersect with each other; otherwise, there will be a short circuit. Your job is to determine if it is feasible to route the metal lines on the PCB surface in a way that avoids short circuits. Let's assume we connect each pair using a straight line of metal. It is a proven fact that you can connect the pairs without intersection (using either straight or curved lines) iff you can connect them using straight lines that do not intersect.

Problem 1.19: How would you determine if a given set of straight lines intersect in a given rectangle or not?

1.20   CONTAINED INTERVALS

In various applications (such as laying out computer chips), it is important to find when a given shape is completely contained inside another shape. Let's do a simpler version of this problem where we are just concerned with line segments along a straight line.

Problem 1.20: Write a function that takes a set of open intervals on the real line (a_i, b_i) for $i \in \{0, 1, \ldots, n-1\}$ and determines if there exists some interval (a_l, b_l) that is completely contained inside another interval (a_m, b_m). If such pairs of intervals exist, then return one such pair.

1.21   VIEW FROM THE TOP

This is a simplified version of a problem that often comes up in computer graphics—you are given a million overlapping line segments of different colors situated at different heights. Implement a function that draws the lines as seen from the top.

1.22   COMPLETION SEARCH

You are working in the finance office for ABC corporation. There are n employees—employee i received $\$s_i$ in compensation last year; the total compensation was $\$S$.

This year, the corporation needs to cut payroll expenses to $\$S'$. The CEO wants to put a cap σ on salaries—every employee who earned more than $\$\sigma$ last year will be paid $\$\sigma$ this year; employees who earned less than $\$\sigma$ will see no change in their salary.

For example, if $(s_1, s_2, s_3, s_4, s_5) = (90, 30, 100, 40, 20)$ and $S' = 210$, then 60 is a suitable value for σ.

Problem 1.22: Design an efficient algorithm for finding such a σ, if one exists.

1.23   MATRIX SEARCH

Let A be an $n \times n$ matrix whose entries are real numbers. Assume that along any column and along any row of A, the entries appear in increasing sorted order.

Problem 1.23: Design an efficient algorithm that decides whether a real number x appears in A. How many entries of A does your algorithm inspect in the worst-case? Can you prove a tight lower bound that any such algorithm has to consider in the worst-case?

1.24   CHECKING SIMPLICITY

A polygon is defined to be simple if none of its edges intersect with each other except for their endpoints.

Problem 1.24: Give an $O(n \log n)$ time algorithm to determine if a polygon with n vertices is simple.

Chapter 2

Sorting

> A description is given of a new method of sorting in the random-access store of a computer. The methods compares very favourably with other known methods in speed, in economy of storage, and in ease of programming.
>
> "Quicksort," C. Hoare, 1962

Sorting—rearranging a collection of items into increasing or decreasing order—is a common problem in computing. Sorting is used to prepro- cess the collection to make searching faster (as we saw with binary search through an array), as well as to identify items that are similar (e.g., stu- dents are sorted on test scores).

Naïve sorting algorithms run in $\Theta(n^2)$ time. There are a number of sorting algorithms which run in $O(n \cdot \log n)$ time—Mergesort, Heapsort, and Quicksort are examples. Each has its advantages and disadvantages: for example, Heapsort is in-place but not stable; Mergesort is stable but not in-place. Most sorting routines are based on a compare function that takes two items as input and returns 1 if the first item is smaller than the second item, 0 if they are equal and -1 otherwise. However it is also possible to use numerical attributes directly, e.g., in Radixsort.

2.1 GOOD SORTING ALGORITHMS

What is the most efficient sorting algorithm for each of the following situations:

  − A small array of integers.

- A large array whose entries are random numbers.
- A large array of integers that is already almost sorted.
- A large collection of integers that are drawn from a very small range.
- A large collection of numbers most of which are duplicates.
- Stability is required, i.e., the relative order of two records that have the same sorting key should not be changed.

2.2   TeraSort

The sorting algorithms alluded to above assume that all the data you need to sort will fit in the RAM. What if your data will not fit in the memory?

Problem 2.2: Sort a file containing 10^{12} 100 byte strings.

2.3   Finding the winner and runner-up

There are 128 players participating in a tennis tournament. Assume that the "x beats y" relationship is transitive, i.e., for all players A, B, and C, if A beats B and B beats C, then A beats C.

Problem 2.3: What is the least number of matches we need to organize to find the best player? How many matches do you need to find the best and the second best player?

2.4   Finding the min and max simultaneously

Given a set of numbers, you can find either the min or max of the set in $N - 1$ comparisons each. When you need to find both, can you do better than $2N - 3$ comparisons?

Problem 2.4: Find the min and max elements from a set of N elements using no more than $3N/2 - 1$ comparisons.

2.5   Efficient trials

You are the coach of a cycling team with 25 members and need to determine the fastest, second-fastest, and third-fastest cyclists for selection to the Olympic team.

You will be evaluating the cyclists using a time-trial course on which only 5 cyclists can race at a time. You can use the completion times from a time-trial to rank the 5 cyclists amongst themselves—no ties are possible. Because conditions can change over time, you cannot compare performances across different time-trials. The relative speeds of cyclists does not change—if A beats B in one time-trial and B beats C in another time-trial, then A is guaranteed to beat C if they are in the same time-trial.

Problem 2.5: What is the minimum number of time-trials needed to determine who to send to the Olympics?

2.6 LEAST DISTANCE SORTING

You come across a collection of 20 stone statues in a line. You want to sort them by height, with the shortest statue on the left. The statues are very heavy and you want to move them the least possible distance.

Problem 2.6: Design a sorting algorithm that minimizes the total distance that the statues are moved.

Figure 2. "Premature optimization is the root of all evil"—D. Knuth

2.7 PRIVACY AND ANONYMIZATION

The Massachusetts Group Insurance Commission had a bright idea back in the mid 1990s—it decided to release "anonymized" data on state employees that showed every single hospital visit they had. The goal was to help the researchers. The state spent time removing identifiers such as name, address, and social security number. The Governor of Massachusetts assured the public that this was sufficient to protect patient privacy. Then a graduate student, Latanya Sweeney, saw significant pitfalls in this approach. She requested a copy of the data and by collating the data in multiple columns, she was able to identify the health records of the Governor. This demonstrated that extreme care needs to be taken in anonymizing data. One way of ensuring privacy is to aggregate data such that any record can be mapped to at least k individuals, for some large value of k.

Problem 2.7: Suppose you are given a matrix M, where each row represents an individual and each column represents an attribute about the individual such as age or gender. Given a set of columns to be deleted, you want to determine if each row has at least k duplicate rows with exactly the same contents in the remaining columns. How would you verify this efficiently?

2.8   VARIABLE LENGTH SORT

Most sorting algorithms rely on a basic swap step. When records are of different lengths, the swap step becomes nontrivial.

Problem 2.8: Sort lines of a text file that has a million lines such that the average length of a line is 100 characters but the longest line is one million characters long.

2.9   UNIQUE ELEMENTS

Suppose you are given a set of names and your job is to produce a set of unique first names. If you just remove the last name from all the names, you may have some duplicate first names.

Problem 2.9: How would you create a set of first names that has each name occurring only once? Specifically, design an efficient algorithm for removing all the duplicates from an array.

Max-heap

Another data-structure that is useful in diverse contexts is the max-heap, sometimes also referred to as the priority queue. (There is no relationship between the heap data-structure and the portion of memory in a process by the same name.) A heap is a kind of a binary tree—it supports $O(\log n)$ inserts and constant time lookup for the max element. (The min-heap is a completely symmetric version of the data-structure and supports constant time lookups for the min element.) Searching for arbitrary keys has $O(n)$ time complexity—anything that can be done with a heap can be done with a balanced BST with the same complexity but with possibly some space and time overhead.

2.10 MERGING SORTED ARRAYS

You are given 500 files, each containing stock quote information for an SP500 company. Each line contains an update of the following form:

```
1232111 131 B 1000 270
2212313 246 S 100   111.01
```

The first number is the update time expressed as the number of milliseconds since the start of the day's trading. Each file individually is sorted by this value. Your task is to create a single file containing all the updates sorted by the update time. The individual files are of the order of 1–100 megabytes; the combined file will be of the order of 5 gigabytes.

Problem 2.10: Design an algorithm that takes the files as described above and writes a single file containing the lines appearing in the individual files sorted by the update time. The algorithm should use very little memory, ideally of the order of a few kilobytes.

2.11 APPROXIMATE SORT

Consider a situation where your data is almost sorted—for example, you are receiving time-stamped stock quotes and earlier quotes may arrive after later quotes because of differences in server loads and network routes. What would be the most efficient way of restoring the total order?

Problem 2.11: There is a very long stream of integers arriving as an input such that each integer is at most one thousand positions away from its correctly sorted position. Design an algorithm that outputs the integers in the correct order and uses only a constant amount of storage, i.e., the memory used should be independent of the number of integers processed.

2.12 RUNNING AVERAGES

Suppose you are given a real-valued time series (e.g., temperature measured by a sensor) with some noise added to it. In order to extract meaningful trends from noisy time series data, it is necessary to perform smoothing. If the noise has a Gaussian distribution and the noise added to successive samples is independent and identically distributed, then the running average does a good job of smoothing. However if the noise can have an arbitrary distribution, then the running median does a better job.

Problem 2.12: Given a sequence of trillion real numbers on a disk, how would you compute the running mean of every thousand entries, i.e., the first point would be the mean of $a[0], \ldots, a[999]$, the second point would be the mean of $a[1], \ldots, a[1000]$, the third point would be the mean of $a[2], \ldots, a[1001]$, etc.? Repeat the calculation for median rather than mean.

2.13   CIRCUIT SIMULATION

While performing timing analysis of a digital circuit, a component is characterized by a Boolean function of the Boolean values at its inputs and the delay of propagating changes from the inputs to the output. For example, a gate may compute the AND function and have a delay of 1 nanosecond from each input to the output or a wire may simply propagate signal from one end to another in 0.5 nanoseconds. In order to simulate how the entire circuit would behave when a set of inputs are given to the circuit, we use "event driven simulation". Here each event represents a change in the signal value and triggers one or more events in the future.

Problem 2.13: You are given a set of nodes, $V_1 \ldots, V_n$ such that the value for each node at time t_0 is 0. An event $\langle t, v, p \rangle$ is a triplet that represents change in the value for node v at time t to potential p (p can be either 0 or 1). You are given a set of input events. Each node v_i also has a function F_i associated with it that maps an input event to a set of output events (output events can happen only after an input event). How would you efficiently compute all the events that will happen as a result of the input events?

Chapter 3

Meta-algorithms

> The important fact to observe is that we have attempted to solve a maximization problem involving a particular value of x and a particular value of N by first solving the general problem involving an arbitrary value of x and an arbitrary value of N.
>
> "Dynamic Programming,"
> R. Bellman, 1957

Dynamic Programming

There are a number of approaches to designing algorithms: exhaustive search, divide-and-conquer, greedy, randomized, parallelization, backtracking, heuristic, reduction, approximation, etc.

Problems which are naturally solved using dynamic programming (DP) are a popular choice for hard interview questions. DP is a general technique for solving complex optimization problems that can be decomposed into overlapping subproblems. Like divide-and-conquer, we solve the problem by combining the solutions of multiple smaller problems but what makes DP efficient is that we are able to reuse the intermediate results and often dramatically reduce the time complexity by doing so[1].

To illustrate the idea, consider the simple problem of computing Fibonacci numbers defined by $F_n = F_{n-1} + F_{n-2}$, $F_0 = 0$, and $F_1 = 1$. A

---

[1]The word "programming" in dynamic programming does not refer to computer programming—the word was chosen by Richard Bellman to describe a program in the sense of a schedule.

function to compute F_n that recursively invokes itself to compute F_{n-1} and F_{n-2} would have a time complexity that is exponential in n. However if we make the observation that recursion leads to computing F_i for $i \in [0, n-1]$ repeatedly, we can save the computation time by storing these results and reusing them. This makes the time complexity linear in n, albeit at the expense of $O(n)$ storage. Note that the recursive implementation requires $O(n)$ storage too, though on the stack rather than the heap and that the function is not tail recursive since the last operation performed is $+$ and not a recursive call.

The key to solving any DP problem efficiently is finding the right way to break the problem into subproblems such that

– the bigger problem can be solved relatively easily once solution to all the subproblems are available, and

– you need to solve as few subproblems as possible.

In some cases, this may require solving a slightly different optimization problem than the original problem. For example, consider the following problem: given an array of integers A of length n, find the interval indices a and b such that $\sum_{i=a}^{b} A[i]$ is maximized.

Let's try to solve this problem assuming we have the solution for the subarray $A[1, n-1]$. In this case, even if we knew the largest sum subarray for array $A[1, n-1]$, it does not help us solve the problem for $A[1, n]$.

Now, consider a variant of this problem. Let

$$\mu_A(i, j) = \max_{k \in [i,j]} \sum_{x=k}^{j} A[x].$$

It is easy to define a recurrence relationship for $\mu_A(i, j)$. This is essentially the largest sequence sum till $j - 1$ added to $A[k]$ (or zero if that sum happens to be negative). Hence $\mu_A(i, j) = \max(0, \mu_A(i, j-1) + A[j])$. Using this relationship, we can tabulate $\mu_A(1, j)$ for $j \in [1, n]$ in linear-time. Once we have all these values, the answer to our original problem is simply $\max_{j \in [1,n]}(\mu_A(1, j))$ which can be computed in another linear pass.

Here are two variants of the subarray maximization problem that can be solved with minor variations of the above approach: find indices a and b such that $\sum_{i=a}^{b} A[i]$ is—(1.) closest to 0 and (2.) closest to t.

A common mistake that people make while solving DP problems is trying to think of the recursive case by splitting the problem into two equal halves, a la Quicksort, i.e., somehow solve the subproblems for arrays $A[1, n/2]$ and $A[n/2 + 1, n]$ and combine the results. However in most cases, these two subproblems are not sufficient to solve the original problem.

3.1 LONGEST NONDECREASING SUBSEQUENCE

In genomics, given two gene sequences, we try to find if parts of one gene are the same as the other. Thus it is important to find the longest common subsequence of the two sequences. One way to solve this problem is to construct a new sequence where for each literal in one sequence, we insert its position into the other sequence and then find the longest nondecreasing subsequence of this new subsequence. For example, if the two sequences are $\langle 1, 3, 5, 2, 7 \rangle$ and $\langle 1, 2, 3, 5, 7 \rangle$, we would construct a new sequence where for each position in the first sequence, we would list its position in the second sequence like so, $\langle 1, 3, 4, 2, 5 \rangle$. Then we find the longest nondecreasing sequence which is $\langle 1, 3, 4, 5 \rangle$. Now, if we use the numbers of the new sequence as indices into the second sequence, we get $\langle 1, 3, 5, 7 \rangle$ which is our longest common subsequence.

Problem 3.1: Given an array of integers A of length n, find the longest sequence $\langle i_1, \ldots i_k \rangle$ such that $i_j < i_{j+1}$ and $A[i_j] \leq A[i_{j+1}]$ for any $j \in [1, k-1]$.

3.2 FROG CROSSING

Figure 3. "Be fearful when others are greedy"—W. Buffett

DP is often used to compute a plan for performing a task that consists of a series of actions in an optimum way. Here is an example with an interesting twist.

Problem 3.2: There is a river that is n meters wide. At every meter from the edge, there may or may not be a stone. A frog needs to cross the river. However the frog has the limitation that if it has just jumped x meters, then its next jump must be between $x - 1$ and $x + 1$ meters, inclusive. Assume the first jump can be of only 1 meter. Given the position of the stones, how would you determine whether the frog can make it to the other end or not? Analyze the runtime of your algorithm.

3.3   CUTTING PAPER

We now consider an optimum planning problem in two dimensions. You are given an $L \times W$ rectangular piece of kite-paper, where L and W are positive integers and a list of n kinds of kites that can be made using the paper. The i-th kite design, $i \in [1, n]$ requires an $l_i \times w_i$ rectangle of kite-paper; this kite sells for p_i. Assume l_i, w_i, p_i are positive integers. You have a machine that can cut rectangular pieces of kite-paper either horizontally or vertically.

Problem 3.3: Design an algorithm that computes a profit maximizing strategy for cutting the kite-paper. You can make as many instances of a given kite as you want. There is no cost to cutting kite-paper.

3.4   WORD BREAKING

Suppose you are designing a search engine. In addition to getting keywords from a page's content, you would like to get keywords from URLs. For example, `bedbathandbeyond.com` should be associated with "bed bath and beyond" (in this version of the problem we also allow "bed bat hand beyond" to be associated with it).

Problem 3.4: Given a dictionary that can tell you whether a string is a valid word or not in constant time and given a string s of length n, provide an efficient algorithm that can tell whether s can be reconstituted as a sequence of valid words. In the event that the string is valid, your algorithm should output the corresponding sequence of words.

The next three problems have a very similar structure. Given a set of objects of different sizes, you need to partition them in various ways. The solutions also have the same common theme that you need to explore all possible partitions in a way that you can take advantage of overlapping subproblems.

Alabama	9	Indiana	11	Nebraska	5	South Carolina	8
Alaska	3	Iowa	7	Nevada	5	South Dakota	3
Arizona	10	Kansas	6	New Hampshire	4	Tennessee	11
Arkansas	6	Kentucky	8	New Jersey	15	Texas	34
California	55	Louisiana	9	New Mexico	5	Utah	5
Colorado	9	Maine	4	New York	31	Vermont	3
Connecticut	7	Maryland	10	North Carolina	15	Virginia	13
Delaware	3	Massachusetts	12	North Dakota	3	Washington	11
Florida	27	Michigan	17	Ohio	20	West Virginia	5
Georgia	15	Minnesota	10	Oklahoma	7	Wisconsin	10
Hawaii	4	Mississippi	6	Oregon	7	Wyoming	3
Idaho	4	Missouri	11	Pennsylvania	21	Washington, DC	3
Illinois	21	Montana	3	Rhode Island	4	Total electors	538

Table 2. Number of Electoral College votes per state and Washington, DC

3.5 TIES IN A PRESIDENTIAL ELECTION

The US President is elected by the members of the Electoral College. The number of electors per state and Washington, DC, are given in Table 2. All electors from each state as well as Washington, DC cast their vote for the same candidate.

Problem 3.5: Suppose there are two candidates in the presidential election. How would you programmatically determine if a tie is a possibility?

3.6 RED OR BLUE HOUSE MAJORITY

Suppose you want to place a bet on the outcome of the coming elections. Specifically, you are betting if the US House of Representatives will have a Democratic or a Republican majority. A polling company has computed the probability of winning for each candidate in the individual elections. You are interested in just one number—what is the probability that the Republican party is going to have a majority in the House?

Problem 3.6: Given that a party needs 223 or more seats to win a majority in the House, how would you compute the probability of a Republican win? Assume each race is independent and that the probability of a Republican winning the race i is p_i.

3.7 LOAD BALANCING

Suppose you want to build a large distributed storage system on the web. Millions of users will store terabytes of data on your servers. One way to design the system would be to hash each user's login id, partition the hash ranges into equal-sized buckets, and store the data for each bucket of users on one server. For this scheme, mapping a user to the server that serves the user is a simple hash computation.

However if a small number of users occupy a large fraction of the storage space, hashing will not achieve a balanced partition. One way to solve this problem is to make the hash buckets have a nonuniform width based on the load in that hash range.

Problem 3.7: You have n users with unique hashes h_1 through h_n and m servers, numbered 1 to m. User i has B_i bytes to store. You need to find numbers K_1 through K_m such that all users with hashes between K_j and K_{j+1} get assigned to server j. Design an algorithm to find the numbers K_1 through K_m that minimizes the load on the most heavily loaded server.

So far we have applied DP to one-dimensional and two-dimensional objects. Here are applications of DP to trees.

3.8   VOLTAGE SELECTION

You are given a logic circuit that can be modeled as a rooted tree—the leaves are the primary inputs, the internal nodes are the gates, and the root is the single output of the circuit.

Each gate can be powered by a high or low supply voltage. A gate powered by a lower supply voltage consumes less power but has a weaker output signal. You want to minimize power while ensuring that the circuit is reliable. To ensure reliability, you should not have a gate powered by a low supply voltage drive another gate powered by a low supply voltage. All gates consume 1 nanowatt when connected to the low supply voltage and 2 nanowatts when connected to the high supply voltage.

Problem 3.8: Design an efficient algorithm that takes as input a logic circuit and selects supply voltages for each gate to minimize power consumption while ensuring reliable operation.

3.9   OPTIMUM BUFFER INSERTION

You are given a tree-structured logic circuit that can be modeled as a rooted tree, exactly as in Problem 3.8. Signals degrade as they pass through successive gates.

You can overcome this degradation by "buffering" gates—buffering enhances its output but does not change its logical functionality.

Problem 3.9: How would you efficiently compute the least number of gates to buffer in the circuit so that after buffering, every path of k or more gates has at least one buffered gate? More formally, given a rooted tree, how would you color the edges of the graph in green or red such that no path from a node to any ancestor contains more than k successive red edges and the number of green edges is minimized?

DP can also be applied to geometric constructions, as illustrated by this problem:

3.10   TRIANGULATION

Let P be a convex polygon with n vertices specified by their x and y co-ordinates. A triangulation of P is a collection of $n-3$ diagonals of P such that no two diagonals intersect, except possibly at their endpoints. Observe that a triangulation splits the polygon's interior into $n-2$ disjoint triangles. Define the cost of a triangulation to be the sum of the lengths of the diagonals that it is made up of.

Problem 3.10: Design an efficient algorithm for finding a triangulation that minimizes the cost.

3.11   MAXIMIZING EXPRESSIONS

The value of an arithmetic expression depends upon the order in which the operations are performed. For example, depending upon how one parenthesizes the expression $5 - 3 \cdot 4 + 6$, one can obtain any one of the following values:

$$
\begin{aligned}
-25 &= 5 - \left(3 \cdot (4 + 6)\right) \\
-13 &= 5 - \left((3 \cdot 4) + 6\right) \\
20 &= (5 - 3) \cdot (4 + 6) \\
-1 &= \left(5 - (3 \cdot 4)\right) + 6 \\
14 &= \left((5 - 3) \cdot 4\right) + 6
\end{aligned}
$$

Given an unparenthesized expression of the form $v_0 \circ_0 v_1 \circ_1 \cdots \circ_{n-2} v_{n-1}$, where $v_0, \ldots, v_{n-1}$ are operands with known real values and $\circ_0, \ldots, \circ_{n-2}$ are specified operations, we want to parenthesize the expression so as to maximize its value.

Problem 3.11: Devise an algorithm to solve this problem in the special case that the operands are all positive and the only operations are $\cdot$ and $+$.

Explain how you would modify your algorithm to deal with the case in which the operands can be positive and negative and $+$ and $-$ are the only operations.

Suggest how you would generalize your approach to include multiplication and division (pretend divide-by-zero never occurs).

Greedy Algorithms

A greedy algorithm is one which makes decisions that are locally optimum and never changes them. This approach does not work generally. For example, consider making change for 48 pence in the old British currency where the coins came in $30, 24, 12, 6, 3, 1$ pence denominations. A greedy algorithm would iteratively choose the largest denomination coin that is less than or equal to the amount of change that remains to be made. If we try this for 48 pence, we get $30, 12, 6$. However the optimum answer would be $24, 24$.

In its most general form, the coin changing problem is NP-hard (*cf.* Chapter 6) but for some coinages, the greedy algorithm is optimum—e.g., if the denominations are of the form $\{1, r, r^2, r^3\}$. *Ad hoc* arguments can be applied to show that it is also optimum for US coins. The general problem can be solved in pseudopolynomial time using DP in a manner similar to Problem 6.1.

3.12 SCHEDULING TUTORS

You are responsible for scheduling tutors for the day at a tutoring company. For each day, you have received a number of requests for tutors. Each request has a specified start time and each lesson is thirty minutes long. You have more tutors than requests. Each tutor can start work at any time. However tutors are constrained to work only one stretch which cannot be longer than two hours and each tutor can service only one request at a time.

Problem 3.12: Given a set of requests for the day, design an efficient algorithm to compute the least number of tutors necessary to schedule all the requests for the day.

3.13 MINIMIZE WAITING TIME

A database has to respond to n simultaneous client SQL queries. The service time required for query i is t_i milliseconds and is known in advance. The lookups are processed sequentially but can be processed in any order. We wish to minimize the total waiting time $\sum_{i=1}^{n} T_i$, where T_i is the time client i takes to return. For example, if the lookups are served in order of increasing i, then the client making the i-th query has to wait $\sum_{j=1}^{i} t_j$ milliseconds.

Problem 3.13: Design an efficient algorithm for computing an optimum order for processing the queries.

3.14 HUFFMAN CODING

In 1951, David A. Huffman and his classmates in a graduate course on information theory at MIT were given the choice of a term paper or a final exam. For the term paper, Huffman's professor, Robert M. Fano, had given the problem of finding an algorithm for assigning binary codes to symbols such that a given set of symbols can be represented in the smallest number of bits.

Huffman worked on the problem for months, developing a number of approaches but none that he could prove to be the most efficient. Finally, he despaired of ever reaching a solution and decided to start studying for the final. Just as he was throwing his notes in the garbage, the idea of using a frequency-sorted binary tree came to him and he quickly proved this method to be the most efficient.

Huffman's solution proved to be a significant improvement over the "Shannon-Fano codes" proposed by his professor Robert M. Fano along with Claude E. Shannon—the inventor of Information Theory.

Let's look at an application of Huffman coding. We want to compress a large piece of English text by building a variable length code book for each possible character. Consider the case where each character in the text is independent of all other characters (we can achieve better compression if we do not make this assumption but for this problem we will ignore this fact).

One way of doing this kind of compression is to map each character to a bit string such that no bit string is a prefix of another (for example, 011 is a prefix of 0110 but not a prefix of 1100).

We can simply encode the text by appending the bit strings for each character in the text. While decoding the string, we can keep reading the bits until we find a string that is in our code book and then repeat this process until the entire text is decoded.

Since our objective is to compress the text, we would like to assign the shorter strings to more probable characters and the longer strings to less probable characters.

Problem 3.14: Given a set of symbols with corresponding probabilities, find a prefix code assignment that minimizes the expected length of the encoded string.

3.15 EFFICIENT USER INTERFACE

A user interface (UI) designer is trying to design a menu system that customers use to trigger certain tasks. He wants to minimize the average amount of time it takes for a customer to perform tasks.

If a menu item is at the i-th position, it takes i units of time for the user to reach there (linear scan) and it takes c units of time to click on it.

Each menu item can have multiple levels of sub-menus and a sub-menu can be reached by clicking on its parent menu item.

The designer is provided with a user study that details how often users want tasks to be triggered. (In a real application, we would also worry about grouping related items in the same sub-menu as well but for this problem we will ignore grouping requirements.)

Problem 3.15: How should the menu system be designed so as to minimize the average UI interaction time if $c = 1$? How would you do it if $c > 1$?

3.16   PACKING FOR USPS PRIORITY MAIL

The United States Postal Service makes fixed-size mail shipping boxes— you pay a fixed price for a given box and can ship anything you want that fits in the box. Suppose you have a set of n items that you need to ship and have a large supply of the $4 \times 12 \times 8$ inch priority mail shipping boxes. Each item will fit in such a box but all of them combined may take multiple boxes. Naturally, you want to minimize the number of boxes you use.

The first-fit heuristic is a greedy algorithm for this problem—it processes the items in the sequence in which they are first given and places them in the first box in which they fit, scanning through boxes in increasing order. First-fit is not optimum but it never takes more than twice as many boxes as the minimum possible.

Problem 3.16: Implement first-fit to run in $O(n \log n)$ time.

3.17   POINTS COVERING INTERVALS

Consider an engineer responsible for a number of tasks on the factory floor. Each task starts at a fixed time and ends at a fixed time. The engineer wants to visit the floor to check on the tasks. Your task is to help him minimize the number of visits he makes. In each visit, he can check on all the tasks taking place at the time of the visit. A visit takes place at a fixed time and he can only check on tasks taking place at exactly that time.

More formally, model the tasks as n closed intervals on the real line $[a_i, b_i]$, $i = 1, \ldots, n$. A set S of visit times "covers" the tasks if $[a_i, b_i] \cap S \neq \emptyset$, for $i = 1, \ldots, n$.

Problem 3.17: Design an efficient algorithm for finding a minimum cardinality set of visit times that covers all the tasks.

3.18   RAYS COVERING ARCS

Let's say you are responsible for the security of a castle. The castle has a circular perimeter. There are n robots that patrol the perimeter—each robot is responsible for a closed connected subset of the perimeter, i.e., an arc. (The arcs for different robots may overlap.) You want to monitor the robots by installing cameras at the center of the castle that look out to the perimeter. Each camera can look along a ray. To save cost, you would like to minimize the number of cameras.

More formally, let $[\theta_i, \phi_i]$, $i = 1, \ldots, n$ be n arcs, where the i-th arc is the set of points on the perimeter of the unit circle that subtend an angle in the interval $[\theta_i, \phi_i]$ at the center.

A ray is a set of points that all subtend the same angle to the origin— we identify a ray by the angle it makes relative to the X-axis. A set R of rays "covers" the arcs if $[\theta_i, \phi_i] \cap R \neq \emptyset$, for $i = 1, \ldots, n$.

Problem 3.18: Design an efficient algorithm for finding a minimum cardinality covering the set of rays.

3.19 k-CLUSTERING

A k-clustering of a set O is a collection $\{O_1, O_2, \ldots, O_k\}$ of nonempty subsets ("clusters") of O which has the following properties: $O = \cup_{i=1}^{k}$ and $O_i \cap O_j \neq \emptyset \Rightarrow i = j)$.

Let d be a function (the "distance") from $O \times O$ to Z^+, where Z^+ is the set of nonnegative integers.

The need to compute a k-clustering, in which elements that are far apart are in different clusters, comes up in many contexts—assigning cities to salesmen, selecting which racks to place magazines in at a bookstore, etc.

Define the *separation* s_C of a k-clustering C to be the distance between the two objects in different clusters which are closest, i.e., $s_C = \min\{d(p, q) | p \in O_i, q \in O_j, i \neq j\}$. Intuitively, the separation is a measure of how good a job the clustering does of keeping things which are far apart in different clusters.

There is a natural greedy algorithm to compute the clustering: start with $|O|$ clusters, i.e., one cluster per element of O. Look for the pair of elements in different clusters which are closest and merge their two clusters; repeat this merge a total of $n - k$ times to obtain k clusters.

This algorithm can be made to run very efficiently using a min-heap to store the distances being considered and a union-find data-structure to represent and merge the subsets.

Problem 3.19: Prove that the resulting cluster has the maximum separation of all possible k-clusterings.

Note that the algorithm above is very simplistic: it does not attempt to balance cluster sizes, look at distances outside of pairwise closest ones, exploit any structure in the distance function (e.g., the triangle inequality), etc. In a realistic setting, these and many more considerations are taken into account.

3.20   PARTY PLANNING

Leona is holding a party and is trying to select people to invite from her friend circle. She has N friends and she knows which pairs of friends already know each other. Leona wants to invite as many friends as possible but she wants each invitee to know at least six other invitees and not know six other invitees.

Problem 3.20: Devise an efficient algorithm that takes as input Leona's N friends and a set of pairs of friends who know each other and returns an invitation list that meets the above criteria.

Chapter 4

Algorithms on Graphs

> Concerning these bridges, it was
> asked whether anyone could
> arrange a route in such a way that
> he would cross each bridge once
> and only once.
>
> ---
>
> "The solution of a problem
> relating to the geometry of
> position," L. Euler, 1741

A graph is a set of vertices and a set of edges connecting these vertices. Mathematically, a directed graph is a tuple (V, E), where V is a set of *vertices* and $E \subset V \times V$ is the set of edges. An undirected graph is also a tuple (V, E); however E is a set of unordered pairs of V. Graphs are often decorated, e.g., by adding lengths to edges, weights to vertices, a start vertex, etc.

Graphs naturally arise when modeling geometric problems, such as determining connected cities. However they are more general since they can be used to model many kinds of relationships.

A graph can be represented in two ways—using an *adjacency list* or an *adjacency matrix*. In the *adjacency list* representation, for each vertex v, a list of vertices adjacent to v is stored. The *adjacency matrix* representation uses a $|V| \times |V|$ Boolean-valued matrix indexed by vertices, with a 1 indicating the presence of an edge. The complexity of a graph algorithm is measured in terms of the number of vertices and edges.

A tree (sometimes called a free tree) is a special kind of graph—it is an undirected graph that is connected but has no cycles. (Many equivalent definitions exist, e.g., a graph is a free tree iff there exists a unique path between every pair of vertices.) There are a number of variants on the basic idea of a tree—e.g., a rooted tree is one where a designated vertex

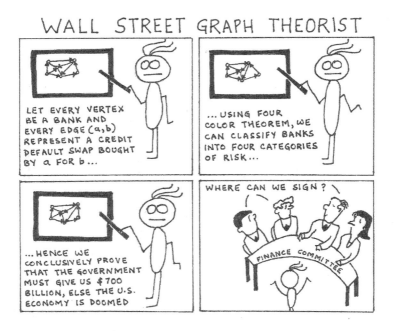

Figure 4. The power of obscure proofs

is called the root, an ordered tree is a rooted tree in which each vertex has an ordering on its children, etc.

Graph Search

Computing vertices which are reachable from other vertices is a fundamental operation. There are two basic algorithms—Depth First Search (DFS) and Breadth First Search (BFS). Both are linear-time—$O(|V| + |E|)$. They differ from each other in terms of the additional information they provide, e.g., BFS can be used to compute distances from the start vertex and DFS can be used to check for the presence of cycles.

4.1   SEARCHING A MAZE

It is natural to apply graph models and algorithms to spatial problems. Consider a black and white digitized image of a maze—white pixels represent open areas and black spaces are walls. There are two special pixels: one is designated the entrance and the other is the exit.

Problem 4.1: Given a two-dimensional matrix of black and white entries representing a maze with designated entrance and exit points, find a path from the entrance to the exit, if one exists.

4.2   ORDER NODES IN A BINARY TREE BY DEPTH

There are various traversals that can be performed on a tree: in-order, pre-order, and post-order are three natural examples.

Problem 4.2: How would you efficiently return an array $A[0 \ldots h]$, where h is the height of the tree and $A[i]$ is the head of a linked list of all the nodes in the tree that are at height i?

4.3   CONNECTEDNESS

A connected graph is one for which, given any vertices u and v, there exists a path from u to v. The notion of connectedness holds for both directed and undirected graphs—for undirected graphs, we sometimes simply say there exists a path between u and v.

Intuitively, some graphs are more connected than others—e.g., a clique is more connected than a tree. To be more quantitative, we could refer to a graph as being $2\forall$-connected if it remains connected even if any single edge is removed. A graph is $2\exists$-connected if there exists an edge whose removal leaves the graph connected.

One application of this idea is in fault tolerance for data networks. Suppose you are given a set of datacenters connected through a set of dedicated point-to-point links. You want to be able to reach from any datacenter to any other datacenter through a combination of these dedicated links. Sometimes one of these links can become temporarily out of service and you want to ensure that your network can sustain up to one faulty link. How can you verify this?

Problem 4.3: Let $G = (V, E)$ be a connected undirected graph. How would you efficiently check if G is $2\exists$-connected? Can you make your algorithm run in $O(|V|)$ time? How would you check if G is $2\forall$-connected?

4.4   PCB WIRING

Consider a collection of p electrical pins. For each pair of pins, there may or may not be a wire joining them. There are w pairs of pins with a wire joining them.

Problem 4.4: Give an $O(p + w)$ time algorithm that determines if it is possible to place some of the pins on the left half of a PCB and the rest on the right half such that each wire is between a pin on the left and a pin on the right. Your algorithm should return a placement, should one exist.

4.5   EXTENDED CONTACTS

You are given a social network. Specifically, it consists of a set of individuals and for each individual, a list of his contacts. (The contact relationship need not be symmetric—A may be a contact of B but B may not be a contact of A.) Let's define C to be an extended contact of A if he is either a contact of A or a contact of an extended contact of A.

Problem 4.5: Devise an efficient algorithm which takes a social network and computes for each individual his extended contacts.

4.6   EULER TOUR

Leonhard Euler wrote a paper titled "Seven Bridges of Köenigsberg" in 1736. It is considered to be the first paper in graph theory. The problem was set in the city of Köenigsberg, which was situated on both sides of the Pregel River and included two islands which were connected to each other and the mainland by seven bridges. Euler posed the problem of finding a walk through the city that would cross each bridge exactly once. In the paper, Euler demonstrated that it was impossible to do so.

More generally, an Euler tour of a connected directed graph $G = (V, E)$ is a cycle that includes each edge of G exactly once; it may repeat vertices more than once.

Problem 4.6: Design a linear-time algorithm to find an Euler tour if one exists.

4.7   EPHEMERAL STATE IN A FINITE STATE MACHINE

A finite state machine (FSM) is a set of states S, a set of inputs I, and a transition function $T : S \times I \mapsto S$. If $T(s, i) = u$, we say that s *leads to* u on application of input i. The transition function T can be generalized to sequences of inputs—if $\iota = \langle i_0, i_1, \ldots, i_{n-1} \rangle$, then $T(s, \iota) = s$ if $n = 0$; otherwise, $T(s, \iota) = T\big(T(s, \langle i_0, i_1, \ldots, i_{n-2} \rangle), i_{n-1}\big)$.

The state e is said to be *ephemeral* if there is a sequence of inputs α such that there does not exist an input sequence β for which $T(T(e, \alpha), \beta) = e$. Informally, e is ephemeral if there is a possibility of the FSM starting at e and getting to a state f from which it cannot return to e.

Problem 4.7: Design an efficient algorithm which takes an FSM and returns the set of ephemeral states.

4.8   TREE DIAMETER

Packets in Ethernet LANs are routed according to the unique path in a tree whose vertices correspond to clients and edges correspond to physical connections between the clients. In this problem, we want to design an algorithm for finding the "worst-case" route, i.e., the two clients that are furthest apart.

Problem 4.8: Let T be a tree, where each edge is labeled with a real-valued distance. Define the diameter of T to be the length of a longest path in T. Design an efficient algorithm to compute the diameter of T.

4.9 TIMING ANALYSIS

A combinational logic network consists of primary inputs and logic gates. Some of the gates may be designated as being primary outputs. Each gate has an output and a number of inputs—these inputs may be primary inputs or the outputs of other gates. A cycle of gates is defined as a sequence of gates $\langle g_0, g_1, \ldots, g_{n-1}, g_0 \rangle$ starting and ending at the same gate such that for each consecutive pair of gates in the sequence, the first gate is an input to the second gate. Cycles of gates are disallowed.

Each gate has a fixed delay. A change at the primary input propagates through the logic network and eventually the output of every gate stops changing.

Problem 4.9: Given a logic network with primary inputs changing, find the smallest time after which all the primary outputs no longer change.

4.10 TEAM PHOTO DAY—1

You are a photographer for a soccer meet. You will be taking pictures of pairs of opposing teams. Each team has 20 players on its roster. Each picture will consist of two rows of players, one row for each of the two teams. You want to place the players so that if Player A stands behind Player B, he must be taller than Player B.

Problem 4.10: Describe an efficient method that takes as input two teams and the heights of the players in the teams and checks if it is possible to place players to take the picture—if it is possible, your function should print which team comes to the front and the order in which the players appear. How would you generalize your approach to determine the largest number of teams that can be photographed simultaneously subject to the same constraints?

4.11 ASSIGNING RADIO FREQUENCIES

If two neighboring radio stations are using the same radio frequency, there would be a region geographically between them where the signal from both stations would be equally strong and the resulting interference would cause neither of the signals to be usable. Hence neighboring radio stations try to pick different frequencies. Consider the problem where we have just two frequencies available and we are given a neighborhood graph of a set of radio stations. We are supposed to assign the frequencies to the radio stations such that the interference is minimized. Suppose we are interested in a simpler problem where we are happy if for any given radio station, the majority of its neighbors use a different frequency from the given station. This can be modeled as a graph coloring problem.

Let $G = (V, E)$ be an undirected graph. A two-coloring of G is a function assigning each vertex of G to *black* or *white*. Call a two-coloring *diverse* if each vertex has at least half its neighbors opposite in color to itself.

Problem 4.11: Does every graph have a diverse coloring? How would you compute a diverse coloring, if it exists?

Advanced Graph Algorithms

Up to this point we looked at basic search and combinatorial properties of graphs. The algorithms we considered were all linear-time complexity and relatively straightforward—the major challenge was in modeling the problem appropriately.

There are essentially four problems on graphs that can be solved efficiently, i.e., in polynomial time. All other problems are either variants of these or very likely, not solvable by polynomial time algorithms.

- Matching—given an undirected graph, find a maximum collection of edges subject to the constraint that every vertex is incident to at most one edge. The matching problem for bipartite graphs is especially common and the algorithm for this problem is much simpler than for the general case. A common variant is the maximum weighted matching problem in which edges have weights and a maximum weight edge set is sought, subject to the matching constraint.

- Shortest paths—given a graph, directed or undirected, with costs on the edges, find the minimum cost path from a given vertex to all vertices. Variants include computing the shortest path for all pairs of vertices, the case where costs are all nonnegative, and constraints on the number of edges.

- Max flow—given a directed graph with a capacity for each edge, find the maximum flow from a given source to a given sink, where a flow is a function mapping edges to numbers satisfying conservation (flow into a vertex equals the flow out of it) and the edge capacities.

- Minimum spanning tree—given a connected undirected graph (V, E) with weights on each edge, find a subset E' of the edges with minimum total weight such that (V, E') is connected.

Each of these has a polynomial time algorithm and can be solved efficiently in practice for very large graphs.

4.12 SHORTEST PATH WITH FEWEST EDGES

In the usual formulation of the shortest path problem, the number of edges in the path is not a consideration.

Heuristically, if we did want to avoid paths with a large number of edges, we can add a small amount to the cost of each edge. However depending on the structure of the graph and the edge costs, this may not result in the shortest path.

Problem 4.12: Design an algorithm which takes as input a graph $G = (V, E)$, directed or undirected, a nonnegative cost function on E and vertices s and t; your algorithm should output a path with the fewest edges amongst all shortest paths from s to t.

4.13 COUNTING SHORTEST PATHS

There may be many shortest paths between two vertices in a graph. It is commonly the case that a single shortest path is required, possibly one with the fewest edges, as in Problem 4.12. Sometimes we want to know the number of shortest paths, e.g., when analyzing the structure of a Boolean function or checking the stability of a system.

Problem 4.13: Develop an efficient algorithm that computes the number of shortest paths between vertices s and t in an undirected graph with unit cost edges.

4.14 RANDOM DIRECTED ACYCLIC GRAPH

You are given a map with a set of cities connected by roads of known lengths.

A storm has made some roads uncrossable. For each road, you know the probability of the road being uncrossable. A given path consisting of a set of roads is considered uncrossable if any of the roads in the path is uncrossable.

Problem 4.14: Find a path between a given pair of cities that is the minimum length path amongst all the paths for which the probability of being crossable is greater than 0.9.

4.15 SHORTEST PATHS IN THE PRESENCE OF RANDOMIZATION

You are given a map to a maze of rooms interconnected by one-way corridors. The map specifies a set of entrance rooms and a treasure room.

Some of the rooms are special—when you arrive at a special room, you are randomly transported out of it through one of the one-way corridors leading out of it. The map designates which rooms are special. You are also told that the way the maze is designed is that once you leave a room, there is no way of coming back to it.

Problem 4.15: Find a strategy which gets you to the treasure room in the minimum expected time.

4.16   TRAVELING SALESMAN WITH A CHOICE

Suppose you are a salesman with a set of cities to visit. If you visit city i, you can make $p(i)$ profit. The cost of going from city i to city j is $c(i, j) > 0$. You want to establish a route for yourself such that you start from a city, visit a set of cities, and then come back to the original city. You can choose to ignore certain cities if you like. Your objective is to maximize the ratio of profit-to-cost.

Problem 4.16: Devise an efficient algorithm for finding a route which maximizes the ratio of the total profit to the total cost.

4.17   ROAD NETWORK

The Texas Department of Transportation is considering adding a new section of highway to the Texas Highway System. Each highway section connects two cities.

The state officials have submitted a number of proposals for the new highway—each proposal includes the pair of cities being connected and the length of the section.

Problem 4.17: Devise an efficient algorithm which takes the existing network, the proposals for new highways, and returns one of the proposed highways which minimizes the shortest driving distance between the cities of El Paso and Corpus Christi.

4.18   STABLE ASSIGNMENT

Consider a department with N graduate students and N professors. Each student has ordered all the professors based on how keen he is to work with them. Each professor has an ordered list of all the students.

Problem 4.18: Devise an algorithm which takes the preferences of the students and the professors and pairs a student with his adviser. There should be no student-adviser pair $(s0, a0)$ and $(s1, a1)$ such that $s0$ prefers $a1$ to $a0$ and $a1$ prefers $s0$ to $s1$.

4.19 ARBITRAGE

You are exploring the remote valleys of Papua New Guinea, one of the last uncharted places in the world. You come across a tribe that does not have money—instead it relies on the barter system. There are N commodities which are traded and the exchange rates are specified by a two-dimensional matrix. For example, three sheep can be exchanged for seven goats; four goats can be exchanged for 200 pounds of wheat, etc.

Problem 4.19: Devise an efficient algorithm to determine whether or not there exists an arbitrage—a way to start with a single unit of some commodity C and convert it back to more than one unit of C through a sequence of exchanges. Assume there are no transaction costs, rates do not fluctuate, and that fractional quantities of items can be sold.

4.20 BIRKHOFF-VON NEUMANN DECOMPOSITION

A crossbar is a piece of networking hardware which has a number of inputs and outputs. It can simultaneously transfer packets from inputs to outputs in a single cycle, as long as no more than one packet leaves an input and no more than one packet arrives at any given output. (Assume all packets are of the same length and take equally long to transfer.)

Problem 4.20: You are given an $N \times N$ matrix of nonnegative integers; $A[i, j]$ encodes the number of packets at input i that need to be transferred to output j. What is the least number of cycles needed to perform the transfer encoded by A?

4.21 CHANNEL CAPACITY

Suppose we have the capability of transmitting one of the five symbols, A, B, C, D, E, through a communication channel. In the absence of errors, we can communicate $\log_2(5)$ bits with each symbol.

Now, suppose the channel is noisy—specifically, the receiver cannot differentiate between the following pairs of symbols: $\Pi = \{(A, B), (B, C), (C, D), (D, E), (E, A)\}$. We can still achieve error-free communication by arranging with the receiver to only transmit two out of the five symbols—e.g., A and C. We cannot transmit more than two symbols and guarantee that we do not make errors because then some pair must be in Π. In this fashion, we are limited to $\log_2(2) = 1$ bit per symbol transmitted.

Problem 4.21: Design a scheme for the given channel by which the transmitter and receiver can achieve more than 1 bit per symbol transmitted.

4.22   TEAM PHOTO DAY—2

This problem is a continuation of Problem 4.10, where we wanted an algorithm to find the maximum number of teams that could be put in one photograph, subject to a placement constraint.

Problem 4.22: Design an efficient algorithm for computing the minimum number of subsets of teams so that the teams in each subset can be organized to appear in one photograph, subject to the placement constraint and each team appears in some subset.

4.23   DANCING WITH THE STARS

You are organizing a celebrity dance charity. Specifically, a number of celebrities have offered to be partners for a ballroom dance. The general public has been invited to offer bids on how much they are willing to pay for a dance with each celebrity.

Some rules governing the dance are—(1.) each celebrity will dance once at the most, (2.) each bidder will dance once at the most, and (3.) the celebrities and the bidders are disjoint.

Problem 4.23: Design an algorithm for pairing bidders with celebrities to maximize the revenue from the dance.

4.24   2-SAT

A Boolean logic expression is said to be in conjunctive normal form (CNF) if complementation is only applied to variables; the operation $+$ is applied to variables or their negation. For example, $(a + b + c') \cdot (a' + b) \cdot (a + c' + d)$ is in CNF. The terms $a + b + c'$, $a' + b$, and $a + c' + d$ are referred to as clauses.

Determining whether an expression in CNF is satisfiable is conjectured to be intractable—i.e., no polynomial time algorithm exists for this problem. However some variants of CNF can be solved in polynomial time.

Problem 4.24: Design a linear-time algorithm for checking if a CNF in which each clause contains no more than two variables is satisfiable.

4.25   THEORY OF EQUALITY

Programs are usually checked using testing—a number of manually written or random test cases are applied to the program and the program's results are checked by assertions or visual inspection.

Formal verification consists of examining a program and analytically determining if there exists an input for which an assertion fails. Formal verification of general programs is undecidable. However there are significant subclasses of general programs for which the verification problem is decidable.

Consider the following problem: given a set of variables $x_1, \ldots, x_n$, equality constraints of the form $x_i = x_j$, and inequality constraints of the form $x_i \neq x_j$, is it possible to satisfy all the constraints simultaneously? For example, the constraints $x_1 = x_2, x_2 = x_3, x_3 = x_4, x_1 \neq x_4$ cannot be satisfied simultaneously.

Such constraints arise in checking the equivalence of loop-free programs with uninterpreted functions.

Problem 4.25: Design an efficient algorithm that takes as input a collection of equality and inequality constraints and decides whether the constraints can be satisfied simultaneously.

Chapter 5

Algorithms on Strings

> A general purpose computer
> program and special purpose
> apparatus for matching strings of
> alphanumeric characters are
> disclosed.
>
> ───────────────────────────
> "Text Matching Algorithm,"
> K. Thompson, 1971

Algorithms that operate on strings are of great practical and founda-
tional importance. Practical applications include web search, compilation, natural language processing, text editors, and DNA analysis. From
a theoretical perspective, any program can be viewed as implementing a
function from $\{0, 1\}$-valued strings to $\{0, 1\}$-valued strings, according to
certain string rewriting rules.

5.1 FIND ALL OCCURRENCES OF A SUBSTRING

A good string search algorithm is fundamental to the performance of
many applications and there are several elegant algorithms proposed for
it, each with its own tradeoffs. As a result, there is no one perfect answer
to it. If someone asks you this question in an interview, the best way to
approach this problem would be to work through one good algorithm in
detail and discuss the breadth of other algorithms for solving this problem.

Problem 5.1: Given two strings s (search string) and T (text), find all
occurrences of s in T.

5.2 STRING MATCHING WITH UNIQUE CHARACTERS

Suppose we are looking for a search string S in another string T. A naïve algorithm would try to match all the characters in S to characters in T at each offset. The worst-case complexity of the naïve algorithm is $\Theta(|S| \cdot |T|)$—consider the case where S is $2n$ 0s and T is $n - 1$ 0s followed by a 1.

Problem 5.2: The worst-case behavior for the naïve algorithm requires many duplicated characters. Suppose no character occurs more than once in the search string. Devise an algorithm to efficiently search for all occurrences of the search string in the text string.

5.3 ROTATE A STRING

Let A be a string of length n. If we have enough memory to make a copy of A, rotating A by i positions is trivial; we just compute $B[j] = A[(i + j) \bmod n]$. If we are given only a constant amount of additional memory c, we can rotate the string by c positions a total of $k = \lceil \frac{n}{c} \rceil$ times but this increases the time complexity to $\Theta(n \cdot k)$.

Problem 5.3: Design a $\Theta(n)$ algorithm for rotating a string of n letters to the left by i positions. You are allowed only a constant number of bytes of additional storage.

5.4 TEST ROTATION

In Problem 5.3, we faced the problem of efficiently implementing rotation with a limited amount of memory. We now consider the problem of testing if one string is a rotation of another.

Problem 5.4: Develop a linear-time algorithm for checking if a string S is a cyclic rotation of another string R. (For example, *arc* is a cyclic rotation of *car*.)

5.5 NORMALIZE URLs

A URL is described canonically in the following way:
`<protocol>://<hostname>:[<port>]/<path>`
    There may be a number of different URL strings that are semantically equivalent. For example, `cnn.com` is equivalent to `http://cnn.com` and `http://www.ece.utexas.edu.//index.html` to `http://www.ece.utexas.edu`. Applications such as web search which deal with URLs need to perform transformations to a URL string to normalize it. The transformations may vary from application to application.

Problem 5.5: Implement a function which takes a URL as input and performs the following transformations on it: (1.) make hostname and protocol lowercase, (2.) if it ends in index.html or default.html, remove the filename, (3.) if protocol field is missing, add "http://" at the beginning, and (4.) replace consecutive '/' characters by a single '/' in the "path" segment of the URL.

5.6 LONGEST PALINDROME SUBSEQUENCE

A palindrome is a string which is equal to itself when reversed. For example, the human Y-chromosome contains a gene with the amino acid sequence $\langle C, A, C, A, A, T, T, C, C, C, A, T, G, G, G, T, T, G, T, G, G, A, G \rangle$, which includes the palindromic subsequences $\langle T, G, G, G, T \rangle$ and $\langle T, G, T \rangle$. Palindromic subsequences in DNA are significant because they influence the ability of the strand to loop back on itself.

Problem 5.6: Devise an efficient algorithm that takes a DNA sequence $D[1, \ldots, n]$ and returns the length of the longest palindromic subsequence.

5.7 PRETTY PRINTING

Consider the problem of arranging a piece of text in a fixed width font (i.e., each character has the same width) in a rectangular space. Breaking words across line boundaries is visually displeasing. If we avoid word breaking, then we may frequently be left with many spaces at the end of lines (since the next word will not fit in the remaining space). However if we are clever about where we break the lines, we can reduce this effect.

Problem 5.7: Given a long piece of text, decompose it into lines such that no word spans across two lines and the total wasted space at the end of each line is minimized.

5.8 EDIT DISTANCES

Spell checkers make suggestions for misspelled words. Given a misspelled string s, a spell checker should return words in the dictionary which are close to s.

One definition of closeness is the number of "edits" it would take to transform the misspelled word into a correct word, where a single edit is the deletion or insertion of a single character.

Problem 5.8: Given two strings A and B, compute the minimum number of edits needed to transform A into B.

5.9 REGULAR EXPRESSION MATCHING

A regular expression is a sequence of characters that defines a set of matching strings. For this problem, we define a simple subset of a full regular expression language:

- Alphabetical and numerical characters match themselves. For example, aW9 will match that string of 3 letters wherever it appears.
- The metacharacters ^ and $ stand for the beginning and end of the string. For example, ^aW9 matches aW9 only at the start of a string, aW9$ matches aW9 only at the end of a string, and ^aW9$ matches a string only if it is exactly equal to aW9.
- The metacharacter . matches any single character. For example, a.9 matches a89 and xyaW9123 but not aw89.
- The metacharacter * specifies a repetition of the single previous period or a literal character. For example, a.*9 matches aw89.

By definition, regular expression r matches string s if s contains a substring starting at any position matching r. For example, aW9 and a.9 match string xyaW9123 but ^aW9 does not.

Problem 5.9: Design an algorithm that takes strings s and r and returns if r matches s. (Assume r is a well-formed regular expression.)

Chapter 6

Intractability

All of the general methods presently known for computing the chromatic number of a graph, deciding whether a graph has a Hamiltonian circuit, or solving a system of linear inequalities in which the variables are constrained to be 0 or 1, require a combinatorial search for which the worst-case time requirement grows exponentially with the length of the input. In this paper, we give theorems which strongly suggest, but do not imply, that these problems, as well as many others, will remain intractable perpetually.

"Reducibility Among Combinatorial Problems," R. Karp, 1972

In engineering settings, you will sometimes encounter problems that can be directly solved using efficient textbook algorithms such as binary search and shortest paths. As we have seen in the earlier chapters, it is often difficult to identify such problems because the core algorithmic problem is obscured by details. More generally, you may encounter problems which can be transformed into equivalent problems which have an efficient textbook algorithm or problems which can be solved efficiently using meta-algorithms such as DP.

It is very often the case however that the problem you are given is intractable—i.e., there may not exist an efficient algorithm for the problem. Complexity theory addresses these problems—some have been proven to not have an efficient solution (such as checking the validity of relationships involving $\exists, +, <, \rightarrow$ on the integers) but the vast majority are only conjectured to be intractable. The CNF-SAT problem (*cf.* Prob-

Figure 5. $P = NP$, by XKCD

lem 6.5) is an example of a problem that is conjectured to be intractable.

When faced with a problem that appears to be intractable, the first thing to do is to prove intractability, typically by efficiently reducing a problem that is intractable to it. Often this reduction gives insight into the cause of intractability.

Unless you are a complexity theorist, proving a problem to be intractable is a starting point, not an end point. Remember something is a problem only if it has a solution. There are a number of approaches to solving intractable problems:

— Brute-force solutions which are typically exponential but may be acceptable, if the instances encountered are small.

— Branch-and-bound techniques which prune much of the complexity of a brute-force search.

— Approximation algorithms which return a solution that is provably close to optimum.

— Heuristics based on insight, common case analysis, and careful tuning that may solve the problem reasonably well.

— Parallel algorithms, wherein a large number of computers can work on subparts simultaneously.

6.1 0-1 KNAPSACK

A thief has to choose from n items. Item i can be sold for v_i dollars and weighs w_i pounds (v_i and w_i are integers). The thief wants to take as valuable a load as possible but he can carry at most W pounds in his knapsack.

Problem 6.1: Design an algorithm that will select a subset of items that has maximum value and weighs at most W pounds. (This problem is called the 0-1 knapsack problem because each item must either be taken or left behind—the thief cannot take a fractional amount of an item or take an item more than once.)

The following two problems exhibit structure that can be exploited to come up with fast algorithms that return a solution that is within a constant factor of the optimum (2 in both cases).

6.2   TRAVELING SALESMAN IN THE PLANE

Suppose a salesman needs to visit a set of cities $A_0, A_1, \ldots, A_{n-1}$. For any ordered pair of cities (A_i, A_j), there is a cost $c(A_i, A_j)$ of traveling from the first to the second city. We need to design a low cost tour for the salesman.

A tour is a sequence of cities $\langle B_0, B_1, \ldots, B_{n-1}, B_0 \rangle$. It can start at any city and the salesman can visit the cities in any order. All the cities must appear in the subsequence $\langle B_0, B_1, \ldots, B_{n-1} \rangle$. (Note that this implies that all the cities in this subsequence are distinct.)

The cost of the tour is the sum of the costs of the n successive pairs $(B_i, B_{i+1 \bmod n})$, $i = 0$ to $n - 1$.

Determining the minimum cost tour is a classic NP-complete problem and the problem remains hard even if we just ask for a tour whose cost is within a given multiple M of the minimum cost tour. However there is a special case for which this problem can be efficiently solved.

Problem 6.2: Suppose all the cities are located in some Euclidean space and the cost of traveling from one city to another is a constant multiple of the distance between the cities. Give an efficient procedure for computing a tour whose cost is guaranteed to be within a factor of two of the cost of an optimum tour.

6.3   FACILITY LOCATION PROBLEM

Let $A_0, \ldots, A_{n-1}$ be a set of n cities. We are trying to select k cities to locate warehouses. We want to choose the k cities in such a way that the cities are close to the warehouses. Let's say we define the cost of a warehouse assignment to be the maximum distance of any city to a warehouse.

The problem of finding a warehouse assignment that has the minimum cost is known to be NP-complete.

Problem 6.3: Design a fast algorithm for selecting warehouse locations that is provably within a constant factor of the optimum solution.

The following two problems are best solved using branch-and-bound with intelligent bounding and branch selection.

6.4 COMPUTING x^n

A straight-line program for computing x^n is a finite sequence

$$x \mapsto x^{i_1} \mapsto x^{i_2} \mapsto \cdots \mapsto x^n$$

constructed as follows: the first element is x; each succeeding element is either the square of some previously computed element or the product of any two previously computed elements. The number of multiplications to evaluate x^n is the number of terms in the shortest such program sequence minus one. No efficient method is known for the problem of determining the minimum number of multiplications needed to evaluate x^n; the problem for multiple exponents is known to be NP-complete.

Problem 6.4: How would you determine the minimum number of multiplications to evaluate x^{30}?

6.5 CNF-SAT

The CNF-SAT problem was defined in Problem 4.24. In that problem, we asked for a linear-time algorithm for the special case where each clause had exactly two literals.

Problem 6.5: Design an algorithm for CNF-SAT. Your algorithm should use branch-and-bound to prune partial assignments that can easily be shown to be unsatisfiable.

The following problems illustrate the use of heuristic search and pruning principles.

6.6 SCHEDULING

We need to schedule N lectures in M classrooms. Some of those lectures are prerequisites for others.

Problem 6.6: How would you choose when and where to hold the lectures in order to finish all the lectures as soon as possible?

6.7 HARDY-RAMANUJAN NUMBER

The mathematician G. H. Hardy was on his way to visit his collaborator S. Ramanujan who was in the hospital. Hardy remarked to Ramanujan that he traveled in taxi cab number 1729 which seemed a dull one and he hoped it was not a bad omen. To this, Ramanujan replied that 1729 was a very interesting number—it was the smallest number expressible as the sum of cubes of two numbers in two different ways. Indeed, $10^3 + 9^3 = 12^3 + 1^3 = 1729$.

Problem 6.7: Given an arbitrary positive integer n, how would you determine if it can be expressed as a sum of two cubes?

6.8 COLLATZ CONJECTURE

Lothar Collatz proposed this remarkable conjecture in 1937: "Define C : $\{1, 2, 3, \ldots, \} \mapsto \{1, 2, 3, \ldots, \}$ as follows: if n is even, $C(n) = n/2$, else $C(n) = 3n + 1$. Then for any choice of n, $C^i(n) = 1$, for some i".

For example, if we start with the number 11 and iteratively compute $C^i(11)$, we get the sequence $11, 34, 17, 52, 26, 13, 40, 20, 10, 5, 16, 8, 4, 2, 1$.

Despite intense efforts, the Collatz conjecture has not been proved or disproved.

Suppose you are given the task of proving or disproving the Collatz conjecture for the first billion integers. A direct approach would be to compute the convergence sequence for each number in this set.

Problem 6.8: How would you prove that Collatz hypothesis works for at least the first N integers? What is the runtime of your algorithm?

The following problems have the property that they can, in principle, both be solved in polynomial time. However the polynomial time solutions are not straightforward and in the context of an interview, a heuristic solution may be preferable.

6.9 NEAREST POINTS IN THE PLANE

Instead of having single integers in the array, if you have integral points in a two-dimensional plane, the problem of finding a closest pair of points becomes significantly more difficult. There are fast exact algorithms for this problem but they are tricky to analyze and implement. Can you design a heuristic for identifying the closest pair of points?

Problem 6.9: You are given a list of pairs of points in the two-dimensional Cartesian plane. Each point has integer x and y coordinates. How would you find the two closest points?

6.10 PRIMALITY CHECKING

Primality checking has received a great deal of attention from mathematicians and theoretical computer scientists and there are a number of highly sophisticated approaches to efficiently solving this problem. One reason for this is that number theory plays a key role in cryptography.

The brute-force approach to checking if n is a prime is to divide n by every smaller number. The size of input here is the number of bits in n and hence the brute-force algorithm has exponential time complexity.

In an interview context, if you are asked to implement primality checking, you are just expected to provide some simple improvements over the basic brute-force approach.

Problem 6.10: Implement a function which takes a number n and returns whether the number is prime or not. What is the runtime of your algorithm?

Chapter 7

Parallel Computing

> The activity of a computer must include the proper reacting to a possibly great variety of messages that can be sent to it at unpredictable moments, a situation which occurs in process control, traffic control, stock control, banking applications, automization of information flow in large organizations, centralized computer service and, finally, all information systems in which a number of computers are coupled to each other.
>
> ───────────────────────────────
> "Cooperating sequential processes," E. Dijkstra, 1965

Parallel computation has become increasingly common. For example, laptops and desktops come with multicore processors in which each core is a complete processor and accesses shared memory. High-end computation is often performed using clusters consisting of individual computers communicating through a network. Parallelism provides a number of benefits:

- High performance—more processors working on a task (usually) means it is completed faster.
- Better use of resources—a program can execute while another waits on the disk or network.
- Fairness—letting different users or programs share a machine rather than have one program run at a time to completion.
- Convenience—it is often conceptually more straightforward to accomplish a task using a set of concurrent programs for the subtasks rather than have a single program manage all the subtasks.

Parallelism can also be used for fault tolerance—for example, if a machine fails in a cluster that is serving web pages, the others can take over.

Concrete applications of parallel computing include graphic user interfaces (a dedicated thread handles UI actions resulting in increased responsiveness), Java virtual machines (a separate thread handles garbage collection which would otherwise lead to blocking), web servers (a single logical thread handles a single client request), scientific computing (a large matrix multiplication can be split across a cluster), and web search (multiple machines crawl, index, and retrieve web pages).

There are two primary models for parallel computation—the shared memory model, in which each processor can access any location in memory and the distributed memory model, in which a processor must explicitly send a message to another processor to access its memory. The former is more appropriate in the multicore setting and the latter is more accurate for a cluster. The questions in this chapter target a shared memory model. We cover some problems related to the distributed memory model such as leader election and host discovery as well as applications such as web search in Chapter 8.

Writing correct parallel programs is challenging because of the subtle interactions between parallel components. One of the key challenges is races—two concurrent instruction sequences access the same address in memory and at least one of them writes to that address. Other challenges to correctness are starvation (a processor needs a resource but never gets it, e.g., Problem 7.5), deadlock (A and B acquire resources M and N respectively and then try to acquire N and M respectively, e.g., Problem 7.10), and livelock (a processor keeps retrying an operation that always fails). Bugs caused by these issues are very difficult to find using testing; debugging them is also very difficult because they may not be reproducible since they are load dependent. It is also often true that it is not possible to realize the performance implied by parallelism—sometimes a critical task cannot be parallelized, making it impossible to improve performance, regardless of the number of processors added. Similarly, the overhead of communicating intermediate results between processors can exceed the performance benefits.

7.1 SERVLET WITH CACHING

Problem 7.1: Design a servlet which implements an online spell correction suggester. Specifically, it takes as input a string s and computes an array of entries in its dictionary which are closest to the string using the edit distance specified in Problem 5.8.

Since computing the edit distances s to each entry in the dictionary is time consuming, you should implement a caching strategy. Specifically, cache the most recently computed result.

7.2   THREAD POOLS

The following class, `SimpleWebServer`, implements part of a simple HTTP server:

```
1   public class SimpleWebServer {
2     final static int PORT = 8080;
3     public static void main (String [] args) throws IOException
          {
4       ServerSocket serversock = new ServerSocket(PORT);
5       for (;;) {
6         Socket sock = serversock.accept();
7         ProcessReq(sock);
8       }
9     }
10  }
```

Problem 7.2: Suppose you find that `SimpleWebServer` has poor performance because `processReq` frequently blocks on IO. What steps could you take to improve `SimpleWebServer`'s performance?

7.3   ASYNCHRONOUS CALLBACKS

It is common in a distributed computing environment for the responses to not return in the same order as the requests were made. One way to handle this is through an "asynchronous callback"—a method to be invoked on response.

Problem 7.3: Implement a `Requestor` class. The class has to implement a `Dispatch` method which takes a `Requestor` object. The `Requestor` object includes a `request` string, a `ProcessResponse(string response)` method, and an `Execute` method that takes a string and returns a string.

Dispatch is to create a new thread which invokes `Execute` on `request`. When `Execute` returns, `Dispatch` invokes the `ProcessResponse` method on the response.

The `Execute` method may take an indeterminate amount of time to return; it may never return. You need to have a time-out mechanism for this: assume the `Requestor` objects have an `Error` method that you can invoke.

7.4   TIMER

Consider a web-based calendar in which the server hosting the calendar has to perform a task when the next calendar event takes place. (The task could be sending an email or an SMS.) Your job is to design a facility that manages the execution of such tasks.

Problem 7.4: Develop a `Timer` class that manages the execution of deferred tasks. Specifically, at creation, the constructor of `Timer` is passed an object which includes a `Run` method and a `name` field (which is a string). The `Timer` class must support—(1.) starting a thread at a given time in the future; the thread is identified by name and (2.) canceling a thread with a given name (you can ignore the request if the thread has already started).

7.5 READERS-WRITERS

Consider an object s which is read from and written to by many threads. (For example, s could be the cache from Problem 7.1.) You need to ensure that no thread may access s for reading or writing while another thread is writing to s. (Two or more readers may access s at the same time.)

One way to achieve this is by protecting s with a mutex that ensures that no thread can access s at the same time as another writer. However this solution is suboptimal because it is possible that a reader $R1$ has locked s and another reader $R2$ wants to access s. There is no need to make $R2$ wait until $R1$ is done reading; instead, $R2$ should start reading right away.

This motivates the first readers-writers problem: protect s with the added constraint that no reader is to be kept waiting if s is currently opened for reading.

Problem 7.5: Implement a synchronization mechanism for the first readers-writers problem.

7.6 READERS-WRITERS WITH WRITE PREFERENCE

Suppose we have an object s as in Problem 7.5. In the solution to Problem 7.5, a reader $R1$ may have the lock; if a writer W is waiting for the lock and then a reader $R2$ requests access, $R2$ will be given priority over W. If this happens often enough, W will starve. Instead, suppose we want W to start as soon as possible.

This motivates the second readers-writers problem: protect s with "writer-preference", i.e., no writer, once added to the queue, is to be kept waiting longer than absolutely necessary.

Problem 7.6: Implement a synchronization mechanism for the second readers-writers problem.

7.7 READERS-WRITERS WITH FAIRNESS

The specifications to both Problems 7.5 and 7.6 can lead to starvation—the first may starve writers and the second may starve readers. The third readers-writers problem adds the constraint that no thread shall be allowed to starve—the operation of obtaining a lock on s always terminates in a bounded amount of time.

Problem 7.7: Implement a synchronization mechanism for the third readers-writers problem. It is acceptable (indeed necessary) that in this solution, both readers and writers have to wait longer than absolutely necessary. (Readers may wait even if s is opened for read and writers may wait even if no one else has a lock on s.)

7.8   PRODUCER-CONSUMER QUEUE

Two threads, the producer P and the consumer Q, share a fixed length array of strings A. The producer generates strings one at a time which it writes into A; the consumer removes strings from A, one at a time.

Problem 7.8: Design a synchronization mechanism for A which ensures that P does not attempt to add a string into the array if it is full and C does not try to remove data from an empty buffer.

7.9   BARBER SHOP

Consider a barber shop with a single barber B, one barber chair, and n chairs for customers who are waiting for their turn for a haircut. If there are no customers, the barber sleeps in his chair. On entering, a customer either awakens the barber or if the barber is cutting someone else's hair, he sits down in one of the chairs for waiting customers. If all of the waiting chairs are taken, the newly arrived customer simply leaves.

Problem 7.8: Assume there is a thread for each customer and for the barber. Model the system using semaphores and mutexes to ensure correct behavior.

7.10   DINING PHILOSOPHERS

In the dining philosophers problem n threads, numbered 0 to $n - 1$, run concurrently. There are n resources, numbered 0 to $n - 1$. Thread i requires resources i and $i + 1 \mod n$ before it can invoke a method m. (The problem gets its name because it models n philosophers sitting at a round table, alternating between thinking, eating, and waiting. There is a single chopstick between each pair of philosophers. To eat, a philosopher must hold two chopsticks—one placed immediately to his left and one immediately to his right.)

Problem 7.10: Implement a synchronization mechanism for the dining philosophers problem.

Chapter 8

Design Problems

> We have described a simple but very powerful and flexible protocol which provides for variation in individual network packet sizes, transmission failures, sequencing, flow control, and the creation and destruction of process-to-process associations.

> "A Protocol for Packet Network Intercommunication," V. Cerf and R. Kahn, 1974

This chapter is concerned with system design problems. Each question can be a large open-ended software project. During the interview, you should provide a high level sketch of such a system with thoughts on various design choices, the tradeoffs, key algorithms, and the data-structures involved.

8.1 MOSAIC

One popular form of computer art is photomosaics where you are given a collection of images called "tiles". Then given a target image, you want to build another image which closely approximates the target image but is actually built by juxtaposing the tiles. Here the quality of approximation is mostly defined by human perception. It is often the case that with a given set of tiles, a user may want to build several mosaics.

Problem 8.1: How would you design a software that produces high quality mosaics with minimal compute time?

8.2   SEARCH ENGINE

Modern keyword-based search engines maintain a collection of several billion documents. One of the key computations performed by a search engine is to retrieve all the documents that contain the keywords contained in a given query. This is a nontrivial task because it must be done within few tens of milliseconds.

In this problem, we consider a smaller version of the problem where the collection of documents can fit within the RAM of a single computer.

Problem 8.2: Given a million documents with an average size of 10 kilobytes, design a program that can efficiently return the subset of documents containing a given set of words.

8.3   IP FORWARDING

There are many applications where instead of an exact match of strings, we are looking for a prefix match, i.e., given a set of strings and a search string, we want to find a string from the set that is a prefix of the search string. One application of this is Internet Protocol (IP) route lookup problem. When an IP packet arrives at a router, the router looks up the next hop for the packet by searching the destination IP address of the packet in its routing table. The routing table is specified as a set of prefixes on the IP address and the router is supposed to identify the longest matching prefix. If this task is to be performed only once, it is impossible to do better than testing each prefix. However an Internet core router needs to lookup millions of destination addresses on the set of prefixes every second. Hence it can be advantageous to do some precomputation.

Problem 8.3: You are given a large set of strings S in advance. Given a query string Q, how would you design a system that can identify the longest string $p \in S$ that is a prefix of Q?

8.4   SPELL CHECKER

Designing a good spelling correction system can be challenging. We discussed spelling correction in the context of the edit distance (Problem 5.8). However in that problem, we just considered the problem of computing the edit distance between a pair of strings. A spell checker must find a set of words that are closest to a given word from the entire dictionary. Furthermore, edit distance may not be the right distance function when performing spelling correction—it does not take into account the commonly misspelled words or the proximity of letters on a keyboard.

Problem 8.4: How would you build a spelling correction system?

8.5 STEMMING

When a user submits the query "computation" to a search engine, it is quite possible he might be interested in documents containing the words "computers", "compute", and "computing" also. If you have several keywords in a query, it becomes difficult to search for all combinations of all variants of the words in the query.

One way to solve this problem is to reduce all variants of a given word to one common root, both in the query string and in the documents. This process is called stemming. An example of stemming would be $\{computers, computer, compute\} \mapsto comput$. It is almost impossible to succinctly capture all possible variants of all words in the English language but a few simple rules can get us a majority of the cases.

Problem 8.5: Design a stemming algorithm that runs fast and does a reasonable job.

8.6 DISTRIBUTED THROTTLING

Let's say you have N machines crawling the world wide web such that the responsibility for a given URL is assigned to the crawler with id equal to Hash(URL) mod N. Downloading a page takes away bandwidth from the server hosting it. Therefore you want to ensure that in any given minute, your crawlers never request more than B bytes from any host.

Problem 8.6: How would you implement crawling under such a constraint?

8.7 IMPLEMENT PAGERANK

PageRank algorithm assigns a rank to web pages based on the number of important pages link to this page. The algorithm essentially amounts to the following:
   1. Build a matrix A based on the hyperlink structure of the web with $A_{ij} = \frac{1}{d_i}$ if there is a link for webpage i to webpage j, and d_i is the total number of unique outgoing links from page i.
   2. Solve for X satisfying

$$X = \epsilon \cdot [\mathbf{1}] + (1 - \epsilon) A^T \cdot X.$$

Here ϵ is a scalar constant (e.g., $\frac{1}{7}$) and $[\mathbf{1}]$ represents a column vector of 1s. The value $X[i]$ is the rank of the i-th page.

The most commonly used approach to solving the above equation is to start with a value of X, where each component is $\frac{1}{n}$ (where n is the number of pages) and then perform the following iteration:

$$X_k = \epsilon \cdot [\mathbf{1}] + (1 - \epsilon) A^T \cdot X_{k-1}.$$

Problem 8.7: How would you design a system that can compute the ranks for a collection of a billion web pages in a reasonable amount of time?

8.8   SCALABLE PRIORITY SYSTEM

Maintaining priority in a distributed system can be tricky. Consider the crawlers for a search engine visiting web pages in some prioritized order or event driven simulation in molecular dynamics. In both cases, we could be dealing with billions of entities with a given priority and we need to do three things efficiently: (1.) find the highest priority entity, (2.) insert new entities with a given priority, and (3.) delete certain entities specified by a unique id.

Problem 8.8: How would you design a system that can implement these requirements when the data cannot fit into a single machine's memory?

8.9   LATENCY REDUCTION

The Pareto distribution is defined as follows:

$$P[X > x] \;=\; 1 - \left(\frac{x_m}{x}\right)^{\alpha}, \text{ if } x > x_m$$
$$=\; 1 \text{ if } x \le x_m.$$

Here α and x_m are parameters of the distribution. It is one of the heavy-tailed distributions that commonly occur in various workloads.

Suppose you are running a service on k servers and that any service request can be processed by any of the servers. A given server can process only one request at a time. Depending on the request r, a server may take time $t(r)$, where $t(r)$ follows a Pareto distribution.

Problem 8.9: You have a service level agreement with your clients which requires that 99% of the requests are serviced in less than one second. How would you design the system to meet this requirement with minimal cost?

8.10   ONLINE ADVERTISING SYSTEM

Jingle, a search engine startup, wants to monetize its search results by displaying advertisements alongside search results.

Problem 8.10: Design an online advertising system for Jingle.

8.11 RECOMMENDATION SYSTEM

Jingle wants to generate more page views on its news site. One idea the product manager has is to put in a sidebar of clickable snippets from articles that are likely to be of interest to the reader.

Problem 8.11: Design a system that automatically generates the sidebar.

8.12 ONLINE POKER

Clump Enterprises has a large number of casinos. Their CEO wants to create a website by which gamblers can play poker online.

Problem 8.12: Design an online poker playing service for Clump Enterprises.

8.13 DRIVING DIRECTIONS

As a part of their charter to collect all the information in the world and make it universally accessible, Jingle wants to develop a driving directions service. Users enter a start and finish address; driving directions service returns directions.

Problem 8.13: Design a driving directions service with a web interface.

8.14 ISBN CACHE

The International Standard Book Number (ISBN) is a unique commercial book identifier based on the 9-digit standard book numbering code developed by Professor Gordon Foster from Trinity University, Dublin. The 10-digit ISBN was ratified by the ISO in 1974; since 2007, ISBNs have contained 13 digits. The last digit in a 10-digit ISBN is the check digit—it is the sum of the first 9 digits, modulo 11; a 10 is represented by an X. For 13 digit ISBNs, the last digit is also a check digit but is guaranteed to be between 0 and 9.

Problem 8.14: Implement a cache for looking up prices of books identified by their ISBN. Use the least-recently-used strategy for cache eviction policy.

8.15 DISTRIBUTING LARGE FILES

Jingle is developing a search feature for breaking news. New articles are collected from a variety of online news sources such as newspapers, bulletin boards, blogs, etc. by a single lab machine at Jingle. Every minute, roughly one thousand articles are posted and each article is a 100 kilobytes in size.

Jingle would like to serve these articles from a datacenter consisting of a thousand servers. For performance reasons, each server should have a copy of articles that were recently added. The datacenter is far away from the lab machine.

Problem 8.15: Suggest an efficient way of getting the articles added in the past five minutes from the lab machine to the servers.

8.16 LEADER ELECTION

You are to devise a protocol by which a collection of hosts on the Internet can elect a leader. Hosts can communicate with each other using TCP connections. For host A to communicate with host B, it needs to know B's IP address. Each host starts off with a set of IP addresses and the protocol code that you implement that will run on a fixed port across all the hosts.

Problem 8.16: Devise a protocol by which hosts can elect a unique leader from all the hosts participating in the protocol. The protocol should be fast, in that it converges quickly; it should be efficient, in that it should not involve too many connections, too many data exchanges, and too much data exchanged.

8.17 HOST DISCOVERY

You are to devise a protocol by which a collection of hosts on the Internet can discover each other. Hosts can communicate with each other using TCP connections. For host A to communicate with host B, it needs to know B's IP address.

Each host starts off with a set of IP addresses and the protocol code that you implement which will run on a fixed port across all the hosts.

Problem 8.17: Devise a protocol by which hosts can discover all the hosts participating in the protocol. The protocol should be fast and efficient like in Problem 8.16.

Chapter 9

Discrete Mathematics

There is required, finally, the ratio between the fluxion of any quantity x you will and the fluxion of its power x^n. Let x flow till it becomes $x + o$ and resolve the power $(x + o)^n$ into the infinite series

$$x^n + nox^{n-1} + \tfrac{1}{2}(n^2 - n)o^2 x^{n-2} + \tfrac{1}{6}(n^3 - 3n^2 + 2n)o^3 x^{n-3} \cdots$$

"On the Quadrature of Curves," I. Newton, 1693

Discrete mathematics comes up in algorithm design in many places such as combinatorial optimization, complexity analysis, and probability estimation. Discrete mathematics is also the source of some of the most fun puzzles and interview questions. The solutions can range from simple application of the pigeon-hole principle to complex inductive reasoning.

Some of the problems in this chapter fall into the category of brain teasers where all you need is one *aha* moment to solve the problem. Such problems have fallen out of fashion because it is hard to judge a candidate's ability based on whether he is able to make a tricky observation in a short period of time. However they are asked enough times that we feel it is important to cover them. Also, these problems are quite a lot of fun to solve.

9.1 COMPUTING THE BINOMIAL COEFFICIENTS

The symbol $\binom{n}{k}$ is short form for $\frac{n(n-1)\dots(n-k+1)}{k(k-1)\dots3\cdot2\cdot1}$. It is the number of ways to choose a k-element subset from an n-element set.

It is not obvious that the expression defining $\binom{n}{k}$ always yields an integer. Furthermore, direct computation of $\binom{n}{k}$ from this expression quickly results in the numerator or denominator overflowing if integer types are used, even if the final result fits in an integer. If floats are used, the expression may not yield an integer.

Problem 9.1: Design an efficient algorithm for computing $\binom{n}{k}$ that has the property that it never overflows if $\binom{n}{k}$ can be represented as an `int`; assume n and k are `ints`.

9.2   CLIMBING STAIRS

You are climbing a staircase with N steps. Every time you can jump over either one step or two steps.

Problem 9.2: How many ways are there to get to the top of the staircase?

9.3   RAMSEY THEORY

In 1930, Frank Ramsey wrote a paper titled "On a problem in formal logic" which initiated an entirely new field of discrete mathematics called "Ramsey Theory" in his honor. He proved what is now called Ramsey's theorem as an intermediate lemma in a bigger proof. The problem below illustrates Ramsey's theorem.

Problem 9.3: There are six guests at a party such that any two guests either know each other or do not know each other. Prove that there is a subset of three guests who either all know each other or all do not know each other.

9.4   500 DOORS

There are 500 closed doors off a corridor. A person walks through the corridor and opens each door. Another person walks through the corridor and closes every alternate door. Continuing in this manner, the i-th person comes and toggles the position of every i-th door starting from door i.

Problem 9.4: How many doors will be open at the end after the 500-th person has passed through the doors?

9.5   HEIGHT DETERMINATION

You are given a number of identical balls and a building with N floors. You know that there is an integer $X < N$ such that the ball will break if it is dropped from any floor X or higher but will remain intact if dropped from a floor below X.

Problem 9.5: Given K balls and N floors, what is the minimum number of ball drops that are required to determine X in the worst-case?

9.6 BETTING ON CARD COLORS

A deck of 52 playing cards is shuffled. The deck is placed face-down on a table. You can place a bet on the color of the top card at even odds. After you have placed your bet, the card is revealed to you and discarded. Betting continues till the deck is exhausted. On any card, you can bet any amount from 0 to all the money you have and the odds are always even.

Problem 9.6: You begin with one dollar. It is known that if you can bet arbitrary fractions of the money you have, the maximum amount of money that you guarantee you can win, regardless of the order in which the cards appear, is $2^{52}/\binom{52}{26} \approx 9.08132955$. However you are allowed to bet only in penny increments. Write a program to compute a tight lower bound on the amount you can win under this restriction.

Invariants

The following problem was popular at interviews in the early 1990s: you are given a chessboard with two squares at the opposite ends of a diagonal removed, leaving 62 squares. You are given 31 rectangular dominoes. Each can cover exactly two squares. How would you cover all the 62 squares with the dominoes?

It is easy to spend hours trying unsuccessfully to find such a covering. This will teach you that a problem may be intentionally worded to mislead you into following a futile path.

There is a simple argument that no covering exists—the two squares removed will always have the same color, so there will be either 30 black and 32 white squares to be covered or 32 black and 30 white squares to be covered. Each domino will cover one black and one white square, so the number of black and white squares covered as you successively put down the dominoes is equal. Hence it is impossible to cover the given chessboard.

This proof of impossibility is an example of invariant analysis. An invariant is a function of the state of a system being analyzed that remains constant in the presence of (possibly restricted) updates to the state. Invariant analysis is particularly powerful at proving impossibility results as we just saw with the chessboard tiling problem. The challenge is finding a simple invariant.

Let's consider a more sophisticated example now, namely the MU puzzle. The following rules may be applied to transform a string over the alphabet $\{M,I,U\}$:

1. If a string ends with an I, a U may be appended ($xI \mapsto xIU$). For example—MI to MIU.
2. A string after a starting M may be completely duplicated ($Mx \mapsto Mxx$). For example—MIU to $MIUIU$.
3. Three consecutive Is (III) may be replaced with a single U ($xIIIy \mapsto xUy$). For example—$MIIIU$ to MUU.
4. Two consecutive Us may be removed ($xUUy \mapsto xy$). For example—$MUUII$ to MII.

Problem: Is it possible to convert MI into MU by repeated application of these four transformation rules?

You can try different strategies to find the right sequence of transformations and after a while you may begin to suspect that it is impossible to perform this conversion. Showing that no sequence of transformations will implement the transformation seems daunting at first—after all, there are infinitely many transformations. However consider the following invariant: the number of Is in any string s derived from MI is never a multiple of three.

We prove the invariant by induction on the number of transformations performed on MI. For the base case, MI has 1 I, which is not a multiple of three.

For the inductive step, transformations 1 and 4 do not change the number of Is, so induction goes through in this case. The number of Is after application of transformation 2 is twice the number of Is. So, if the number of Is was not a multiple of three, i.e., was of the form $3 \cdot n + 1$ or $3 \cdot n + 2$, then the number of Is after transformation 2 is either $2 \cdot (3 \cdot n + 1) = 3 \cdot (2 \cdot n) + 2$ or $2 \cdot (3 \cdot n + 2) = 3 \cdot (2 \cdot n + 1) + 1$, neither of which is a multiple of 3. Transformation 3 reduces the number of Is by three and induction goes through in this case too.

Since MU has 0 Is, which is a multiple of three, it is impossible to get from MI to MU.

9.7   EVEN OR ODD

Let A be a multiset of integers. Consider the following process: randomly select two elements of A. If they are both even or both odd, remove them from the set and insert a new even integer; if not, remove just the even integer.

Problem 9.7: What can you say about the last remaining integer as a function of the numbers of even and odd integers initially in A?

9.8 GASSING UP

Consider a circular route that connects n cities. You need to visit all the n cities and come back to the starting city. In each city, a certain amount of gasoline is kept for you such that the total amount of gasoline on the route is exactly equal to the amount of gasoline needed to go around the circular route once.

Problem 9.8: Is it always possible to find a starting point on the route such that you can start there with an empty tank and complete the route? How can you efficiently find this city?

9.9 COMMON KNOWLEDGE

An explorer comes to an island with 100 inhabitants. Exactly half the inhabitants have blue eyes and half the inhabitants have green eyes. The green eyes are indicative of a disease that brings all the island inhabitants in danger. There is an understanding on the island that whenever someone learns that they have green eyes, they must leave the island; they never leave the island for any other reason. The inhabitants are too polite to inform anyone else of eye color. There are no other means for the inhabitants to observe the color of their eyes on the island.

The inhabitants assemble each day at exactly 9:00 AM, they see each other, and then go back to their own houses. They never see anyone else for the rest of the day. Furthermore, they are capable of instant logical reasoning.

The explorer visits one of their daily assemblies and says, "That's interesting—some of you have blue eyes and some of you have green eyes".

Problem 9.9: What would follow after this event? In particular, why does this observation sadden the inhabitants?

The explorer seems to have added no new knowledge to the system since each inhabitant can already tell that amongst the inhabitants, some have blue eyes and some have green eyes.

9.10 HERSHEY BAR

A Hershey bar is modeled as $m \times n$ rectangle of $m \cdot n$ pieces. You can take a bar and break it along a horizontal or vertical axis into two bars.

Problem 9.10: How would you break a 4×4 bar into 16 pieces using as few breaks as possible?

9.11 $n \times n$ CHOMP

Consider an $n \times n$ rectangle in the upper right quadrant in the Cartesian plane, with the lower leftmost point at $(0,0)$. The block $(0,0)$ is known to contain poison. Two players take turns at taking a bite out of the rectangle. A bite removes a square and all squares above and to the right. The first player to eat the square at $(0,0)$ loses.

Problem 9.11: Assuming the players have infinite computational resources at their disposal, who will win the game?

9.12 $n \times 2$ CHOMP

Solve Problem 9.11 if the rectangle is of dimension $n \times 2$.

Problem 9.12: Assuming the players have infinite computational resources at their disposal, who will win the game?

9.13 $m \times n$ CHOMP

Solve Problem 9.11 if the rectangle is of dimension $m \times n$.

Problem 9.13: Assuming the players have infinite computational resources at their disposal, who will win the game?

9.14 PICKING UP COINS–I

There are fifty coins in a line—these could be pennies, nickels, dimes, or quarters. Two players, F and S, take turns at choosing one coin each—they can only choose from the two coins at the ends of the line. The game ends when all the coins have been picked up. The player whose coins have the higher total value wins. Each player must select a coin when it is his turn, so the game ends in fifty turns.

Problem 9.14: If you want to ensure you do not lose, would you rather be F or S?

9.15 PICKING UP COINS–II

Problem 9.14 does not ask for the optimum profit. Let's explore the strategies that would maximize the winnings.

Problem 9.15: Derive an efficient algorithm for computing the maximum amount of money F can win.

9.16   SPACE-TIME INTERSECTIONS

Adam starts climbing a mountain at 9:00 AM on Saturday. He reaches the summit at 5:00 PM. He camps at the summit overnight and descends the mountain on Sunday. He begins and ends at the same time and follows exactly the same route. His speeds may vary and he may take breaks at different places.

Problem 9.16: Prove that there is a time and a place such that Adam is at exactly the same place at the same time on Saturday as he is on Sunday.

Chapter 10

Probability

Therefore, that will be the most
probable system of values of
the unknown quantities
p, q, r, s, etc., in which the sum
of the squares of the differences
between the observed and
computed values of the
functions V, V', V'', etc. is a
minimum, if the same degree of
accuracy is presumed in all the
observations.

"Theory Of The Motion Of The
Heavenly Bodies Moving
About The Sun In Conic
Sections," C. Gauss, 1809

Probability comes often in algorithms and software engineering, either
when you are trying to model a random event, such as a client request
or design an efficient algorithm, such as Quicksort. Given the richness of
the subject, it provides a large number of interesting puzzles and interview questions.

To a first approximation, a probability measure is a function p from
subsets of a set E of events to $[0, 1]$ that has the properties that $p(E) = 1$
and $p(A \cup B) = p(A) + p(B)$ for disjoint A and B. Various properties and
notations can be given around these concepts. For example, it is easy to
prove that $p(A \cup B) = p(A) + p(B) - p(A \cap B)$.

A random variable X is a function from E to $(-\infty, \infty)$; it can be identified with a cumulative distribution function $F_X : \Re \mapsto [0, 1]$, where
$f_X(\tau) = p(X^{-1}((-\infty, \tau]))$. When X takes a finite or countable set of val-

ues, we can talk about the probability of X taking a particular value, i.e., $p(X = \tau_i)$. If X takes a continuous range of values and F_X is differentiable, we talk of $f_X(\tau) = \frac{dF_X}{d\tau}$ as being the probability density function.

The expected value $E[X]$ of a random variable X taking a finite set of values $T = \{\tau_0, \tau_1, \ldots, \tau_{n-1}\}$ is simply $\sum_{\tau_i \in T} \tau_i \cdot p(X = \tau_i)$, i.e., it is the average value of X, weighted by probabilities. The notion of expectation generalizes to countable sets of values. For a random variable taking a continuous set of values, the sum is replaced with an integral and the weighting function is the probability density function. The variance $\text{var}(X)$ of a random variable X is the expected value of $(|X - E[X])^2$. Some of the key results in probability have to do with bounds on the probability of events, e.g., the Chebyshev bound which says that $Pr\left(|X - E[X]| \geq k\sqrt{\text{var}(X)}\right) \leq \frac{1}{k^2}$.

There are a number of famous classes of random variables–the Bernoulli random variable takes only two values, 0 and 1; it is used, for example, in modeling coin tosses. The Poisson random variable takes nonnegative values—it models the number of events in a fixed period of time, e.g., the number of HTTP requests in a minute. The Gaussian random variable takes all real values—the sum of a series of identically distributed independent random variables tends to Gaussian.

For the most part, probability corresponds to our intuition; there are however notable exceptions. For example, at first glance, it would seem impossible for there to exists three 6-sided dice A, B, C such that A is more likely to roll a higher number than B, B is more likely to roll a higher number than C, and C is more likely to roll a higher number than A. However if A has sides $2, 2, 4, 4, 9, 9$, B has sides $1, 1, 6, 6, 8, 8$, and dice C has sides $3, 3, 5, 5, 7, 7$, then the probability that A rolls a higher number than B is $\frac{5}{9}$, the probability that B rolls a higher number than C is $\frac{5}{9}$, and the probability that C rolls a higher number than A is $\frac{5}{9}$.

10.1 OFFLINE SAMPLING

Let A be an array of n distinct elements. We want to compute a random subset of k elements.

Problem 10.1: Design an algorithm that returns a subset of k elements; all subsets should be equally likely. Use as few calls to the random number generator as possible and use only $O(1)$ additional storage. (You can return the result in the same array as input.)

10.2 RESERVOIR SAMPLING

You are building a packet sniffer for your network that should be able to provide a uniform sample of packets for any network session. You always want to get k packets irrespective of the length (assuming each session is longer than k).

Problem 10.2: Compute a random subset of size k from a set of unknown size which is presented as a sequence of elements.

10.3 ONLINE SAMPLING

Compute a random subset of size k from the integers in the interval $[0, n-1]$. You should return the result in an array of length k. You may use only constant additional storage. All subsets should be equally likely and all permutations of the array should be equally likely.

10.4 RANDOM PERMUTATIONS—1

Consider estimating the probability of winning a game of blackjack, assuming the cards were shuffled perfectly uniformly before dealing hands and everyone is playing rationally. One way to do this would be to generate a few random permutations and compute the chances of winning in each case where you are dealt the given cards. Here it would be important that the process you use to generate a random permutation can generate any permutation with equal probability. This can be tricky.

Problem 10.4: Does the following process yield a uniformly random permutation of A? "For $i \in \{1, 2, \ldots, n\}$, swap $A[i]$ with a randomly chosen element of A." (The randomly chosen element could be i itself.)

10.5 RANDOM PERMUTATIONS—2

In Problem 10.4, we saw that generating random permutations is not as straightforward as it seems.

Problem 10.5: Design an algorithm that creates random permutations of $\{1, 2, \ldots, n\}$. Each permutation should be equally likely. You are given a random number generation function; use as few calls to it as possible.

10.6 FORMING A TRIANGLE FROM RANDOM LENGTHS

Suppose you pick two numbers $u1$ and $u2$ uniformly randomly and independently in the interval $[0, 1]$. These numbers divide the interval into three segments—the first of length $\min(u1, u2)$, the second of length $\max(u1, u2) - \min(u1, u2)$, and the third of length $1 - \max(u1, u2)$. What is the probability that these three segments can be assembled into a triangle?

Repeat the computation for the case where we pick $u1$ uniformly randomly from $[0, 1]$ and then $u2$ uniformly randomly from $[1 - u1, 1]$.

Can you determine which of the above two methods of generating u_1 and u_2 is more likely to produce a triangle without computing the exact probabilities?

10.7 BALLS AND BINS

Suppose you have n web servers talking to m clients such that each client picks a server uniformly at random. If you do not end up wasting your server capacity, this is a nice way of pairing servers to clients since you do not need to centralize anything. But there is a chance that some of your servers are idle while clients are waiting to be served. How likely is it that there will be servers that are not doing anything? This problem is often modeled using balls and bins.

Problem 10.7: If you throw m balls into n bins randomly, how would you compute the expected number of bins that do not have any balls?

10.8 RANDOM PERMUTATIONS

Suppose we create a random permutation of $\langle 1, 2, \ldots, n \rangle$ as in Problem 10.5, i.e., each permutation has equal probability.

Problem 10.8: What is the expected number of numbers that get mapped to themselves? What is the expected length of the largest increasing subsequence $\mu = \langle x_1, \ldots, x_l \rangle$ in a randomly chosen permutation, where x_1 is the first element of the permutation and $x_k, k > 1$ is the first element that is larger than x_{k-1}.

10.9 UNIFORM RANDOM NUMBER GENERATION

Sometimes you may not have the perfect random number generator you need. For example, it would require a bit of thinking to devise an algorithm to pick one out of five friends who gets to be the designated driver by a coin flip such that the process is fair to everyone.

Problem 10.9: How would you implement a random number generator that generates a random integer between a and b, given a random number generator that produces either zero or one with equal probability. What would be the runtime of this algorithm, assuming each call to the given random number generator takes $O(1)$ time?

10.10 NONUNIFORM RANDOM NUMBER GENERATION

Suppose you want to write a load test for your server. You looked at the inter-arrival time of requests to your server over a period of one year and from this data you have computed a histogram of the distribution of the inter-arrival time of requests. Now, in your load test you want to generate requests for your server such that the inter-arrival times come from the same distribution that you have seen in your data. How would you generate these inter-arrival times?

Problem 10.10: Given the probability distribution of a discrete random variable X and a uniform $[0, 1]$ random number generator, how would you generate instances of X that follow the given distribution?

Figure 6. *FINANCIAL ENGINEERING*: an oxymoron widely used *circa* 2008.

10.11   EXPECTED NUMBER OF DICE ROLLS

Bob repeatedly rolls an unbiased 6-sided dice. He stops when he has rolled all the six numbers on the dice. How many rolls will it take, on an average, for Bob to see all the six numbers?

Option pricing

A call option gives the owner the right to buy something—a share, a barrel of oil, an ounce of gold—at a predetermined price at a predetermined time in the future. If the option is not priced fairly, an arbitrageur can either buy or sell the option in conjunction with other transactions and come up with a scheme of making money in a guaranteed fashion. A fair price for an option would be a price such that no arbitrage scheme can be designed around it.

We now consider problems related to determining the fair price for an option for a stock, given the distribution of the stock price for a period of time.

10.12   OPTION PRICING—DISCRETE CASE

Consider an option to buy a stock S that currently trades at $100. The option is to buy the stock at $100 in 100 days.

Suppose we know there are only two possible outcomes—S will go to $120 or to $70.

An arbitrage is a situation where you can start with a portfolio (x_s shares and x_o options) which has negative value (since you are allowed to short shares and sell options, both x_s and x_o may be negative) and regardless of the movement in the share price, the portfolio has positive value.

For example, if the option is priced at $26, we can make money by buying one share for $100 and selling four options—the initial outlay on the portfolio is $100 - 4 \times 26 = -4$. If the stock goes up, our portfolio is worth $120 - 20 \times -4 = \$80$. If the stock goes down, the portfolio is worth $70. In either case, we make money with no initial investment, i.e., the option price allows for an arbitrage.

Problem 10.12: For what option price(s), are there no opportunities for arbitrage?

10.13   OPTION PRICING WITH INTEREST

Consider the same problem as Problem 10.12, with the existence of a third asset class, a bond. A $1 bond pays $1.02 in 100 days. You can borrow money at this rate or lend it at this rate.

Problem 10.13: Show there is a unique arbitrage-free price for the option and compute this price.

10.14   OPTION PRICING—CONTINUOUS CASE

Problem 10.14: Suppose the price of Jingle stock 100 days in the future is a normal random variable with mean $300 and deviation $20. What would be the fair price of an option to buy a single share of Jingle at $300 in 100 days worth today? (Ignore the impact of interest rates.)

10.15   OPTIMUM BIDDING

Consider an auction for an item in which the reserve price is set by the seller to be a random variable X that is uniformly distributed in the range $[0, 400]$. You can place a bid B; if your bid is greater than or equal to the reserve price, you win the auction and have to pay B. You can then sell the item for an 80% markup over what you paid for it.

Problem 10.15: How much should you offer for the item?

10.16   ONCE OR TWICE

Suppose you are playing a game against a dealer. In order to play the game, you must pay \$1. The dealer gets a random card from a full deck. You are shown a randomly selected card from another full deck. You have the choice of taking the card or exchanging it for another card which is also randomly selected from a full deck. You win the game if and only if the face value of your card is larger than that of dealer. If you win, you get w dollars. (The face value of an ace is 1; the face values of Jack, Queen, and King are $12, 13,$ and $14,$ respectively.)

Problem 10.16: What would be the value of w such that it is a fair game, i.e., for a rational player, the expected gain is 0.

10.17   SELECTING A RED CARD

A deck of 52 playing cards is shuffled. The deck is placed face-down on a table. You are trying to select a red card. You can either examine or select the card that is currently at the top of the deck. If you choose to examine the top card, its value is revealed and it is set face-up. If you choose to select the top card, the game ends there—you win if you select a red card and lose if the card is black. Once you examine a card, it cannot be selected. If you have turned over 51 cards, you must select the last card.

Problem 10.17: What is the strategy that optimizes the likelihood of your selecting a face card?

10.18   SELECTING THE BEST SECRETARY

Suppose you are to choose a secretary from a pool of n secretaries who you interview in a random order. Given any two secretaries, you can tell who is better and the "is better" relationship is transitive. Once you interview a secretary, you can select her as your secretary and the selection process stops. Alternately, you can move on to the next one (but cannot go back to a previous secretary).

Problem 10.18 : Can you come up with a strategy that results in your selecting the best secretary with probability greater than $\frac{1}{n}$? What strategy maximizes the probability of selecting the best secretary?

10.19 DIFFERENTIATING BIASES

Two coins that are identical in appearance are placed in a black cloth bag. One is biased towards heads—it comes up heads with probability 0.6. The other is biased towards tails—it comes up heads with probability 0.4. For both coins, the outcomes of successive tosses are independent.

Problem 10.19 : You select a coin at random from the bag and toss it 5 times. It comes up heads 3 times—what is the probability that it was the coin that was biased towards tails? How many times do you need to toss the coin that is biased towards tails before it comes up with a majority of tails with probability greater than $\frac{99}{100}$?

10.20 THE COMPLEXITY OF AND-OR FORMULAS

Suppose we want to evaluate an expression of the form $(A \wedge B) \vee (C \wedge D))$, where $\wedge$ and $\vee$ are Boolean AND and OR respectively and A, B, C, D are Boolean variables. It is natural to use *lazy evaluation*, i.e., when evaluating $A \wedge B$, if we evaluate A first and it evaluates to false, then we skip evaluating B.

We now define a restricted set of expressions: L_0 expressions are just Boolean variables; an L_{k+1} expression is of the form $((\phi_0 \wedge \phi_1) \vee (\psi_0 \wedge \psi_1))$, where $\phi_0, \phi_1, \psi_0, \psi_1$ are L_k expressions. All Boolean variables appearing in an L_k expression are distinct.

We want to design an algorithm for evaluating an L_k expression and want to minimize the number of variables that it reads. We do not care how much time the algorithm spends traversing the expression.

Problem 10.20 : Prove that a deterministic algorithm—one in which the choice of the next variable to read is a deterministic function of the values read so far—must read all 4^k variables in the worst-case. Can you design a randomized algorithm that reads fewer variables on an average, regardless of the values assigned to the variables?

Chapter 11

Programming

> First, since we are
> programmers, we naturally
> designed the system to make it
> easy to write, test, and run
> programs.
>
> "The UNIX Time-Sharing
> System," D. Ritchie and
> K. Thompson, 1974

The focus of this book is algorithm design problems that arise in software interviews. However basic programming questions are an integral part of software interviews for many companies.

You should be ready to answer questions on any skill you claim on your resumé. In particular, do not write that you know something, unless you are confident that you can answer questions about it. For example, if your knowledge of Perl comes from cutting-and-pasting Perl code from the web to find large duplicate files, then do not include Perl in your resumé.

We begin this chapter by reviewing basic concepts such as primitive types, arrays, linked lists, asymptotic complexity, etc. Although it is likely that you are familiar with this material, as you will see, it can still be the source of challenging interview problems. Then we classify commonly asked questions, provide references for places to read about them, and give sample problems. A more comprehensive list of such problems is available on the companion website.

Bit Fiddling

The following problems involve manipulation of bit-level data. Bit fiddling questions are often asked in interviews and one important thing to note here is that it is very easy to introduce (and miss) errors in code that manipulates bit-level data—when you play with bits, expect to get bitten.

11.1 COMPUTING THE PARITY OF A LONG

The parity of a sequence of bits is 1 if the number of 1s in the sequence is odd; otherwise, it is 0. By keeping the parity of every word of data, you can check for single bit errors in storage or transmission. It is fairly straightforward to write a code that computes the parity of a long.

Problem 11.1: How would you compute parity if you had to perform the computation for a very large number of longs?

11.2 REVERSING THE BITS IN A LONG

There are several variants of the parity problem posed above, e.g., computing the number of bits set to 1 in a long. Here is a bit fiddling problem that is concerned with restructuring:

Problem 11.2: Write a function which takes a long x and returns a long that has the bits of x reversed.

11.3 RUN-LENGTH ENCODING

Consider the problem of compressing black and white bitmap images. A $n \times m$ pixel black-and-white image can be represented in $n \times m/8$ bytes, where each pixel is represented by a single bit. If you know that the image consists of large blocks which have the same color, then one way to compress the image is by just counting the length of alternate sequence of ones and zeroes. For example, 111111000011 becomes $6, 4, 2$.

Problem 11.3: How would you most efficiently do run-length encoding on a large bit sequence represented as a byte array?

Arrays

The simplest data-structure is the array, which is a contiguous block of memory. Given an array A which holds n objects, $A[i]$ denotes the i-th object stored in the array. Retrieving and updating $A[i]$ takes constant time. However the size of the array is fixed, which makes adding more than n objects impossible. Deletion of the object at location i can be handled by having an auxiliary Boolean associated with the location i indicating whether the entry is valid or not. Insertion of an object into an array of length n can be handled by allocating a new array with additional memory and copying over the entries from the original array. This makes the worst-case time of insertion high but if the new array has, for example, twice the space of the original array, the average time for insertion is constant since the expense of copying the array is infrequent.

11.4 PERMUTING THE ELEMENTS OF AN ARRAY

A permutation of length n is a 1-1 onto mapping π from $\{0, 1, \dots, n-1\}$ to itself. We can represent a permutation using an array Π: set $\Pi[i] = \pi(i)$. A permutation can be applied to an array A of n elements: $\Pi(A)$ is defined by $\Pi(A[i]) = A[\Pi[i]]$. Applying a permutation to a given array is easy if you have additional storage to write the resulting array.

Problem 11.4: Given an array A of integers and a permutation Π, compute $\Pi(A)$ using only constant additional storage.

11.5 INVERT A PERMUTATION

Every 1-1 onto mapping is invertible, i.e., if f is 1-1 onto, then there exists a unique function f^{-1} such that $f^{-1}(f(x)) = x$. In particular, for any permutation Π, there exists a unique permutation Π^{-1} that is the inverse of Π.

Given a permutation represented by an array A, you can compute its inverse B by simply assigning $B[A[i]] = i$ for all values of i.

Problem 11.5: Given an array A of ints representing a permutation Π, update A to represent Π^{-1} using only constant additional storage.

11.6 REVERSE ALL THE WORDS IN A SENTENCE

Given a string containing a set of words separated by white space, we would like to transform it to a string in which the words appear in the reverse order. For example, "Alice likes Bob" $\mapsto$ "Bob likes Alice". We do not need to keep the original string.

Problem 11.6: Implement a function for reversing the words in a string that is in-place, i.e., uses only constant additional storage.

Linked Lists

The next basic data-structure we consider is the linked list. A singly linked list is a data-structure that contains a sequence of nodes such that each node contains an object and a reference to the next node in the list. The first node is referred to as the head and the last node is referred to as the tail; the tail's next field is a reference to null. (There are many variants, e.g., in a doubly linked list, each node has a link to its predecessor; similarly, a sentinel node or a self-loop can be used in place of null.)

11.7 REVERSING A SINGLY LINKED LIST

Suppose you were given a singly linked list of integers sorted in ascending order and you need to return a list with the elements sorted in descending order. Suppose memory is scarce but you can reuse nodes in the original list.

Problem 11.7: Give a linear-time nonrecursive procedure that reverses a singly linked list. The procedure should use no more than constant storage beyond that needed for the list itself.

11.8 CHECKING FOR CYCLICITY

While a linked list is supposed to be a sequence of nodes ending in a null, it is possible to introduce a cycle in a linked list by making the next field of an element reference to one of the earlier nodes.

Problem 11.8: Given a reference to the head of a singly linked list, how would you determine whether this list ends in a null or reaches a cycle of nodes? (You do not know the length of the list.)

11.9 DELETION FROM A SINGLY LINKED LIST

Given a node in a singly linked list, deleting it in constant time appears impossible because its predecessor's next field has to be updated. Surprisingly, it can be done with one small caveat—the node to delete cannot be the last one in the list and it is easy to copy the value part of a node.

Problem 11.9: Let v be a node in a singly linked list. Node v is not the tail; delete it in $O(1)$ time.

Complexity Analysis

The runtime of an algorithm depends on the size of its input. One common approach to capture the runtime dependency is by expressing asymptotic bounds on the worst-case runtime as a function of the input size. Specifically, the runtime of an algorithm on an input of size n is $O(f(n))$ if for sufficiently large n, the runtime is not more than $f(n)$ times a constant. The big-O notation simply indicates an upper bound; if the runtime is proportional to $f(n)$, the complexity is written as $\Theta(f(n))$. (Note that the big-O notation is widely used where Θ is more appropriate.)

Generally speaking, if an algorithm has a runtime that is a polynomial, i.e., $O(n^k)$ for some fixed k, where n is the size of the input, it is considered to be efficient; otherwise, it is inefficient. Notable exceptions exist—for example, the simplex algorithm for linear programming is not polynomial but works very well in practice; the AKS primality checking algorithm is polynomial but has a high k.

As an example, searching an unsorted array of integers of length n, for a given integer, has an asymptotic complexity of $\Theta(n)$ since in the worst-case, the given integer may not be present.

Similarly, consider the naïve algorithm for primality which tries all numbers from 2 to the square root of the input. What is its complexity? In the best case, the input is divisible by 2. However in the worst-case, the input may be a prime, so the algorithm performs $\sqrt{n}$ iterations. Furthermore, since the number n requires only $\log_2 n$ bits to encode, this algorithm's complexity is actually exponential in the size of the input.

As a rule, algorithms should be designed with the goal of reducing the worst-case complexity rather than average-case complexity for several reasons—(1.) it is very difficult to define meaningful distributions on the inputs, (2.) pathological inputs are more likely than statistical models may predict (for example, worst-case input for a naïve implementation of Quicksort is one where all entries are the same, which is not at all unlikely), and (3.) malicious users may exploit bad worst-case performance to create denial-of-service attacks.

11.10 BINARY SEARCH

Binary search, which is the subject of a number of problems in Chapter 1, is a technique for searching for a given key in a sorted array.

Problem 11.10: What is the time complexity of the following implementation of binary search?

```
1    boolean search(array A, int K) {
2      if (A.size() == 0)
3        return false;
4
5      if (A.size() == 1)
6        return (A[0] == K);
7
8      int m = A.size()/2;
9
10     return (A[m] == K) ? true :
11                ( (A[m] < K) ?
12                     search(A[m+1::A.size()], K) :
13                     search(A[0::m], K)
14                );
15   }
```

It is not uncommon in some companies to quiz the candidates about their knowledge of computer science directly rather than asking them to solve problems. In the rest of this chapter, we cover a number of areas and provide a list of questions that can help a candidate prepare for such an interview. The answers to these questions can be easily found in standard textbooks for that field. Hence instead of providing answers to these questions we point our readers to textbooks that we consider a good reference for that field.

11.11 PROGRAMMING LANGUAGES

Basics

We like *The C Programming Language* by Kernighan and Ritchie for C; for Java, *Java Precisely* by Sestoft covers the core language and libraries succinctly.

- What are the types in C, Java, C++, and Perl? How many bits does it take to represent the basic types?
- What do floating point numbers look like in memory? Specifically, how many bits are there in a double and what sequence to the bits appear in?
- What is two's-complement notation?
- How would you implement a bit-vector class?
- Does the check x == x + 1 always return false for integer x?
- What does a C struct look like in memory? What does a C++ object look like in memory? What does a Java object look like in memory?
- What is the difference between an interpreted and a compiled language?
- What is garbage collection?
- How would you determine if call stack grows up or down relative to memory addresses?
- Give an example of a memory leak in Java.
- What is tail recursion? How can it be removed automatically?
- Is the natural recursive program for computing $n!$ tail recursive?
- Your manager reads an online article that says it is $10\times$ faster to code in Python than in C++. He wants you to code exclusively in Python from now on. What would you say to him?
- What does an executable look like as a sequence of bytes?

Libraries

A programmer who regularly implements complex algorithms such as KMP string matching or Dijkstra's shortest path computation quickly will not advance very far. Solutions to such problems are well-known and have high quality, thoroughly tested, and debugged implementations, often available as open source. Programmers should know and use these libraries.

- Give an example of a function which is in the C standard library.
- Give an example of a commonly used function which is not in the C standard library.
- What library would you use to determine the current date in Java?
- What library would you use in Java if you had to implement a tinyurl service?
- How does STL implement sets?
- How does the library code compute trigonometric functions?
- The strtok(char *s1, char *s2) function in the C standard library successively returns occurrences of the characters in s2 in string s1; it returns null if there are no more occurrences. What makes this a dangerous function to use in a multithreaded program?

11.12 DEBUGGING AND TESTING

Debugging and testing are topics which are not usually the focus of university teaching. We highly recommend *The Practice of Programming* by Kernighan and Pike, which teaches much more than just writing code—it covers testing, debugging, portability, performance, and design alternatives.

- What was your last bug? What was your hardest bug?
- How would you debug a distributed program?
- A program works sometimes and fails other times—why?
- A program works sometimes and fails other times on the exact same input—why?
- How would you determine where a program spends most of its time?
- How does JUnit make the process of testing easier?
- List five ways in which C code can be nonportable. What can you do to make the code portable?
- Write tests for implementation of an isupper function.
- Should you test private methods? Should you test one line methods?
- If you find and fix an error by adding debug code, should you remove the debug code afterwards? Should you leave them in with a conditional compilation flag or with a runtime flag?
- What is a buffer overflow and how can hackers exploit it?
- How can you use Valgrind to solve segfault problems?
- How does Valgrind catch access uninitialized memory?

11.13 BEST PRACTICES

Our favorite best practices book is *Effective Java* by Bloch—it covers many topics: object-oriented programming, design patterns, code organization, concurrency, and generics are just a few examples. *Effective C++* by Meyer is highly thought of for C++. *Design Patterns: Elements of Reusable Object-Oriented Software* by Gamma *et al.* is a very popular introduction to patterns.

- Give an example of a problem you solved where you made good use of object-oriented programming.
- What is the factory pattern? What is the publish-subscribe model?
- Give an example of how inheritance violates encapsulation.
- What do Java bounded wildcards buy you?
- Why should you always override the equals and hash function methods for Java classes?

11.14 PROGRAMMING LANGUAGE IMPLEMENTATION

We recommend *Programming Languages Pragmatics* by Scott—it covers both theory and practice of programming languages and is very up-to-date.

- Give an example of a language which cannot be parsed by any computer.
- What problems does dynamic linkage solve? What problems does it introduce?
- What is a functional language?
- What is a virtual function?
- How is method dispatch implemented in Java?
- What is automatic garbage collection and how is it implemented?
- What is a type-safe language?
- What is the difference between a lexer and a parser?
- Give an example of a language which cannot be recognized by a lexer.
- Give an example of a language which cannot be parsed by a parser.

11.15 OPERATING SYSTEMS

Modern Operating Systems by Tanenbaum is widely used; one of its claims to fame is that Linux was developed from the Minix OS developed in an earlier version of this book.

- What is a system call?
- How is a system call different from a library call?

- What is a device driver?
- What is livelock? What is deadlock? Give examples of each.
- What is a race? What can you do to prevent races?
- What is a mutex? What are semaphores? How are they implemented?
- Give examples of system calls that are not related to input-output.
- Give examples of library functions that call a system function all the time, none of the time, and some of the time.
- What is the time lag between the system call on the client side and the receipt of the packet on the server on a local area network?
- How fast can you write a gigabyte of data from RAM to disk?
- How does TCP/IP work?

11.16   TOOLS

Building and maintaining programs

There is a paucity of books on programming tools; one book we have used is *Essential Open Source Toolset* by Zeller and Krinke.

- What version control system do you use?
- What coverage tool do you use?
- What build system do you use?
- What documentation system do you use?
- What bug tracking system do you use?
- How is branching implemented in a version control system?
- Are deltas in the branching for a revision tree stored out forwards or backwards? What are the benefits of each approach?
- What are the advantages and disadvantages of a version control system that locks files?

Shell tools

There are scores, if not hundreds of books on the Unix shell and related tools. We have enjoyed *LINUX 101 Hacks* by Natarajan. It introduces these tools through useful hacks, such as the use of `find` to find all files that have not been modified in the past 100 days and are larger than 100 megabytes in size, sorting the password file on the third field, etc.

- Write a regular expression for identifying social security numbers in a file.
- Write a command that prints out lines in a text file which contain the strings `foo` and `bar` in any order.
- Write a command which replaces every occurrence of a `foo` followed by a `bar` (with possibly some other characters in between) by `widget`.

- Given a text file with two columns of integers, i.e., two integers encoded in ASCII per line, write a filter which sorts lines in the file by the second integer.
- How would you take two documents in PDF and create a new document which consists of the pages of the two original documents interleaved in order?
- How would you write a program which checks every hour if a network connection is up?
- How would you write a program which checks the price of a Nikon D40 DLSR each day on amazon.com?

11.17 COMPUTER ARCHITECTURE

Computer Architecture: A Quantitative Approach and *Computer Organization and Design, The Hardware/Software Interface*, both by Patterson and Hennessy, are the definitive works in this field.

- What is pipelining? Describe a 5-stage pipeline.
- What is a multi-issue processor?
- What is the difference between a superscalar and a VLIW processor? Where is each appropriate?
- What is a multicore machine?
- What is the significance of the privileged bit?
- How is kernel mode different from running as root?
- What do big-endian and little-endian notations mean?
- You rewrite some machine code to reduce the number of instructions to perform a computation and performance drops. Can you explain this?
- You benchmark a 3.0 gigahertz Pentium 4 and find it to be noticeably slower than a 2.4 gigahertz Pentium Pro—Why?
- You find the same computation on the same operating system with the same load takes longer on hot days—Why?
- How large and fast are the register file, L1 cache, L2 cache, main memory, and disk on current machines?
- How many instructions are in-flight in a modern core?
- What is branch prediction?
- Why is prediction based on the program counter insufficient?
- What is prefetching? What is a reasonable criterion for prefetching?

11.18 SYSTEMS

Professional programmers use many software systems everyday and it is reasonable to expect that they should have some understanding of how these systems work.

- Describe how an operating system is implemented. Specifically describe how Linux implements processes and I/O.
- How does a web browser work? Specifically, describe how auto-completion (such as in a search engine query box) is implemented.
- How does the Internet work? Specifically describe the roles of the TCP/IP protocol, routers, and DNS.
- How is a social networking site built? Specifically comment on scalability, spam prevention, and resilience to denial-of-service.

Part II

The Interview

Chapter 12

Strategies For A Great Interview

A typical one hour interview with a single interviewer consists of five minutes of introductions and questions about the candidate's resumé. This is followed by five to fifteen minutes of questioning on basic programming concepts.

The core of the interview is one or two detailed algorithm design questions where the candidate is expected to present a detailed solution on a whiteboard or paper. Depending on the interviewer and the question, the solution may be required to include syntactically correct code in a language that the candidate is comfortable with.

The reason for asking such questions is that algorithms and associated data-structures underlie all software. They are often hidden in library calls. They can be a small part of a code base dominated by IO and format conversion. But they are the crucial component in terms of performance and intricacy.

The most important part of interview preparation is to know the material and practice solving problems. However the nontechnical aspects of interviewing cannot be underplayed either. There are a number of things that could go wrong in an interview and it is important to have a strategy to deal with them.

12.1 Before the interview

One of the best ways of preparing for an interview is mock interviews. Get a friend to ask you questions from this book (or any other source) and have you solve the problems on a whiteboard or paper. Ask your friend to take notes and give you detailed feedback, both positive and negative. Also ask your friend to provide hints from the solution if you are stuck. This will help you overcome any fear or problem areas well in advance.

12.2 APPROACHING THE PROBLEM

No matter how well prepared you are, there is a good chance that the solution to an interview problem will not occur to you immediately. When this happens, there are several things you can do.

Clarify the question: This may seem obvious but it is amazing how many interviews go badly because the candidate spends most of the time trying to solve the wrong problem. If a question seems exceptionally hard, there is a good chance you have misunderstood the question.

The best way of clarifying the question is to state a concrete instance of the problem. For example, if the question is *"find the first occurrence of a number greater than k in a sorted array"*, you could ask the following *"if the input array is* $[2, 20, 30]$ *and k is 3, then are you supposed to return 1 (index of 20)?"*

Work on small examples: Consider Problem 9.4. This problem may seem pretty hard at first. But if you start working out which doors are going to be open for up to the fifth door, you will see that only door 1 and door 4 are open. This may suggest to you that the door is open only if its index is a perfect square. Once you have this realization, it is relatively easy to prove the correctness of this assertion. This may not be true for all the problems. However there is a large class of problems where after working out the solution for a few small examples, you may see a pattern emerge.

Spell out the brute-force solution: Problems that are put to you in an interview tend to have an obvious brute-force solution that has a large runtime compared to more sophisticated solutions. For example, instead of trying to work out a dynamic programming solution for a problem (such as Problem 3.4), try all the possible configurations. There are several advantages to this: (1.) it helps you explore opportunities for optimization and hence reach a better solution, (2.) it gives you an opportunity to demonstrate some problem solving and coding skills, and (3.) it establishes that both you and the interviewer are thinking about the same problem. Be warned that this strategy can sometimes be detrimental if it takes too long to describe even the brute-force approach and leaves you with less time to work on the optimal solution.

Think out loud: One of the worst things you can do in an interview is to freeze up while solving the problem. It is always a good idea to think out loud while searching for a solution. On one hand, this increases the chances of you finding the right solution because it forces you to put your thoughts in a coherent manner. On the other hand, this helps the interviewer guide your thought process in the right direction. In the very least, even if you are not able to reach the solution, this leaves the interviewer with the impression that you have the intellectual ability to attack an unknown problem.

Search for isomorphic problems: Even if you may not have seen the exact problem, you may have seen another problem with similar mathematical structure. See if this seems like a good fit for general algorithmic techniques, such as, divide-and-conquer, dynamic programming, greedy, etc. Can you map the problem to a graph? Can you map it to an objective function and a set of constraints, such as an integer linear program?

12.3   PRESENTING THE SOLUTION

Once you have a solution, it is important to present it well and do a comprehensive job at it. A lot of these things become simpler if you use a higher level language such as Java. However you should use the language with which you are most familiar. In most scenarios, it is perfectly fine to write a pseudocode as well. Here are some thoughts that could help:

Test for corner cases: For a number of problems, your general idea may work for the majority of the cases but there may be a few obscure inputs where your algorithm (or code) would fail. For example, you could write a binary search code that crashes if the input is an empty array or you may do arithmetic without considering the possibility of integer overflow. It is important to check for these things carefully. One way of doing this is to construct a few test cases and work out the output of your algorithm for them. In many cases, the code to handle some obscure corner cases may be too complicated. In such cases, you should at least mention to the interviewer that you are aware of the problem and you could try to address it if they are interested.

Function signature: Several candidates tend to get this wrong and getting your function signature wrong reflects badly on you. For example, it would be bad if you are writing the code in C language and your function returns an array but you fail to return the size of the array along with the pointer. Another place where function signatures could be important is knowing when to pass parameters by value versus by reference.

Memory management: If you allocate memory in your function, you must ensure that in every execution path, this memory is de-allocated. In general, it is best to avoid memory management operations all together. If you must do this, consider use of scoped pointers.

Syntax: In almost all cases, the interviewers are not evaluating you on the correctness of the syntax of your code. The editors and compilers do a great job at helping you get the syntax right. However you cannot underplay the possibility of an interviewer leaving with the impression that you got most of the syntax wrong since you do not have much experience writing code. Hence once you are done writing your code, you should make a pass over it to avoid any obvious syntax errors before claiming you are done.

12.4 KNOW YOUR INTERVIEWERS

If the organization can share some information about the background of your interviewers, it can help you a great deal. For fresh graduates, it is also important to think from the perspective of the interviewers. Hence we highly recommend reading the next chapter on interviewing from the perspective of an interviewer.

It is also important to note that once you ace the interview, you will have an offer and you would have an important decision to make— is this the organization where you want to work? Interviews are the best time to collect this information. Based on your interaction with the interviewers, you can get a pretty good idea of their intellect as well as how pleasant the organization could be. Most interviews end with the interviewers letting the candidates ask questions. You should make the best use of this time by (1.) getting the information you would need and (2.) communicating to the interviewer that you are interested in the job. Prepare a list of questions in advance that both gets you helpful information as well as shows your knowledge and interest in the organization.

12.5 GENERAL CONVERSATION

Often interviewers will spend some time asking questions about your past projects, dissertation, etc. The point of this conversation is:

Can the candidate clearly communicate a complex idea: This is one of the most important skills for working in an engineering team. If you have a grand idea to redesign a big system, can you communicate it to your colleagues and bring them on board? It is best to practice how you want to present some of your best work in advance. Being precise, clear, and having concrete examples can go a long way here. For candidates who have to communicate in a language that is not their first language, it may be important to speak slowly and perhaps use the whiteboard to augment their words.

Is the candidate passionate about his work: We always want our colleagues to be passionate, full of energy, and inspiring to work with. If you are so passionate about your work that your eyes light up while describing your work, it can go a long way in terms of establishing you as a great colleague. Hence when you are asked to describe a project from the past, it is best to pick something that you are passionate about rather than a project that was complex but did not interest you.

Is there a potential interest match with some project: During a general conversation, the interviewer may gauge areas of strengths for a potential project match. If you know the requirements of the job, you may want to steer the conversation in that direction. However in the computing industry, things change so fast that most teams prefer a strong generalist.

Also, it is a good idea to maintain a homepage with links to your projects and articles; things that can help interviewers learn more about you.

12.6 OTHER GRANDFATHERLY ADVICE

Keep a positive spirit: A cheerful optimistic attitude can go a long way. There is really no point complaining how difficult your journey was or how you are not a morning person.

Grooming: Most software companies have a relaxed dress-code, so new graduates may wonder if they will look foolish by overdressing. The damage done when you are more casual than expected is far more than the minor embarrassment you may feel being overdressed. Therefore it is always a good idea to err on the side of caution and dress formally for your interviews. At the very minimum, be clean and well-groomed.

Keep money and perks out of the interview: Money is a big factor in any job but it is best left to be discussed with the Human Resources division after an offer is made; the same is true for vacation time, day care support, etc.

Be aware of your body language: Think of a friend or coworker who is slouched all the time or absent-mindedly does things that may offend others.

Chapter 13

Conducting An Interview

For someone at the beginning of their career, interviewing can feel like a huge responsibility. If you hire a bad candidate, it can be very expensive for the organization, not just because the employee would not be productive but more so because the employee would be a drain on the productivity of everyone else who is trying to train and mentor the employee. Firing someone after a bad hiring decision is extremely painful and detrimental to the morale of both the team and the individual. On the other hand, if you discard good candidates too often, it can be problematic for a rapidly growing organization, not to mention the moral responsibility of not crushing someone's dreams and aspirations unnecessarily. Here are some thoughts that could potentially help you make this process a little easier.

13.1 OBJECTIVE

The ultimate goal of any interview is to determine if a given candidate takes up the job and is appropriately trained, what are the chances that the candidate will be a successful employee of the company. Usually this means you want incredibly smart people who can get things done. It is important to design the whole process with this as the central theme. Ideally, your interviews should be designed such that you score a good candidate 1.0 and a bad candidate 0.0. A common mistake made by novice interviewers is to not be decisive. Unless the candidate walks on water or completely disappoints the interviewer, the novice interviewers try not to make a decision and score the candidates somewhere in the middle. This essentially means that the interview was a wasted effort. One way of making this easier for the interviewers is to imagine if this candidate replaces someone productive in their team. If this feels like a good change, then you should give the candidate a high score, otherwise, a low score.

A secondary objective of the interview process might be to turn the candidate into a good brand ambassador for your organization. Even if the candidate is not a good fit for your organization, they may know others who would be. It is important for the candidate to have an overall positive experience during the process. It is fairly obvious that it is a bad idea to ask a candidate a problem and then start checking email or insult the candidate over a mistake they made but you would be surprised how often this happens in some organizations.

13.2   WHAT TO ASK

One important question you should ask yourself is how much training time your work environment allows. For example, in a startup, it may be very important that a new person is productive right from the first week whereas some organizations allow a month of training time and yet another set of organizations allow for a few months of training and ramp up time. For example, in a startup, it would be important to test the candidate on the specific technologies you are using and the specific areas you are working on whereas in most large organizations, the best thing to do is not emphasize on the domain knowledge and test the candidate on their basic problem solving abilities and fundamentals of computer science.

Most big organizations have a fairly structured interview process where specific interviewers are responsible for probing specific areas. For example, you may be asked to evaluate the candidate on either their coding skills, algorithm knowledge, critical thinking, or the ability to design complex systems. We hope that this book gives you access to a fairly large collection of problems to choose from for each of the categories. As you approach the decision of picking one problem from a set of problems, keep the following in mind:

   – No single point of failure—if you are going to ask just one question, you should not pick a problem where the candidate would pass the interview if they get one particular insight. The best of the candidates can miss one simple insight. There should be at least two or three opportunities for the candidates to redeem themselves. For example, the problems in the dynamic programming section can almost always be solved through (1.) a greedy algorithm that is fast but suboptimum or (2.) a brute-force algorithm that is slow but optimum. In such cases, even if the candidate cannot get the key insight, they can still demonstrate some problem solving abilities.

   – No unnecessary domain knowledge—it is not a good idea to quiz a candidate on advanced graph algorithms if the job does not require it and the candidate does not claim any special knowledge of the field. (The exception to this rule is if you want to test the candidate's response to a high-stress situation.)

— Cover multiple areas—even if you are responsible for testing the candidate on just algorithms, you could easily pick a problem that also exposes some aspects of design and coding.

— Possible multiple solutions—if a given problem has multiple good solutions, the chances of a good candidate coming up with a good solution increases. It also gives you more freedom as an interviewer to maneuver the interviewee in the direction of one of the good solutions. Also, a great candidate may finish with one solution soon enough to discuss other approaches and the tradeoffs involved.

Often new interviewers have an incorrect notion of how tough or easy a problem is for a thirty minute or one hour interview. It is usually a good idea to calibrate the toughness of a problem by asking one of your colleagues to solve it and see how much difficulty they have with it.

13.3 CONDUCTING THE INTERVIEW

Conducting a good interview is like juggling a lot of pieces together. At high level, you want to ask your question and evaluate the candidate's responses. Since so many things can happen in an interview that could help you make a decision, it is important to take notes. At the same time, it is important to keep a conversation going with the candidate and help them out wherever they get stuck. What works best is to have a series of hints worked out prior to the interview and you provide these hints progressively as needed. Coming up with the right set of hints may require some thinking. You do not want to give away the problem, yet find a way for the candidate to make progress. There are a few situations that can throw you off board:

A candidate that gets stuck and shuts up: Some candidates can get intimidated by the problem or the process and just shut up. Usually, in such situations, the candidate's performance may not reflect their true caliber. In such situations, it is important to put the candidate at ease by mentioning that the problem is tough and a good way of proceeding would be to think out loud, so you can guide their thinking.

A verbose candidate: The other class of candidates that can render an interview ineffective is the candidates who go on in tangential directions and keep on talking without making progress. Here also it is important to take control of the conversation and assert that this line of conversation is not making any progress towards the problem.

An overconfident candidate: It is not uncommon to meet candidates who weaken their own case by insisting that their wrong answer is correct. In order to give the candidate a fair chance, it is important to demonstrate to the candidate that they are making a mistake, so they can correct it. Often the best way of doing this is to construct a test case where the candidate's solution breaks down.

13.4   SCORING AND REPORTING

At the end of an interview, most times the interviewers have a good idea of how they want to score the candidate. But, in general, it is a good idea to keep notes and revisit them before making a final decision. It is often a good idea to standardize how you score based on things like which hints you had to give to make progress or how many of your intended questions was the candidate able to get to. While isolated minor mistakes can be ignored in most cases, sometimes when you look at all the mistakes together, a coherent picture of weakness in a certain area may emerge, such as consistent lack of attention to details or unfamiliarity with the syntax of a language.

In cases of indecision, we have found that it is always better to err on the side of caution and wait for the next candidate instead of making a bad hiring decision. The ultimate litmus test is always imagining the candidate replacing a valuable member of your team and whether or not that seems like a welcome change.

Part III

Solutions

Chapter 1

Searching

Solution 1.1: One of the fastest ways to invert a fast-growing mono-tone function (such as the square function) is to do a binary search in a precomputed table of the function. Since the square root for the largest 32-bit unsigned integer can be represented in 16 bits, we build an array of length 2^{16} such that i-th element in the array is i^2. When we want to compute square root for a given number n, we look for the largest number in the array that is still smaller than n. Because the square root is relatively small, it is faster to compute it on the fly than to precompute it.

```
1   unsigned int sqrt_search(unsigned int input) {
2     int begin = 0;
3     int end = 65536;
4     while(begin + 1 < end){
5       int mid = begin + (end - begin) / 2;
6         unsigned int mid_sqr = mid * mid;
7       if (mid_sqr == input) {
8         return mid;
9       } else if (mid_sqr > input) {
10        end = mid;
11      } else {
12        begin = mid;
13      }
14    }
15    return begin;
16  }
```

Solution 1.2:

```
1   public class BinSearch {
2     static int search( int [] A, int K ) {
3       int l = 0;
4       int u = A.length -1;
5       int m;
6       while ( l <= u ) {
```

```
7          m = (1+u)/2;
8          if (A[m] < K) {
9            l = m + 1;
10         } else if (A[m] == K) {
11           return m;
12         } else {
13           u = m-1;
14         }
15       }
16       return -1;
17     }
18 }
```

Solution 1.3: A straightforward way to find an element larger than a given value k is to look for k via a binary search and then, if k is found, walk the array forward (linearly) until either the first element larger than k is encountered or the end of the array is reached. If k is not found, a binary search will end up pointing to either the next largest value after K in the array, in which case no further action is required or the next smallest value in which case the next element is the next largest value.

The worst-case runtime of this algorithm is $\Theta(n)$—the input of all values matching K, except for the last one (which is greater than K), is the worst-case.

The solution to this problem is to replace the linear scan with a binary search in the second part of the algorithm, which leads to the desired element to be found in $O(\log n)$ time.

Solution 1.4: Since the array contains distinct integers and is sorted, for any $i > 0$, $A[i] \geq A[i-1] + 1$. Therefore $B[i] = A[i] - i$ is also nondecreasing. It follows that we can do a binary search for 0 in B to find an index such that $A[i] = i$. (We do not need to actually create B, we can simply use $A[i] - i$ wherever $B[i]$ is referenced.)

Solution 1.5: The key idea here is to simultaneously do a binary search for the end of the array as well as the key. We try to look for $A[2^k]$ in the k-th step and catch exceptions for successive values of k till either we hit an exception or we hit a number greater than or equal to b. Then we do a binary search for b between indices 2^{k-1} and 2^k. The runtime of the search algorithm is $O(\log n)$. In code:

```
1 int BinarySearchInUnboundedArray(int * A, int b) {
2   int k = 0;
3   while(true) {
4     int c;
5     try {
6       c = A[(1 << k) -1];
7       if (c == b) {
8         return (1 << k) -1;
```

```
 9            } else if (c >= b) {
10               break;
11            }
12         }
13         catch (exception e) {
14            break;
15         }
16         k++;
17      }
18      // Now do a binary search between indices 2^(k−1) and (2^k)
           −1.
19      int begin = 1 << (k −1);
20      int end = (1 << k) − 1;
21      while(begin + 1 > end) {
22         int mid = begin + (end − begin) / 2;
23         try {
24            if (A[mid] == b) {
25               return mid;
26            } else if (A[mid] < b){
27               begin = mid;
28            } else {
29               end = mid;
30            }
31         }
32         catch (exception e) {
33            end = mid;
34         }
35      }
36      // Nothing matched b
37      return −1;
38   }
```

Solution 1.6: In the first step, we build an array of 2^{16} integers that is initialized to 0 and for every number in the file, we take its 16 most significant bit to index into this array and increment that number. Since there are less than 2^{32} numbers in the file, there is bound to be one number in the array that is less than 2^{16}. This tells us that there is at least one number missing among the possible numbers with those upper bits. In the second pass, we can focus only on the numbers that match this criterion and use a bit-vector of size 2^{16} to identify one of the missing numbers.

Solution 1.7: The simplest algorithm is a "loop join", i.e., walking through all the elements of one array and comparing them to the elements of the other array. This has $O(m \cdot n)$ time complexity, regardless of whether the arrays are sorted or unsorted:

```
1   for each unique element in A
2       for each unique element in B
3           if A = B
4               include A in output
```

However since both the arrays are sorted, we can make some optimizations. First, in the right array, we can use binary search to find whether the element exists rather than scanning the entire array:

```
1   for each unique element in A
2       use binary search to find A in B
3       if found, include A in output
```

Now our algorithm should be $O(n \cdot \log_2 m)$. We should choose the larger set for the inner loop (i.e., binary search) since if $n \ll m$ then $m \log(n) \gg n \log(m)$.

This is the best solution if one set is much smaller than the other. However it is not optimal for cases where the set sizes are similar because we are not using the fact that both arrays are sorted to our advantage. In that case, a linear scan through both the arrays in tandem will work best as shown in this Python code:

```
1   def TryLinearIntersect(n, m, a, b):
2       # construct sorted sets of random numbers of size n and m
3       A = []
4       for i in range(n):
5           A.append(random.randint(a, b))
6       A.sort()
7
8       B = []
9       for j in range(m):
10          B.append(random.randint(a, b))
11      B.sort()
12
13      return LinearIntersect(A, B)
14
15  def LinearIntersect(A, B):
16      output = []
17      ACounter = 0
18      BCounter = 0
19      lastMatch = None
20      while ACounter < len(A) and BCounter < len(B):
21          if A[ACounter] == B[BCounter] and A[ACounter] !=
                lastMatch:
22              lastMatch = A[ACounter]
23              output.append(lastMatch)
24              ACounter = ACounter + 1
25              BCounter = BCounter + 1
26          elif A[ACounter] < B[BCounter]:
27              ACounter = ACounter + 1
28          else:
29              BCounter = BCounter + 1
30      return output
```

The runtime for this algorithm is $O(m + n)$.

Solution 1.8: A simple way to approach this problem is to hash each word based on its sorted representation (i.e., "logarithm" and "algorithm" would both be hashed as "aghilmort"). This ensures that all the anagrams of a given word map to the same hash value.

```
1   def anagrams(dictionary):
2       output = []
3       map = {}
4       # for each word
5       for word in dictionary:
6           # sort the letters
7           sorted_word = sortchars(word)
8           # add the word to the list held in a dictionary
9           # under its sorted key
10          if sorted_word not in map:
11              map[sorted_word] = [word]
12          else:
13              map[sorted_word].append(word)
14      # for each dictionary key
15      for k in map.keys():
16          # return the list if it has more than one item
17          if len(map[k]) > 1:
18              output.append(map[k])
19      return output
20
21  def sortchars(word):
22      l = list(word)
23      l.sort()
24      return ''.join(l)
```

A sample run:

```
>> anagrams(("algorithm", "god", "logarithm", "dog", "snute"))
[['algorithm', 'logarithm'], ['god', 'dog']]
```

Solution 1.9: This could be easily done in $O(n^2)$ time by searching for all possible values of i and j such that $A[i] + A[j] = K$.

We could do significantly better by storing the values from the array in a hash table. Then for each new value, we check to see if its complement (i.e., K minus the value) has already been seen and if so, what is the index? Here is a Python implementation of this concept using Python's built-in dictionary object as the hash table:

```
1   def PairSum(arr, K):
2       h = {}
3       for i in range(len(arr)):
4           complement = K - arr[i]
5           h[arr[i]] = i
6           if complement in h:
7               return h[complement], i
```

This gives the following results, where the return values of the function are the two indices of elements that add up to K:

```
ar1 = [2, 3, 4, 5, 6, 7, 8, 7]

PairSum(ar1, 4)  = (0, 0)
PairSum(ar1, 5)  = (0, 1)
PairSum(ar1, 10) = (3, 3)
PairSum(ar1, 13) = (4, 5)
PairSum(ar1, 15) = (5, 6)
PairSum(ar1, 17) = None
```

This algorithm runs in $O(n)$ time since it makes only a single pass through the list and the work done inside the loop is constant (assuming we have a nice hash function that gives us a constant time hash insert and lookup).

Solution 1.10: Here essentially we need to efficiently represent two multisets (one for characters in the anonymous letter and one for characters in the magazine) and see if one is a subset of the other.

The most direct way of doing this would be to build a hash table M, where the key is a character and its value is the number of times it appears in the magazine. Once this is built, we can scan the anonymous letter character by character and decrement the corresponding count in M. If the count goes to zero, we delete the character from M. We can write the anonymous letter with characters in the magazine iff we can go over the entire anonymous letter and find every character in M with a positive count.

If the characters are coded in ASCII, we could do away with M and use a 256 entry integer array A, with $A[i]$ being set to the number of times the character i appears in the magazine.

One way to improve performance of the approach outlined above when the magazine is very long is to process the magazine in segments; in this way, if the letter can be written with a relatively small initial prefix of the magazine, the whole magazine does not have to be processed. The segments may be of fixed size or a doubling strategy may be employed. This does not help the worst-case complexity (since it may not be possible to write the letter with the characters in the magazine and this cannot be determined without inspecting the entire magazine) but speeds up the best-case and possibly the average-case.

Solution 1.11: Here essentially each user is associated with a set of attributes and we need to find users associated with a given set of attributes quickly. A hash table would be a perfect solution here but we need a hash function over the set of attributes. There are a couple of good ways of doing this. If the number of attributes is small, then we can represent the set as a bit-vector, where each bit represents a specific attribute. Once we have this canonical representation of set, then it is easy to use any hash function that transforms this bit-vector into a desired hash space.

However if the space of possible attributes is large, then the best way to represent a set canonically would be to sort the attributes. For this sorting, any arbitrary ordering of attributes will work. We can represent the sorted list of attributes in a string concatenating all the attributes.

Incidentally, if we want to group users based on similar rather than identical attributes, the problem becomes significantly more difficult. A common approach is min-hashing. Essentially, we construct a set of k independent hash functions (k is chosen based on how similar we want the sets to be). Then for each set s we define

$$M_k(s) = \min_{a_i \in s} h_k(a_i).$$

If two sets s_1 and s_2 have similar set of attributes then with high probability $M_k(s_1) = M_k(s_2)$. Based on this, we map each set of attributes s to a sequence of hashes $M_1(s) \ldots M_k(s)$. Now the problem has been reduced to pairing users that have the same hash sequence, which is similar to the original problem. Here k can be varied appropriately to increase or decrease the probability of match for a pair of slightly different attribute sets.

Solution 1.12: The idea here is very similar to hashing. Consider a very simple hash function $F(x) = x \bmod (n + 1)$. We can build a bit-vector of length $n + 1$ that is initialized to 0 and for every element in A, we set bit $F(A[i])$ to 1. Since there are only n elements in the array, there has to be at least one bit in the vector that is not set. That would give us the number that is not there in the array.

An even simpler approach is to find the max (or min) element in the array and return one more (less) than that element. This approach will not work if the extremal elements are the largest (smallest) values in the set that the entries are drawn from.

Solution 1.13: Since the energy is only related to the height of the robot, we can ignore x and y co-ordinates. Let's say that the points where the robot goes in successive order have heights $h_1, \ldots, h_n$. Let's assume that the battery capacity is such that with full battery, the robot can climb up B meters. Then the robot will run out of battery iff there exist integers i and j such that $i < j$ and $h_j - h_i > B$. In other words, in order to go from point i to point j, the robot needs to climb more than B points. So, we would like to pick B such that for any $i < j$, we have $B \geq h_j - h_i$.

If we did not have the constraint that $i < j$, then we could just compute B as $\max(h) - \min(h)$ but this may be an overestimate: consider the case when the robot is just going downwards.

We can compute the minimum B in $O(n)$ time if we keep the running min as we do a sweep. In code:

```
 1  double BatteryCapacity(vector<double> h) {
 2    if (h.size() < 2) {
 3      return 0;
 4    }
 5    double min = h[0];
 6    double result = 0;
 7    for (int i = 1; i < h.size(); ++i) {
 8      if (h[i] - min > result) {
 9        result = h[i] - min;
10      }
11      if (min > h[i]) {
12        min = h[i];
13      }
14    }
15    return result;
16  }
```

Solution 1.14: Let's first consider just the strict majority case. This problem has an elegant solution when you make the following observation: if you take any two distinct elements from the stream and throw them away, the majority element remains the majority of the remaining elements (we assumed there was a majority element to begin with). The reasoning goes as follows: let's say the majority element occurred m times out of n elements in the stream such that $m/n > 1/2$. The two distinct elements that we choose to throw can have at most one of the majority elements. Hence after discarding them, the ratio of the previously majority element could be either $m/(n-2)$ or $(m-1)/(n-2)$. It is easy to verify that if $m/n > 1/2$, then $m/(n-2) > (m-1)/(n-2) > 1/2$.

Now, as we read the stream from beginning to the end, as soon as we encounter more than one distinct element, we can discard one instance of each element and what we are left with in the end must be the majority element.

```
 1  string FindMajority(stream* s) {
 2    string candidate, next_word;
 3    int count = 0;
 4    while (s->GetNext(&next_word)) {
 5      if (count == 0) {
 6        candidate = next_word;
 7        count = 1;
 8      } else if (candidate == next_word) {
 9        count++;
10      } else {
11        count--;
12      }
13    }
14    return candidate;
15  }
```

The code above assumes there is a majority word in the stream; if no word has a strict majority, it still returns a string but there are no meaningful guarantees on what that string would be.

Solution 1.15: This is essentially a generalization of Problem 1.14. Here instead of discarding two distinct words, we discard k distinct words at any given time and we are guaranteed that all the words that occurred more than $1/k$ times the length of the stream before discarding continue to have more than $1/k$ fraction of copies. For implementing this strategy, we need to keep a hash table of current k candidates. Here is an example code:

```
1   void FindFrequentItems(stream* s, hash_map<string, int>*
        word_set, int k) {
2     word_set->clear();
3     string word;
4     while(s->GetNextWord(&word)) {
5       hash_map<string, int>::iterator i = word_set->find(word);
6       if (i == word_set->end()) {
7         if (word_set->size() == k) {
8           // Hash table is full, decrement all counts, which
9           // is equivalent to discarding k distinct words.
10          for (hash_map<string, int>::iterator j = word_set->
              begin();
11              j != word_set->end();
12              ++j) {
13            --(j->second);
14            if (j->second ==0){
15              word_set->erase(j);
16            }
17          }
18        } else {
19          (*word_set)[word] = 1;
20        }
21      } else {
22        i->second++;
23      }
24    }
25  }
```

It may seem the above code is taking $O(n.k)$ time since the inner loop may take k steps (decrementing count for all k entries) and the loop goes on for n times. However if you note that each word in the stream can only be erased once, then the total time spent erasing everything is $O(n)$ and the rest of the steps inside the loop run in constant time.

The above code provides us with a $k-1$ size set of words that is a superset of the words that occur more than n/k times. In order to get the exact set, we need to make another pass over the stream and count the number of times each word in the hash table actually occurs so that we keep only the words which occur more than n/k times.

Solution 1.16: A recursive solution is natural:

```
1   Node* SearchBST(Node* root, int key) {
2     if (root == NULL) {
3       return NULL;
4     } else if (root->key == key) {
5       return root;
6     } else if (root->key < key) {
7       return SearchBST(root->left, key);
8     } else {
9       return SearchBST(root->right, key);
10    }
11  }
```

Recursion adds the overhead of function calls. The code above is not literally tail recursive, which means that an optimizing compiler is unlikely to remove the recursive calls; however there still is a straightforward iterative solution:

```
1   Node* SearchBST(Node* root, int key) {
2     while(root != NULL) {
3       if (root->key == key) {
4         return root;
5       } else if (root->key < key) {
6         root = root->left;
7       } else {
8         root = root->right;
9       }
10    return NULL;
11  }
```

Solution 1.17: This is similar to Problem 1.16 but you just have to continue your binary search till the end even if you find the element that you were looking for and also keep track of the last element that met the criteria.

```
1   Node* SearchBST(Node* root, int key) {
2     Node* result = NULL;
3     while(root != NULL) {
4       if (root->key > key) {
5         result = root;
6         root = root->left;
7       } else {
8         root = root->right;
9       }
10    }
11    return result;
12  }
```

Solution 1.18: This problem requires some creative use of the binary search idea. Let's say that the two arrays are $A1$ and $A2$ and say that l of the k smallest elements of the union come from the first array and $l - k$ elements come from the second array. If this were indeed true, then we would see that $A1[l - 1] \le A2[k - l]$ and $A2[l - k] - 1 \le A1[l]$ (barring some corner cases where we reach the end of the array).

The other interesting observation we can make is that if $A1[l - 1] > A2[k - l]$, then we should use at least one more element from the second array in the k smallest elements. Similarly, if $A2[l - k - 1] > A1[l]$, then we should use at least one more element from the first array. Using these two inequalities, we can essentially do a binary search on l. Note that this problem gives you plenty of corner cases to worry about. In code:

```
1   int FindOrderStat(const vector<int>& a1,
2                     const vector<int>& a2,
3                     unsigned int k) {
4     // Check the validity of input.
5     assert(a1.size() + a2.size() >= k);
6     assert(k > 0);
7     // Find an index begin <= l < end such that a1[0]..a1[l-1]
8     // and a2[0]..a2[k-l-1] are the smallest k numbers.
9     unsigned int begin = max(0, k - a2.size());
10    unsigned int end = min(a1.size(), k);
11    while(begin  < end) {
12      unsigned l = begin + (end - begin)/2;
13      // Can we include a1[l] in the k smallest numbers?
14      if((l < a1.size()) && (k-l > 0) && (a1[l] < a2[k-l-1])) {
15        begin = l + 1;
16      } else if ((l > 0) && (k-l < a2.size()) && (a1[l-1] > a2[
            k-l])) {
17        // This is the case where we can discard a[l-1]
18        // from the set of k smallest numbers.
19        end = l;
20      } else {
21        // We found our answer since both the inequalities were
              false.
22        begin = l;
23        break;
24      }
25    }
26    if (begin == 0) {
27      return a2[k - 1];
28    } else if (begin == k) {
29      return a1[k-1];
30    } else {
31      return max(a1[begin -1], a2[k - begin -1]);
32    }
33  }
```

Solution 1.19: Consider two lines $y = a_i + b_i x$ and $y = a_j + b_j x$ such that $a_i > a_j$. The i-th line intersects the line $x = 0$ at $(0, a_i)$ and the j-th line intersects the line $x = 0$ at $(0, a_j)$. Similarly, these lines intersect $x = 1$ at

$(1, a_i + b_i)$ and $(1, a_j + b_j)$. Lines i and j intersect iff

$$((a_i > a_j)\&(a_i + b_i < a_j + b_j))|((a_i < a_j)\&(a_i + b_i > a_j + b_j)).$$

In other words, for the lines to intersect, if $a_i < a_j$, then it must be the case that $(a_i + b_i < a_j + b_j)$ or vice versa (ignoring the trivial case where they intersect on one of the boundaries).

Hence if we sort the pairs (a_i, b_i) by a_i and test that for successive pairs (a_i, b_i) and (a_j, b_j) if $a_i + b_i < a_j + b_j$, we know that they do not intersect. If we do find a violation of this inequality, then we have found one of the intersecting pairs.

Sorting takes $O(n \log n)$ time and comparing successive pairs takes $O(n)$ time. Hence this can be done in $O(n \log n)$ time.

Solution 1.20: One way to solve this is to sort the intervals by their lower boundary and see if their upper boundary is also sorted in the same order. If not, we are sure to find some pair of indices l, m where $a_l \leq a_m$ and $b_l \geq b_m$. This would be the pair we are looking for. If the upper boundaries are also sorted, then we are guaranteed that no interval is completely contained in another interval. Since this involves sorting followed by a linear scan, we can get this done in $O(n \log n)$ time.

Solution 1.21: The key idea here is to sort the endpoints of the lines and do a sweep from left to right. As we do the sweep, we maintain a list of lines that intersect the current position as well as the highest line and its color. In order to quickly lookup the highest line among the set of intersecting lines, we can keep an ordered binary tree data-structure and to lookup the lines by the endpoint quickly, we can maintain a hash table.

Solution 1.22: Define $F(\sigma)$ to be $\sum_{i=1}^{n} \min(s_i, \sigma)$. We are looking for a value of σ such that $F(\sigma) = S'$. Clearly, F monotonically increases with σ. Also, since $0 \leq S' \leq S$, the value of σ is going to be between 0 and $\max(s_i)$. Hence we can perform a binary search like operation for finding the correct value of σ between 0 and $\max(s_i)$.

Assume that the $s_1, \cdots, s_n$ are already sorted, i.e., for all i, $s_i \leq s_{i+1}$. Compute the running sum $z_k = \sum_{i=1}^{k} s_i$.

Now, suppose $s_k \leq \sigma \leq s_{k+1}$. Consequently,

$$F(\sigma) = (n - k) \cdot \sigma + z_k.$$

Using the above expression, we can search for the value of k such that $F(s_k) \leq S' \leq F(s_{k+1})$ by performing binary search for k (since the runtime of this solution is already $\Theta(n \log n)$, we can do a linear search as well for simplicity). Once we have found the right value of k, we can compute the value of y by simply solving the equation for $F(\sigma)$ above.

The most expensive operation for this entire solution is sorting the s_is, hence the runtime is $O(n \log n)$. However if we are given the s_is in advance and we are allowed preprocessing, then for each value of S', the search would just take $O(\log n)$ time.

Solution 1.23: A solution to this problem is discussed in the context of finding Hardy-Ramanujan numbers (Problem 6.7).

Solution 1.24: Given two line segments in a two-dimensional plane, we can test for intersection easily in constant time. Given n line segments of a polygon, we can find if any of the segments intersect in $O(n^2)$ time by simply testing each pair. However doing this in $O(n \log n)$ time requires a fairly complex algorithm.

Consider two line segments and the two farthest vertical lines that each intersect with both the line segments (one vertical line is the leftmost vertical line that still intersects with both lines and the other one is the rightmost). The two line segments would intersect iff their vertical ordering changes between the two vertical lines.

The key idea is to use a sweep line, a vertical line that moves from left to right through each endpoint. We order the polygon vertices (endpoints of line segments) from left to right first by increasing the x co-ordinate, then by increasing the y co-ordinate. Now, imagine a vertical line moving from left to right through these $2n$ endpoints.

For each position of this vertical line, we keep an ordered list of intersecting line segments. The list is sorted by the y co-ordinate of the first endpoint of the line segment. As we reach the starting points of the new line segments, we insert them by doing a binary search for them. As we reach the end of a line segment, we remove it from the list. The sorted list can be maintained using a balanced BST.

When any line segment ends, we test if its vertical ordering changed compared to the other lines in the list (which can be done in constant time by just comparing the nearest two lines). The lines intersect iff the ordering changed for some line segment.

Chapter 2

Sorting

Solution 2.1: In general, Quicksort is considered one of the most efficient sorting algorithms since it has a runtime of $\Theta(n \log_2 n)$ and it sorts in-place (sorted data is not copied to some other buffer). So, for a large set of random integers, Quicksort would be our choice.

Quicksort has to be implemented carefully—for example, in a naïve implementation, an array with many duplicate elements leads to quadratic runtimes (and a high likelihood of stack space being exhausted because of the number of recursive calls)—this can be managed by putting all keys equal to the pivot in the correct place. Similarly, it is important to call the smaller subproblem first—this, in conjunction with tail recursion ensures that the stack depth is $O(\log_2 n)$.

However there are cases where other solutions are more preferable:

- Small set—for a very small set (for example, 3-4 integers), a simple implementation such as insertion sort is easier to code, and runs faster.
- Almost sorted array—if every element is known to be at most k places from its final location, a min-heap can be used to get an $O(n \log_2 k)$ algorithm (Problem 2.11); alternatives are bubble sort and insertion sort.
- Numbers from a small range, small number of distinct keys—counting sort, which records for each element, the number of elements less than it. This count can be kept in an array (if the largest number is comparable in value to the size of the set being sorted) or a BST, where the keys are the numbers and the values are their frequencies.
- Many duplicates—we can add the keys to a BST, with linked lists for elements which have the same key; the sorted result can be derived from an in-order walk of the BST
- Stability is required—most useful sorting algorithms are not stable.

Mergesort, carefully implemented, can be made stable; another solution is to add the index as an integer rank to the keys to break
ties.

Solution 2.2: When sorting data that cannot fit into the RAM of a single
machine, we have to partition the data into smaller blocks that would fit
in the memory, sort each block individually, and then combine the blocks.
If a cluster of machines is available, the blocks can be sorted in parallel
or they can be read in sequence on a single machine and then stored on
the disk.

There are two popular approaches for doing this. If we know the
rough distribution of the data in advance (e.g., it is distributed uniformly), it can be partitioned into contiguous subranges of approximately equal size in the first pass. This has the advantage that once the
individual blocks are sorted, we can combine them just by concatenation.

Another slightly more expensive approach that does not require any
knowledge of distribution is to read the input data in sequence till the
memory is full, sort it, write it, and then read the next block till we are
done with the file. This requires us to merge the sorted blocks in the
end like Mergesort. Here, since we could be potentially merging a large
number of sorted files, using a min-heap is helpful. Essentially, we keep
the smallest unread entry from each file in the heap, then we extract the
min element from the heap, replace it with the next entry from the same
file, and write out the min value to the output file.

The Unix `sort` program is very robust; it makes use of the disk when
needed and can combine a set of files into a single sorted file.

Solution 2.3: First, we consider the problem of finding the best player.
Each game eliminates one player and there are 128 players; so, 127
matches are necessary and also sufficient.

To find the second best, we note that the only candidates are the players who are beaten by the player who is eventually determined to be the
best—everyone else lost to someone who is not the best.

To find the best player, the order in which we organize the matches is
inconsequential—we just pick pairs from the set of candidates and who-
ever loses is removed from the pool of candidates. However if we proceed in an arbitrary order, we might start with the best player, who de-
feats 127 other players and then the players who lost need to play 126
matches amongst themselves to find the second best.

We can do much better by organizing the matches as a binary tree—
we pair off players arbitrarily who play 64 matches. After these matches,
we are left with 64 candidates; we pair them off again arbitrarily and they
play 32 matches. Proceeding in this fashion, we organize the 127 matches
needed to find the best player and the winner would have played only

7 matches. Therefore we can find the second best player by organizing 6 matches between the 7 players who lost to the best player, for a total of 134 matches.

Solution 2.4: Split the numbers into pairs of two and then group the higher values of the pairs into one set and the lower values into another set. Find the min of the lower group and the max of the higher group.

Solution 2.5: Let's start with five time-trials with no cyclist being in more than one of these five initial time-trials. Let the rankings be $A1, A2, A3, A4, A5,$ $B1, B2, B3, B4, B5,$ $C1, C2, C3, C4, C5,$ $D1, D2, D3, D4, D5,$ and $E1, E2, E3, E4, E5,$ where the first cyclist is the fastest. Note that we can eliminate $A4, A5, B4, B5, C4, C5, D4, D5, E4, E5$ at this stage.

Now, we race the winners from each of the initial time-trials. Without loss of generality, assume the outcome is $A1, B1, C1, D1, E1$. At this point, we can eliminate $D1$ and $E1$ as well as $D2, D3$ and $E2, E3$. Furthermore, since $C1$ was third, $C2$ and $C3$ cannot be in the top three; Similarly, $B3$ cannot be a contender.

We need to find the best and the second best from $A2, A3, B1, B2, C1$, which we can determine with one more time-trial, for a total of seven time-trials.

Note that we need time-trials to determine the overall winner, and the sequence of time-trials to determine the winner is essentially unique—if some cyclist did not participate in the first five time-trials, he would have to participate in the sixth one. But then one of the winners of the first five time-trials would not participate in the sixth time-trial and he might be the overall winner. The first six time-trials do not determine the second and the third fastest cyclists, hence a seventh race is needed.

Solution 2.6: Whenever the swap operation for the objects being sorted is expensive, one of the best things to do is indirect sort, i.e., sort references to the objects first and then apply the permutation that was applied to the references in the end.

In the case of statues, we can assign increasing indices to the statues from left to right and then sort the pairs of statue height and index. The indices in the sorted pairs would give us the permutation to apply. While applying permutation, we would want to perform it in a way that we move each statue the minimum possible distance. We can achieve this if each statue is moved exactly to its correct destination exactly once (no intermediate swaps).

Solution 2.7: The simplest way of doing this would be to define a lexicographic ordering over the rows (where we ignore the contents of deleted columns) and sort the rows. Once the rows are sorted, we can count the number of duplicate rows for each unique row easily in a linear pass. In case it is expensive to swap the rows (since each row contains large amounts of data), it might be more efficient to hash the contents of the row and sort the hash values instead.

Solution 2.8: Almost all sorting algorithms rely on swapping records. However this becomes complicated when the record size varies. One way of dealing with this problem is to allocate for the maximum possible size for each record—this can be very wasteful if there is a large variation in the sizes.

Here also indirect sort can be helpful—keep the records in a compact form in the memory and build another array of pointers to the records. Then we just sort the pointers using the compare function on the de-referenced pointers and finally write the data by de-referencing the sorted pointers.

Solution 2.9: An efficient way of eliminating duplicates from any set of records, where a "less-than" operation can be defined, is to sort the records and then eliminate the duplicates in a single pass over the data.

Sorting can be done in $O(n \log n)$ time; the subsequent elimination of duplicates takes $O(n)$ time. If the elimination of duplicates is done in-place, it would be more efficient than writing the unique set in a separate array since we would achieve better cache performance. Here is the code that does in-place duplicate removal:

```
1   size_t EliminateDuplicates(int* array, size_t length) {
2       size_t j = 1;
3       for (size_t i = 1; i < length; i++) {
4           if (array[i] != array[j-1]) {
5               array[j] = array[i];
6               j++;
7           }
8       }
9       return j;
10  }
```

Another efficient way is to use hash tables where we store each record into a hash table as the key with no value and then write out all the keys in the hash table. Since hash table inserts can be done in $O(1)$ time and iterating over all the keys also takes only (n) time, this solution scales much better than the sorting approach. However, in practice, for small size of inputs, the sorting approach might work faster since it can be done in-place.

Solution 2.10: While merging k sorted arrays, we need to repeatedly pick the smallest element amongst the smallest remaining records from each array. A min-heap is ideal for maintaining a set of records when we repeatedly insert and query for the smallest record (both extract-min and insert would take $O(\log k)$ time). Hence we can do the merge in $O(n \log k)$ time, where n is the total number of records in the input. Here is the code for this:

```
 1  bool  Greater(const  pair<int, int>& a,
 2                 const  pair<int, int>& b) {
 3    if (a.first > b.first) {
 4      return true;
 5    } else if (a.first == b.first && a.second > b.second) {
 6      return true;
 7    } else {
 8      return false;
 9    }
10  }
11
12  void  MergeSortedVectors(
13      const  vector<vector<int> >& sorted_input,
14      vector<int>* output) {
15    // The  first  number  is  the  smallest  number  remaining  and
16    // the  second  number  represents  array  from  which  it  was
              taken.
17    vector<pair<int, int> > min_heap;
18    // We keep  an  index  of  the  numbers  read  from  each  array.
19    vector<int> current_read_index(sorted_input.size());
20    for (int i = 0; i < sorted_input.size(); i++) {
21      if (sorted_input[i].size() > 0) {
22        min_heap.push_back(make_pair(sorted_input[i][0], i));
23        current_read_index[i] = 1;
24      }
25    }
26
27    make_heap(min_heap.begin(), min_heap.end(), Greater);
28
29    while (min_heap.size() > 0) {
30      pair<int, int> min = min_heap[0];
31      pop_heap(min_heap.begin(), min_heap.end(), Greater);
32      min_heap.pop_back();
33      output->push_back(min.first);
34      if (current_read_index[min.second] <
35          sorted_input[min.second].size()) {
36        // There  are  more  inputs  to  be  read.  Read  the  next
                number
37        // and  insert  it  in  the  heap.
38        min.first = sorted_input[min.second][current_read_index
                [min.second]];
39        current_read_index[min.second]++;
40        min_heap.push_back(min);
41        push_heap(min_heap.begin(), min_heap.end(), Greater);
42      }
43    }
44  }
```

Solution 2.11: The easiest way of looking at this problem is that we need to store the numbers in memory till all the numbers smaller than this number have arrived. Once those numbers have arrived and have been written to the output file, we can go ahead and write this number. Since we do not know how the numbers are shuffled, it is hard to tell when all the numbers smaller than a given number have arrived and have been written to the output. However since we are told that no number is off by more than one thousand positions from its correctly sorted position, if more than a thousand numbers greater than a given number have arrived and all the numbers smaller than the given number that arrived have been written, we can be sure that there are no more other smaller numbers that are going to arrive. Hence it is safe to write the given numbers.

This essentially gives us the strategy to always keep 1001 numbers in a min-heap. As soon as we read a new number, we insert the new number and then extract the min from the heap and write the output.

Solution 2.12: While it takes $O(k)$ time to compute the average of a window of size k, the successive averages for the sliding window can be computed inexpensively by maintaining the sum over the sliding window. When the window is slid by one position, the new sum can be computed like this: $sum_{i+1} = sum_i + x[i + k + 1] - x[i]$. Hence the entire running average can be computed in $O(n)$ time.

Computing the running median is a bit more involved but the same idea is applicable there as well. When we slide the window by one position, we delete the first element from the list and insert the next element. Therefore we need to maintain a set in a way that allows us to find the median easily in the presence of inserts and deletes. This can be achieved with a balanced BST (an AVL tree or a red-black tree could do the job). Both insert and delete are $O(\log k)$ operations. Finding the median after an update amounts to looking for the successor or predecessor of the existing median depending on whether the update involved an element that was larger or smaller than the current median. Therefore we can compute the running median in $(n \log k)$ time for the entire series.

Alternately, we could just use an order-statistic tree which is simply a balanced BST with some additional information stored at each node. Specifically, in an order-statistic tree, each node records the number of nodes in the subtree stored at that node. Inserts and deletes can be done in $O(\log n)$ time and retrieving an element with a given rank (which covers the median case) can also be implemented in $O(\log n)$ time.

Solution 2.13: Event driven simulation is a classic problem and is used in a number of simulation applications including digital circuits. The main idea here is that at any given point, we know all the future events that are going to happen as a direct result of events that have happened so far. Until the first event in these set of events happens, nothing else is going to happen. Hence we can advance time to this event without doing any new work.

In practice, this essentially amounts to maintaining a queue of events that are going to happen as a direct result of past events, find the event with the smallest time in this set, delete it from the set, compute the events that this event would trigger, and then insert them in the event queue. For this application again, a min-heap works most efficiently.

Chapter 3

Meta-algorithms

Solution 3.1: Let s_i be the length of the longest nondecreasing subsequence of A that ends at $A[i]$ (specifically, $A[i]$ is included in this subsequence). Then we can write the recurrence

$$s_i = \max \left(\max_{j:A[j]\leq A[i],j<i} (s_j + 1), 1 \right).$$

Using this strategy, fill up a table for s_i. If we want the sequence as well, for each i, in addition to storing the length of the sequence, we can store the index of the last element of sequence that we extend to get this sequence. Here is an implementation of the idea:

```
1   void longestNondecreasingSequence(
2       const vector<int>& input, vector<int>* output) {
3       assert(output != NULL);
4       output->clear();
5       if (input.size() == 0) {
6           return;
7       }
8       vector<int> longestSequenceLength(input.size(), 1);
9       vector<int> previous_index(input.size(), -1);
10      longestSequenceLength[0] = 1;
11      int max_length = 1;
12      int longest_sequence_end = 0;
13      for (int i = 1; i < input.size(); i++) {
14          int length = 1;
15          int prev_index = -1;
16          for (int j = 0; j < i; j++) {
17              if (input[j] <= input[i] &&
18                  longestSequenceLength[j] + 1 > length) {
19                  length = longestSequenceLength[j] + 1;
20                  prev_index = j;
21              }
22          }
23          longestSequenceLength[i] = length;
```

```
24        previous_index[i] = prev_index;
25        if (max_length < length) {
26          max_length = length;
27          longest_sequence_end = i;
28        }
29      }
30      assert(output != NULL);
31      output->clear();
32      // Build the reverse of the longest sequence by going
            backwards from the end.
33      while(longest_sequence_end >= 0) {
34        output->push_back(input[longest_sequence_end]);
35        longest_sequence_end = previous_index[
              longest_sequence_end];
36      }
37      std::reverse(output->begin(), output->end());
38    }
```

Solution 3.2: Let $P[x]$ be true iff there is a stone in the river at x meters.

Let's define $F[x][y]$ to be a Boolean variable that is true iff it is possible for the frog to reach x meters from the shore with the last jump being y meters. We can say that $F[0][y]$ is true iff $y = 0$. Also, $F[x][y]$ can be true iff $P[x]$ is true (there is a stone there) and that either $F[x - y][y]$, $F[x - y][y + 1]$, or $F[x - y][y - 1]$ is true. Using DP, we can compute the values of $F[n][y]$ for all possible values of y. One interesting thing to note here is that while jumping the first n meters, the largest jump size could be at most $\sqrt{2n}$. Hence we just need to worry about values of $y \leq \lceil \sqrt{2n} \rceil$. This gives us a runtime of $O(n^{1.5})$. Here is a possible implementation:

```
1   bool isReachable(const vector<bool>& p) {
2     if (p.size() == 0) {
3       return true;
4     }
5     // Max attainable jump size.
6     int m = sqrt(2 * p.size());
7     vector<vector<bool> > f(p.size() + 1);
8     // The first block can only be reached with jump of
9     // size 1 and no block can be reached with jump of
10    // size 0.
11    for (int j = 0; j <= m; j++) {
12      f[0].push_back(false);
13    }
14    for (int i = 1; i < p.size(); i++) {
15      f[i].push_back(false);
16    }
17    if (p[0]) {
18      f[0][1] = true;
19    }
20    for (int i = 1; i < p.size(); i++) {
21      for (int j = 1; j <= m; j++) {
22        f[i].push_back(false);
23        if (p[i] && i - j >= 0) {
```

```
24              if (f[i−j][j]) {
25                f[i][j] = true;
26              } else if (j > 0 && f[i−j][j−1]) {
27                f[i][j] = true;
28              } else if (j + 1 < m && f[i−j][j+1]) {
29                f[i][j] = true;
30              }
31            }
32            if (f[i][j] == true && i + j + 1 > p.size() ) {
33              //From this point the frog can cross the river in
34              // a single jump.
35              return true;
36            }
37          }
38        }
39        return false;
40 }
```

Solution 3.3: Since the machine we have can only cut a piece of paper into two pieces either vertically or horizontally and all the final pieces have integer length and width, this significantly limits the space we have to explore. Let $V(x, y)$ be the maximum value we can extract out of a paper of width x and height y. Let $U(x, y)$ be the price of a paper of dimension x, y without cutting (if we cannot sell it as is, the value is set to 0).

We assert that

$$V(x, y) = \max$$
$$\left(\max_{a \in [0,x]} \left(V(a, y) + V(x - a, y)\right), \right.$$
$$\max_{b \in [0,y]} \left(V(x, b) + V(x, y - b)\right),$$
$$\left. U(x, y)\right).$$

In other words, the value of the paper is the max of the cost of the two vertically cut pieces or the two horizontally cut pieces or the paper as is. Using this recurrence relationship, we can use DP to compute the values of V of interest in $O(a \cdot b + n)$ time.

```
1 float computeMaxCost(int width, int length, vector<PaperPrice
     > prices) {
2   vector<vector<float> > V;
3   for (int i = 0; i <= width; i++) {
4     V.push_back(vector<float>(length + 1, 0));
5   }
6   for (int i = 0; i < prices.size(); i++) {
7     if (prices[i].length <= length && prices[i].width <=
         width) {
```

```
8        if (V[prices[i].width][prices[i].length] < prices[i].
           price) {
9            V[prices[i].width][prices[i].length] = prices[i].
               price;
10       }
11     }
12   }
13
14   for (int i = 1; i <= width; i++) {
15     for (int j = 1; j <= length; j++) {
16       for (int k = 1; k < i; k++) {
17         if (V[i][j] < V[i-k][j] + V[k][j]) {
18           V[i][j] = V[i-k][j] + V[k][j];
19         }
20       }
21       for (int k = 1; k < j; k++) {
22         if (V[i][j] < V[i][k] + V[i][j-k]) {
23           V[i][j] = V[i][k] + V[i][j-k];
24         }
25       }
26     }
27   }
28
29   float result = V[width][length];
30   return result;
31 }
```

Solution 3.4: This is a straightforward DP problem. If the input string S has length n, we build a table T of length n such that $T[k]$ is a Boolean that tells us if the substring $S(0, k)$ can be broken into a set of valid words.

We can build a hash table of all the valid words such that we can determine if a string is a valid word or not in constant time. Then $T[k]$ is true iff there exists a $j \in [0, k-1]$ such that $T[j]$ is true and $S(j, k)$ is a valid word.

This will just tell us if we can break a given string into valid words but would not give us the words themselves. With a little more bookkeeping, we can achieve that. Essentially, in table T along with the Boolean value, we can also store the beginning index of the last word in the string.

If we want all possible decompositions, we can store all possible values of j that gives us a correct break with each position. However the number of possible decompositions can be exponential here. For example, consider the string "itsitsitsits...".

Solution 3.5: We need to determine if there is a subset of states whose Electoral College votes add up to $\frac{538}{2} = 269$. This is a version of the 0-1 knapsack problem described in Problem 6.1 and the DP solution to that problem can be used.

Solution 3.6: Number the individual elections from 1 to 446. Let $T(a, b)$ be the probability that exactly b Republicans win out of elections $\{1, 2, \ldots, a\}$.

Let X_i be the event that a Republican wins the i-th race. Then $T(a, b) = Pr(\sum_{i \leq a} X_i = b)$. There are two ways in which the first a random variables sum up to b: the a-th random variable is 1 and the first $a - 1$ variables sum up to $b - 1$ or the a-th random variable is 0 and the first $a - 1$ random variables sum up to b. Since these events are exclusive, the probability $T(a, b)$ is the sum of the probabilities of these two events. To be precise,

$$T(a, b) = T(a - 1, b - 1) \cdot p_a + T(a - 1, b) \cdot (1 - p_a).$$

The base cases for the recursion are $T(0, 0) = 1$ and $T(0, b) = 0$, for $b > 0$. Therefore T can be computed using DP. Since both a and b take values from 0 to the number of races and computing $T(a, b)$ from earlier values takes constant time, the complexity is quadratic in the number of races.

Solution 3.7: Let $L(a, b)$ be the maximum load on a server when users with hash h_1 through h_a are assigned to servers S_1 through S_b in an optimal way so that the max load is minimized. We observe the following recurrence:

$$L(a, b) = \min_{x \in \{1, \ldots, a\}} \left(\max \left(L(x, b - 1), \sum_{i=x+1}^{a} (B_i) \right) \right).$$

In other words, we find the right value of x such that if we pack the first x users in $b - 1$ servers and the remaining in the last server, the max load on a given server is minimized.

Using this relationship, we can tabulate the values of L till we get $L(n, m)$. While computing $L(a, b)$ when the values of L is tabulated for all lower values of a and b, we need to find the right value of x to minimize the load. As we increase x, $L(x, b - 1)$ in the above expression increases and the term $\sum_{i=x+1}^{a}(B_i))$ decreases. Hence in order to find x that minimizes their max, we can do a binary search for x which can be done in $O(\log a)$ time. Therefore we can compute the load in $O(mn \log(n))$ time.

Solution 3.8: Let $V(g)$ be the voltage level assigned to gate g. Let $I(g)$ be the set of all gates that are inputs to g. Let $P(g)$ be the minimum possible power that can be achieved by a legal assignment of voltages, wherein we choose a low voltage for gate g. Let $Q(g)$ be the minimum possible power that can be achieved when g is assigned a high voltage. We can write the following recurrence relationship for P and Q:

$$P(g) = 1 + \sum_{r \in I(g)} Q(r)$$

$$Q(g) = 2 + \sum_{r \in I(g)} \min \left(P(r), Q(r) \right).$$

Using these equations, we can tabulate the values of P and Q for all gates and our answer is going to come from the maximum of the values of P and Q for the gate at the root of the tree. Since we perform constant operations per gate, the overall complexity is $O(G)$, where G is the number of gates.

Solution 3.9: We can formulate this DP in a manner similar to Solution 3.8. For each node, we tabulate k values. Let $N(u, l)$ be the minimum number of buffers needed for the subtree rooted at node u, if the first buffer above this node appears l or more hops away. The recurrence relationship can be defined by

$$N(n, l) = \sum_{c \in I(n)} \min \left(1 + N(c, k), N \left(c, \min(l + 1, k) \right) \right).$$

We can tabulate the value of N for all nodes from the leaf to the root for all values of $l \leq k$. Then $N(r, k)$, where r is the root, is the minimum number of buffers needed. Since we perform $O(k)$ operations per gate, the overall complexity is $O(G \cdot k)$, where G is the number of gates.

Solution 3.10: Let's label the vertices of the polygon $1, \ldots, n$, starting from an arbitrary vertex and walking clockwise. Let $C(p_1, \ldots, p_k)$ be the cost of triangulating the polygon formed by vertices p_1 through p_k. Let $L(a \cdot b)$ be the length of the straight line drawn from vertex a to vertex b.

Now, we know that if the number of vertices in the polygon is three or less, the cost is zero. Consider an edge $\langle p_i, p_{i+1} \rangle$. One of the triangles must contain this edge. The third vertex of the triangle is going to be another vertex, say p_j. Then the cost of triangulation is going to be the cost of triangle $\langle p_i, p_{i+1}, p_j \rangle$ and the cost of triangulation of the smaller polygons formed by removing this triangle (which may be 1 or 2 polygons depending upon whether $j = i + 2$ or not). For any pair of points a and b, let $L(a, b)$ be the length of the line segment joining a and b. Then we can write the following recurrence relationship:

$$A(p_1, \ldots, p_k) = \min_{x:3 \leq x \leq k} \Big($$
$$A(p_3, \ldots, p_x)$$
$$+ A(p_x, \ldots, p_k, p_1) + L(p_1, p_2) + L(p_1, p_x) + L(p_2, p_x) \Big).$$

If we tabulate the cost of triangulation of each polygon that is a result of picking subsequent points on the original polygon, we would need to do this for roughly n^2 polygons. If we have already tabulated the value for all smaller polygons, it will take us $O(n)$ time for doing so. Hence we can compute the minimum cost in $O(n^3)$ time.

Solution 3.11: We focus on the case where all the operands are nonnegative integers and the only operations are $\cdot$ and $+$.

Represent the expression $v_0 \circ_0 v_1 \circ_1 \cdots \circ_{n-2} v_{n-1}$ by arrays $V = [v_0, \ldots, v_{n-1}]$ and $\circ_0, \ldots, \circ_{n-2}$.

Let $\text{Max}[i, j]$ denote the maximum value achievable by some parenthesization for the subexpression $v_i \circ_i v_i \circ_i \cdots \circ_j v_j$, where $\text{Max}[i, j]$ is just $V[i]$.

The key to solving this problem is to recognize that if operation $\circ_i$ is performed last, the subexpressions $v_0 \circ_0 v_1 \circ_1 \cdots \circ_{i-2} v_{i-1}$ and $v_{i+1} \circ_{i+1} \cdots \circ_{n-2} v_{n-1}$ must be parenthesized to be maximized individually.

In particular, the maximum value must be achieved for some value of i in $[0, n-2]$, so

$$\text{Max}[0, n-1] = \max_{i \in [0, n-2]} \text{Max}[0, i] \circ_i \text{Max}[i+1, n-1].$$

The total number of recursive calls is $O(\binom{n}{2})$ and each call requires $O(n)$ additional computation to combine the results, leading to an $O(n^3)$ algorithm.

Efficiently computing this recurrence requires that intermediate results be cached. In code:

```
1   public class Parens {
2
3       int [] V;
4       char [] Op;
5
6       int [][] Max;
7       boolean [][] valid;
8
9       public Parens(int [] V, char [] Op) {
10          this.V = V;
11          this.Op = Op;
12      }
13
```

```
14    public int maxExpr(int begin, int end) {
15
16      if ( valid[begin][end] ) {
17        return Max[begin][end];
18      }
19
20      if ( begin == end ) {
21        Max[begin][end] = V[begin];
22        valid[begin][end] = true;
23        return V[begin];
24      }
25
26      if ( begin + 1 == end ) {
27        Max[begin][end] = (Op[begin] == '+') ?
28                          V[begin] + V[end] :
29                          V[begin] * V[end];
30        valid[begin][end] = true;
31        return Max[begin][end];
32      }
33
34      int max = Integer.MIN_VALUE;
35      int candidateMax = 0;
36      for ( int i = begin + 1; i < end; i++ ) {
37        int lMax = maxExpr( begin, i );
38        int rMax = maxExpr( i+1, end);
39        if ( Op[i] == '+' ) {
40          candidateMax = lMax + rMax;
41        } else {
42          candidateMax = lMax * rMax;
43        }
44        max = (max < candidateMax) ? candidateMax : max;
45      }
46      Max[begin][end] = max;
47      valid[begin][end] = true;
48      return max;
49    }
50
51    public int maxExpr() {
52      int N = V.length;
53      Max = new int [N][N];
54      valid = new boolean [N][N];
55      return  maxExpr(0,N-1);
56    }
57
58    public static void main( String[] args ) {
59
60      int [] v1 = {1,2,3,3,2,1};
61      char [] o1 = {'+','*','*','+', '+'};
62
63      Parens exp1 = new Parens(v1, o1);
64      System.out.println("Max_value_of_expression_is:" + exp1.
          maxExpr() );
65    }
66 }
```

For the more general cases, we need to keep track of the minimum and maximum values as well as the positive and negative values closest to zero. This makes the code more complicated but does not change the character and the complexity of the algorithm.

Solution 3.12: We schedule tutors greedily: as soon as there is a request that cannot be handled by the previously assigned tutors, we choose a new tutor.

While it is simple to implement this scheme, it is not completely trivial to prove that it is optimum, i.e., we cannot cover all the requests with fewer tutors.

In order to prove the optimality we will define the notion of slack. Consider a set of requests $j_1, \ldots, j_n$ such that the requests are ordered by the time they need to be done. Let $S(j)$ and $E(j)$ be the starting and ending time for request j. Let $t_i, \ldots, t_m$ be the times when we assign a tutor, ordered by time.

Define the time the last tutor assigned has available after his last request is fulfilled as the slack in the schedule.

We claim that greedy scheduling is the optimum scheduling. We can prove this using induction over the number of requests; for our induction hypothesis, in addition to the claim that the number of tutors is minimized, we claim that the schedule maximizes the slack. For $n = 1$, the greedy algorithm will send exactly one tutor at the start time of the request; clearly this is the strategy that uses the minimum number of tutors and no more slack is possible.

Let's assume that this statement is true for all values of $n \leq k$. Now we can prove this for $n = k+1$ as follows: consider the requests $j_1, \ldots, j_k$ sorted by their start time. Consider that $t_1, \ldots, t_m$ are the times when we scheduled the tutors to cover these requests based on the greedy strategy. Now, when we add the next request j_{k+1} to the list, either it can be covered by slack or it may require a new tutor.

In the case the new request can be covered by the slack, clearly this is the optimum solution (if we needed at least m tutors to cover the first k requests, we cannot cover the $k + 1$ requests with fewer tutors). Also, in this case, since the schedule for the first k requests maximized the slack, we cannot have a better schedule with m tutors that cover all $k + 1$ requests and have a bigger slack.

In case we need to pick an additional tutor for the $k + 1$-th request, it must be that the m-th tutor did not have the slack to cover the last request. If there is another way to cover the requests with m or less tutors, then we can use the same set of tutors to cover the first k requests and get a bigger slack, which contradicts our assumptions. Also, since the $(m + 1)$-th tutor will start exactly when the last request starts, this schedule must maximize the slack.

Solution 3.13: Let's say that the time for the i-th customer to be serviced is c_i. Then the waiting time for the customer c_i would be $\sum_{j=1}^{i} t_{c_j}$. Hence sum of all the wait times would be

$$\sum_{i=0}^{n} \sum_{j=1}^{i} t_{c_j} = \sum_{i=0}^{n} t_{c_i} \cdot i.$$

Since we want to minimize the total wait time for all the customers and c_is must take values from 1 through n, it follows that the customers who take the smallest time must get served first. Hence we must sort the customers by their service time and then serve them in the order of increasing service time.

Solution 3.14: Huffman coding is an optimum solution to this problem (there could be other optimum codes as well). Huffman coding proceeds in three steps:
1. Sort symbols in increasing order of probability and create a binary tree node for each symbol.
2. Create a new node by combining the smallest probability nodes as children and assigning it the probability of the sum of its children.
3. Remove the children from consideration and add the new node into the sorted list of nodes to be combined and repeat the entire process till we have a single rooted binary tree.

Once we have the rooted tree, we can assign all the left edges as 0 and the right edges as 1. All the original symbols would be the leaf nodes in this tree and the path from root to the leaf node would give us the bit sequence for that symbol.

Now, we need to prove (1.) this encoding is optimum and (2.) find a fast implementation of this algorithm.

For implementing this idea, we can maintain a min-heap of candidate nodes that can be combined in any given step. Since each combination step requires two *extract-min* and one *insert* operation that can be done in $O(\log n)$ time, we can find the Huffman codes in $O(n \log n)$ time.

We can prove the optimality of Huffman codes inductively. For a single code, obviously Huffman codes are optimum. Let's say that for any probability distribution among n symbols, Huffman codes are optimum. Given this assumption, we will prove it is true for $n + 1$. Suppose there is another encoding that has a smaller expected length of code for some probability distribution for $n + 1$ symbols.

For any encoding, we can map the codes to a binary tree by creating the null string to root and adding a left edge for each 0 and a right edge for each 1. We can make several observations about this binary tree:
- Each symbol must map to a leaf node; otherwise, our prefix assumption will be violated.

- There cannot be a nonleaf node that has less than two children (otherwise, we can delete the node and bring its child one level up and hence reduce the expected code length).
- If we sort the binary tree leaves in order of their path lengths, the two longest paths must have the same length (since the parent of the leaf with the longest path must have another child).
- The two nodes with the longest paths in the tree must be assigned to the two symbols with the smallest probability (otherwise, we can swap symbols and achieve smaller expected code length).
- If we remove the two smallest probability symbols and replace them with one symbol that has its probability equal to the sum of the probabilities of the replaced symbols, the optimum prefix coding must have the same expected code length as this tree when we delete the two lowest probability nodes (otherwise, we can use this new optimum tree and replace it with the old tree).

Now consider that the symbols have probabilities $p_1 \leq p_2 \leq \ldots \leq p_{n+1}$. Let $O(p_1, \ldots, p_{n+1})$ be the optimum expected code length for this probability distribution and $H(p_1, \ldots, p_{n+1})$ be the expected code length for Huffman coding. So, we can easily see that

$$O(p_1, \ldots, p_{n+1}) = O(p_1, \ldots, p_{n-1}, p_n + p_{n+1}) + p_n + p_{n+1}.$$

The way we construct Huffman codes we know that

$$H(p_1, \ldots, p_{n+1}) = H(p_1, \ldots, p_{n-1}, p_n + p_{n+1}) + p_n + p_{n+1}.$$

By our inductive assumption, $H(p_1, \ldots, p_{n-1}, p_n + p_{n+1}) = O(p_1, \ldots, p_{n-1}, p_n + p_{n+1})$. Hence $H(p_1, \ldots, p_{n+1}) = O(p_1, \ldots, p_{n+1})$. In other words, Huffman coding is optimum for $n + 1$ symbols.

Solution 3.15: This problem is very similar in structure to the Huffman coding problem above, if $c = 1$. If we represent each click on the submenu operation as a 1 and each scan down operation as a 0, then the path to reach a menu item can be represented as a string of 0s and 1s. The time it would take to reach each menu item is proportional to the length of this string. And finally, we cannot have two actions mapped to two strings such that one is a prefix of the other. Hence if we use Huffman coding algorithm to come up with the bit-strings for each action and then build the menu system based on these strings, we would achieve the minimum expected time to interact with the menu.

When $c > 1$, it is similar to the case where there is an asymmetric cost for a 0 and a 1 in the code (for example, it requires more power to transmit a 1 than a 0). There is no known polynomial time solution for this case. Below we describe an algorithm that will take $O(2^n \cdot n \cdot \log n)$ time:

1. Sort each operation by the probability of its occurrence.
2. Iterate over all possible binary tree structures with n leaves. Map each left edge in the binary tree as a scan down operation and each right edge as a clock to open sub-menu operation.
   a) For each leaf, compute the time it takes to reach the node (number of left edges + c times the number of right edges in the path to the node).
   b) Sort the nodes in the order of time it takes to reach it.
   c) Map the actions to the nodes such that the highest probability action is mapped to the lowest visit time. Compute the expected visit time to the nodes.
3. Find the tree structure that has the lowest expected time to visit.

The number of unique binary trees with n leaves is roughly $O(2^n)$.

Solution 3.16: This can be trivially done in $O(n^2)$ time if we do a linear scan for the boxes for each new object to find the first box where it would fit.

In order to speed things up, we can maintain a list of boxes where a certain capacity is available for the first time. For each box, we keep a record which contains the remaining box capacity and the box number. We will maintain a sorted list of boxes, first by box capacity, then by box number. When we receive a new item, we look for the first record with capacity greater than or equal to the item's weight. We put it in the corresponding box, update its capacity, and reinsert it at the correct position. In order to maintain a sorted list, we can use a balanced binary tree such that find, delete, and insert are all $O(\log n)$ operations.

Solution 3.17: A covering set S must contain at least one point x such that $x \le b_{min} = \min\{b_i\}$. Any such point covers the subset of intervals $[a_i, b_i]$, $a_i \le b_{min}$. Of course, b_{min} itself covers all such intervals and so there exists a minimum cardinality covering that contains b_{min} and no other points to its left. Consequently, the following procedure computes a minimum covering set S:

```
1  I = {1,2,...,n};
2  S = {};
3  while (I != {}) {
4      bmin = min{b[i] | i in I}
5      S = S + {bmin};
6      I = I - {i|a[i] <= bmin};
7  }
```

Using a balanced BST, we can implement the search for minimum, insertion, and deletion in $O(\log n)$ time, yielding an $O(n \log n)$ algorithm.

Solution 3.18: If there is some point on the circle that is not contained in at least one of the n arcs, then the problem is identical to Problem 3.17. So, suppose this is not so. Without loss of generality, we may assume that a minimum cardinality covering set S contains only right endpoints of arcs, i.e., "clockwise" right endpoints. There are n such endpoints. If we choose a given right endpoint and eliminate all the arcs that are covered by it, the remaining problem is identical to that in Problem 3.17. This means we can solve the arc-covering problem by n calls to the algorithm in Solution 3.17, yielding an $O(n^2 \log n)$ algorithm.

Solution 3.19: Suppose our algorithm computes the clustering $C = \{O_1, O_2, \ldots, O_k\}$. Suppose C is not optimum, i.e., there is another clustering $P = \{P_1, P_2, \ldots, P_k\}$ which lowers the separation. Since C and P are distinct, there must be some pair of objects a, b that are assigned to the same cluster in C but different clusters in P—otherwise, either C and P would be identical or some P_i would be empty, which was explicitly disallowed.

Let u, v be the last pair of objects that we merged in our algorithm. Suppose x, y were the next pair our algorithm would have merged if we had performed one more iteration, i.e., computed a $k + 1$-clustering. Observe that $d(x, y)$ is the separation of C since x and y are a pair of closest objects not in the same cluster.

Now, our algorithm has put a and b in the same cluster, there is some set of pairs of the form $\{(a, \delta_1), (\delta_1, \delta_2), \ldots, (\delta_{l-1}, \delta_l), (\delta_l, b)\}$ that our algorithm selected. (It may be that the set is simply $\{(a, b)\}$ if we directly selected $d(a, b)$.) Since a and b are in different clusters in P, one of these pairs, call it e, must be in distinct P_i and P_j. Therefore the separation of P is at most $d(e)$, which is no more than $d(u, v)$. Now $d(u, v)$ is no more than $d(x, y)$, which is the separation of C. Therefore the separation of P is no more than that of C, contradicting the choice of P. Therefore C has the maximum separation of all k-clusterings.

Solution 3.20: We compute the optimum invitation list by iteratively removing people who cannot meet Leona's constraints until there is no one left to remove—the remaining set is the unique maximum set of people that Leona can invite.

Specifically, we iteratively remove anyone who has fewer than six friends in the current set or anyone who has fewer than six people they do not know in the current set. The process must converge since we start with a finite number of people and remove at least one person in each iteration. The remaining set satisfies Leona's constraints by construction.

It remains to show that the remaining set is maximum. In fact, we show something stronger, namely that it is the unique maximum set that satisfies Leona's constraints.

We do this by proving that people who are removed could never be in a set that satisfies the constraints. We do this by induction on the order in which the people were removed.

The first person P_1 removed was removed because either P_1 had fewer than six friends in the entire set or the number of people P_1 did not know was fewer than six—clearly P_1 cannot belong to any set that satisfies the constraints, let alone the maximum set.

Inductively, assume the first $i-1$ persons removed could not belong to any set that satisfies the constraints.

Consider P_i, the i-th person we remove. It must be that either fewer than six people know P_i in the current set or P_i does not know fewer than six people in the current set. But by induction, the current set includes any maximum set, so the i-th person removed cannot belong to a maximum set and induction goes through.

Chapter 4

Algorithms on Graphs

Solution 4.1: Model the maze as an undirected graph. Each vertex corresponds to a white pixel. We will index the vertices based on the coordinates of the corresponding pixel; so, vertex $v_{i,j}$ corresponds to the matrix entry (i, j). Edges model adjacent pixels; so, $v_{i,j}$ is connected to vertices $v_{i+1,j}$, $v_{i,j+1}$, $v_{i-1,j}$, and $v_{i,j-1}$, assuming these vertices exist— vertex $v_{a,b}$ does not exist if the corresponding pixel is black or the co- ordinates (a, b) lie outside the image.

Now, run a DFS starting from the vertex corresponding to the en- trance. If at some point, we discover the exit vertex in the DFS, then there exists a path from the entrance to the exit . If we implement recur- sive DFS then the path would consist of all the vertices in the call stack corresponding to previous recursive calls to the DFS routine.

This problem can also be solved using BFS from the entrance vertex on the same graph model. The BFS tree has the property that the com- puted path will be a shortest path from the entrance. However BFS is more difficult to implement than DFS since in DFS, the compiler implic- itly handles the DFS stack, whereas in BFS, the queue has to be explicitly coded up. Since the problem did not call for a shortest path, it is better to use DFS.

Solution 4.2: If you traverse the binary tree in BFS order, then you are guaranteed to hit all the nodes at the same depth consecutively. So, you can build the linked list of all the nodes as you discover them in BFS order. While traversing the tree, we also need to know when we move from nodes of depth k to nodes of depth $k+1$. This can be easily achieved by keeping track of the depth when inserting nodes in the queue.

Solution 4.3: First, we consider the problem of checking if G is 2∃- connected. If $G' = (V, E - \{(u, v)\})$ is connected, it must be that a path

144

exists between u and v. This is possible iff u and v lie on a cycle in G. Thus G is $2\exists$-connected iff there exists a cycle in G.

We can check for the existence of a cycle in G by running DFS on G. As soon as we discover an edge from a gray vertex back to a gray vertex which is not its immediate predecessor in the search, a cycle exists in G and we can stop.

The complexity of DFS is $(|V| + |E|)$; however in the case described above, the algorithm runs in $O(|V|)$ time. This is because an undirected graph with no cycles can have at most $|V| - 1$ edges.

Now, we consider the problem of checking if G is $2\forall$-connected. Clearly, G is not $2\forall$-connected iff there exists an edge e such that $G' = (V, E - \{e\})$ is disconnected. The latter condition holds iff there is no cycle including edge e.

We can find an edge (u, v) that is not on a cycle with DFS. Without loss of generality, assume u is discovered first. Observe that the removal of (u, v) disconnects G iff there are no back-edges between v or v's descendants to u or u's ancestors.

Define $l(v)$ to be the minimum of the discovery time $d(v)$ of v and $d(w)$ for w such that (t, w) is a back-edge from t, where t is a descendant of v.

We claim $l(v) < d(v)$ iff there is a back-edge between v or one of v's descendants to u or one of u's ancestors. If $l(v) < d(v)$, then there is a path from v through one of its descendants to an ancestor of v, i.e., v lies on a cycle. If $l(v) = d(v)$, there is no way to get from v back to u; hence removal of (u, v) disconnects u and v.

Now, we show how to compute $l(v)$ efficiently: once we have processed all of v's children, then $l(v) = \min\left(d(v), \min_{x \text{ child of } v} l(x)\right)$. This computation does not add to the asymptotic complexity of DFS since it is just a constant additional work per edge, so we can check $2\forall$-connectedness in linear-time.

Solution 4.4: Assuming the pins are numbered from 0 to $p - 1$, create an undirected graph G on p vertices $v_0, \ldots, v_{p-1}$. Add an edge between v_i to v_j if pins i and j are connected by a wire.

Assume for simplicity, G is connected; if not, the connected components can be analyzed independently.

Run BFS on G starting with v_0. Assign v_0 arbitrarily to lie on the left half. All vertices at an odd distance from v_0 are assigned to the right half.

When performing BFS on an undirected graph, all newly discovered edges will either be from vertices which are at a distance d from v_0 to undiscovered vertices (which will then be at a distance $d + 1$ from v_0) or from vertices which are at a distance d to vertices which are also at a distance d. First, assume we never encounter an edge from a distance k vertex to a distance k vertex. In this case, each wire is from a distance

k vertex to a distance $k + 1$ vertex, so all wires are between the left and right halves.

If any edge is from a distance k vertex to a distance k vertex, we stop—the pins cannot be partitioned into left and right halves as desired. The reason is as follows: let u and v be such vertices. Consider the first common ancestor a in the BFS search of u and v (such an ancestor must exist since the search started at v_0). The paths $p_{a,u}$ and $p_{a,v}$ in the BFS tree from a to u and v are of equal length; therefore the cycle formed by going from a to u, then through the edge (u, v), and then back to a from u via $p_{a,v}$ has an odd length. The vertices in an odd length cycle cannot be partitioned into two sets such that all edges are between the sets.

Solution 4.5: It is natural to model the network as a graph: vertices correspond to individuals and an edge exists from A to B if B is a contact of A.

For an individual x, we can compute the set of x's contacts by running graph search (DFS or BFS) from x. Running graph search for each individual leads to a $O(|V| \cdot (|V| + |E|))$ algorithm for transitive closure.

Another approach which has complexity $O(|V|^3)$ but which may be more efficient for dense graphs is to run an all-pairs shortest path algorithm with edge weights of 1. If there is a path from u to v, the shortest path distance from u to v will be finite; otherwise, it will be ∞. We can further improve the shortest path calculation by simply recording whether there is a path from u to v or not; in this way, we need a Boolean matrix rather than an integer matrix encoding the distances between the vertices.

Solution 4.6: Let v be any vertex in G. Consider an Euler tour T of G. Each time the tour enters v, it must exit v by a different edge. Furthermore, each edge must be entered exactly once and exited exactly once. Hence we can put incoming edges and outgoing edges in a 1-1 correspondence, so the in-degree and out-degree of v must be equal.

Conversely, let the in-degree and out-degree of every vertex v in G be equal. Construct an Euler tour as follows: start with an arbitrary vertex. Use DFS to explore from this vertex until a simple cycle is found. Such a cycle must exist since we can never get trapped in a vertex—if we entered a newly discovered vertex, we can always exit it because of the constraint that in-degree equals out-degree.

Continue doing this till all the edges have been partitioned into disjoint simple cycles. Now, merge these cycles as follows: start with any cycle. For any vertex on the current cycle, find a cycle that it is in, which is not the current cycle, and add a detour to this new cycle. Iteratively add cycles to the current cycle.

We claim that all disjoint cycles must be merged by this process. If not, there must be an edge (p, q) on a simple cycle S that is not in the cycle C our process has converged to, where p appears in C (such an edge exists because the graph is connected). We can merge the edges of S to our cycle about p, thereby contradicting the maximality of C.

The algorithm for constructing the cycles is just DFS and the merge process is also linear-time, so the algorithm is linear-time.

Solution 4.7: Model the FSM as a graph—each state s corresponds to a distinct vertex v_s. The edge set consists of precisely those edges which correspond to potential transitions between states; specifically, $(v_s, v_t) \in E$ iff $\exists i\, T(s, i) = t$. We will refer to states and vertices interchangeably.

Now, consider the directed acyclic graph (DAG) of strongly connected components (SCCs) for this graph. Any state not in an SCC (which is the sink of this DAG) may transition out of the SCC which it is in and once it is out, it will not return. Conversely, all states within the sink SCCs can return to themselves, so the states in the sink SCCs are precisely the nonephemeral states; the complement of this set is the desired set of ephemeral states.

The SCC DAG of a graph can be computed in linear-time from the graph model and the graph itself can be constructed in linear-time from the FSM, so the whole computation is linear.

Solution 4.8: We can compute the diameter by running BFS from each vertex and recording the largest shortest path distance. This has $O(|V| \cdot (|V| + |E|)) = O(|V|^2)$ complexity since $|E| = |V| - 1$ in a tree.

We can achieve better time complexity by using divide-and-conquer. Let r be any vertex. We take r to be the root of the tree T. Suppose r has degree m and the subtrees rooted at r's children are $T_1, T_2, \ldots, T_m$. Let $d_1, d_2, \ldots, d_m$ be their diameters and $h_1, h_2, \ldots, h_n$ their heights.

Let λ be a longest path in T. Either it passes through r or it does not. If it does not pass through r, it must be entirely within one of the m subtrees and hence the longest path length in T is the maximum of $d_1, d_2, \ldots, d_m$. If it does pass through r, it must be between a pair of vertices in distinct subtrees that are farthest from r. The distance from r to the vertex in T_i that is farthest from it is simply $f_i = h_i + 1$. The longest length path in T is the larger of the maximum of $d_1, d_2, \ldots, d_m$ and the two largest f_is.

If we process the subtrees one at a time, update $\max_i\{d_1, d_2, \ldots, d_i\}$, and the largest and second largest of the f_is, the time complexity is proportional to the size of the tree, i.e., $O(|V|)$.

Solution 4.9: Assume the inputs to the network stabilize at time 0. We are trying to bound when the primary outputs stabilize.

Suppose gate g has a delay $D(g)$. It will stabilize at no more than $D(g)$ time after all its inputs have stabilized. Therefore we can compute when each gate has stabilized by processing gates in topological order, starting from the primary inputs—for each gate, we can bound when it stabilizes since we have already bounded when its inputs have stabilized. Topological ordering for a graph can be computed in $O(n + m)$ time, where n and m are the number of vertices and edges in the graph.

The value we compute is an upper bound and may not be tight because of logical relationships between signals—for example, if one of the inputs to an AND gate is 0, then the output of the AND gate will be independent of the changes at its other inputs.

Solution 4.10: Let A and B be n-dimension real vectors; write $A < B$ if $A[i] < B[i]$ for each i. The $<$ relation is transitive.

Let $\langle x_1, x_2, \ldots, x_{20} \rangle$ be the heights of the players in Team X and $\langle y_1, y_2, \ldots, y_{20} \rangle$ be the heights of the players in Team Y. The key observation is that Team X can be placed in front of Team Y iff SORT$\langle x_1, \ldots, x_{20} \rangle <$ SORT$\langle y_1, \ldots, y_{20} \rangle$.

Now, we define a DAG G with vertices corresponding to the teams as follows: there is an edge from vertex X to Y iff SORT$(X) <$ SORT(Y).

Every sequence of teams where the successive teams can be placed in front of each other corresponds to a path in G. To find the longest such sequence, we simply need to find the longest path in the DAG G. We can do this, for example, by topologically ordering the vertices in G; the longest path terminating at vertex v is the maximum of the longest paths terminating at v's fanins concatenated with v itself.

The topological ordering computation is $O(|V| + |E|)$ and dominates the computation time.

Solution 4.11: The most obvious approach is to start with an arbitrary two-coloring. If it is diverse, we are done.

At this point, a natural approach would be to look for a nondiverse vertex v and flipping v's color but this can result in some of v's neighbors becoming nondiverse.

To prove that this approach works, we look at *diverse* edges—edges between vertices of different colors. We claim that a coloring that maximizes the number of diverse edges is also diverse.

If not, suppose x is not diverse. Without loss of generality, suppose x is white. Then by changing x's color to black, the number of diverse edges strictly increases (since x had more white neighbors than black neighbors).

Therefore a coloring which maximizes the number of diverse edges yields a diverse graph. Such a coloring must exist: because the graph is finite, there are only a finite number of colorings. We can construct a coloring by starting with an arbitrary coloring and applying the argument above, i.e., finding nondiverse vertices and flipping their color.

Solution 4.12: Usually Dijkstra's shortest path algorithm uses scalar values for edge length. However it can easily be modified to the case where edge weight is a vector if *addition* and *comparison* can be defined over the vectors. In this case, if the edge cost is c, we say the length of the edge is given by the vector $\langle c, 1 \rangle$. We define addition to be just component-wise addition. Hence if we sum up the edge lengths over a path, we essentially get the total cost and the number of edges in the path. The compare function can be just the lexicographic (first by the total cost, then by the number of edges). With this, we can run Dijkstra's shortest path algorithm and find the shortest path that requires the least number of edges.

Solution 4.13: We can compute the number of shortest paths by performing a BFS-type computation starting at u.

Consider the set of vertices S_{k-1} such that for any vertex $a \in S_{k-1}$, the shortest distance between u and a is $k-1$. Now, consider a vertex v such that the shortest distance between u and v is k. If we know the number of shortest paths between u and any vertex in S_{k-1}, we can easily infer the number of shortest paths between u and v by summing up this number for all vertices $a \in S_{k-1}$ that also have an edge to v. This is because each distinct path from u to a also gives us a distinct path from u to v by simply adding the edge from a to y to the path.

BFS runs in linear-time and, assuming we store the number of shortest paths from intermediate vertices, the computation for a distance k node is proportional to the number of its outgoing edges. Hence the complete algorithm runs in linear-time.

Solution 4.14: This is an NP-complete problem and hence there is no efficient algorithm known for it. However if the probabilities assigned to each edge come from a small set of numbers or if we are willing to approximate the probabilities, then this can be solved efficiently.

It is natural to solve this problem using dynamic programming—we iteratively compute the matrix $M_p^k(s, t)$ which is the shortest path distance between vertices s and t such that the probability of a path existing with that distance is at least p and the number of edges in the path is exactly k.

Given $M_p^k(s, t)$, we can compute $M_p^{k+1}(s, t)$ using the recurrence

$$M_p^{k+1}(s, t) = \min p' \min_{u \in \text{fanin}(t)} \left(M_{p'}^k(s, u) \cdot M_{p/p'}^1(u, t) \right).$$

There are an infinite number of values for p: any real number in $[0, 1]$. In reality, there are only a finite number of paths, so we only need to consider those probabilities. However the number of paths in a graph can be exponential and each path can have a distinct probability, so it is not realistic to consider the possible set of values for p. Instead, we can take the approach of binning: we compute M_p^k for a range of values for p, e.g., $p = \frac{n}{100}$, $n = 0$ to 100.

Solution 4.15: Let's model the map as a graph $G = (V, E)$ such that each room i is represented by vertex $v_i \in V$ and an edge $(v, v_j) \in E$ exists iff there is a way to go from room i to room j. Let $l(e)$ be the length of the corridor represented by the edge e.

     The key idea here is to assign each room an expected time to the treasure room when we follow the optimal strategy. Let's say for room i, the expected time to the treasure room is $t(i)$. Then for a nonspecial room i, we would always pick the next room to be the one that gives us the smallest expected time to the treasure room. Hence for nonspecial room i

$$t(i) = \min_{j:(i,j)\in E} \Big(l((i,j)) + t(j) \Big).$$

On the other hand, for the special rooms, the expected time is going to be the average of the expected times through all the outgoing edges. Hence for special room i

$$t(i) = \text{avg}_{j:(i,j)\in E} \Big(l((i,j)) + t(j) \Big).$$

Also, if the treasure room is vertex s, then $t(s) = 0$. Using these relationships, we can compute $t(i)$ for each vertex i by initializing $t(i) = \infty$ for all nodes $i \neq s$ and $t(s) = 0$. Then we apply the relaxation for each node based on one of the two above equations. Since this graph is a DAG, after $|V|$ steps of relaxation, we would reach a fixed point. This algorithm would have a runtime of $O(|E| \cdot |V|)$ since each relaxation phase takes $|E|$ time. This can be further improved by inverting the graph, doing a topological sort of the graph by starting at node s, and then computing $t(i)$ for node i in topological order.

     Once we have all the values of t computed, if we are in any room where we have to make a choice, we choose the corridor that minimizes the expected time to the treasure room.

Solution 4.16: Consider a directed graph $G = (V, E)$, where the vertices correspond to the cities. Each pair of cities is connected by an edge.

     Every plan corresponds to a cycle in the graph and vice versa. So, we need to find a cycle which maximizes the ratio of profit for all jobs on the cycle to the cost of performing the jobs on the cycle.

     Let $\rho_{\max}$ be the maximum ratio achievable. We can find $\rho_{\max}$ by guessing a ratio ρ and seeing whether it is too large or too small.

     Let ρ be any positive real number. Give each edge $e = (i, j)$ a weight of $\rho \cdot c(e) - p(j)$, where $c(e)$ is the cost of taking edge e and $p(j)$ is the profit of visiting node j.

If the graph has a negative cycle with this weight function, we claim that $\rho < \rho_{max}$.

Let C be such a cycle. Then we know that $\rho c(C) - p(C) < 0$, where we have extended c and p to sequences of edges in the natural way. Therefore for cycle C, we have $p(C)/c(C) > \rho$, i.e., $\rho < \rho_{max}$.

Conversely, if all the cycles in the graph have a positive weight, it must be that $\rho > \rho_{max}$. Since if $\rho_{max} \leq \rho$, let C be a cycle whose profit-to-cost ratio is ρ_{max}. Then $p(C)/c(C) = \rho_{max} \leq \rho$ which implies $p(C) - \rho c(C) \leq 0$, contradicting the absence of nonpositive weight cycles.

There is a straightforward algorithm for computing the presence of negative weight cycles which runs in $O(|V| \cdot |E|)$ time. We can perform binary search to find ρ_{max} with 0 as a lower bound and $\max_{e \in E} p(e)/c(e)$. The search can be terminated when we have determined ρ_{max} to a specified tolerance of ϵ.

Clearly, it is not advantageous to make any move unless the profit-to-cost ratio is greater than one. We can bound the maximum possible profit-to-cost ratio by finding the edge that maximizes the ratio of profit of visiting its destination to the cost of traversing the edge. Suppose this cost is R, then we need to perform the search between 1.0 and R for the optimum ratio. In order to narrow down the search to an interval of size ϵ, we would need $(\log(R - 1) - \log(\epsilon))/\log 2$ steps. Since each step involves finding a negative cycle, it can be done in $O(|V| \cdot |E|)$ time using the Bellman-Ford algorithm.

Solution 4.17: The straightforward solution would be to compute the shortest path from A to B for each proposal.

Note that we cannot add all the proposals at once; otherwise, we may end up with a shortest path which uses multiple proposals.

Instead we use an all-pairs shortest path algorithm on the original graph to get a matrix $S(u, v)$ of shortest path distances for each pair of vertices. Each proposal p is a pair of cities x, y. The best we can do by using proposal p is $\min\big(S(A, B), S(A, x) + A(y, B)\big)$. This computation is constant time, so we can evaluate all the proposals in time proportional to the number of proposals after we have computed the shortest path for each pair. All-pairs shortest path can be computed in $O(|V| \cdot |E| \log |V|)$ time by multiple calls to Dijkstra's algorithm or in $O(|V|^3)$ time using the Floyd-Warshall algorithm.

Solution 4.18: This is a classical problem and is solved using a "proposal algorithm".

Each student who does not have an adviser "proposes" to the most-preferred professor to whom he has not yet proposed.

Each professor then considers all the students who have proposed to him and tells the one he most prefers, "I accept you" and "no" to the rest. The professor is then provisionally matched to a student.

In each subsequent round, each student who does not have an adviser proposes to one professor to whom he has not yet proposed (regardless of whether the professor has already accepted a student or not) and the professor once again replies with one "accept" and rejects the rest.

This may mean that professors who have already accepted a student can "trade-up" and students who have already been accepted by a professor can be "jilted".

This algorithm has two key properties:

- It converges to a state where everyone is paired. Everyone gets accepted at some point. Once a professor accepts a student, he always has a student. There cannot be a professor and a student both unpaired since the student must have proposed to that professor at some point (since a student will eventually propose to everyone, if necessary) and being unpaired, the professor would have accepted.
- The pairings are stable. Let Riemann be a student and Gauss be a professor. Suppose they are each paired but not to each other. Upon completion of the algorithm, it is not possible for both Riemann and Gauss to prefer each other over their current pairings. If Riemann prefers Gauss to his current professor, he must have asked Gauss before he asked his current professor. If Gauss accepted Riemann's proposal, yet is not paired to Riemann at the end, he must have dumped him for someone he preferred more and therefore does not like Riemann more than his current student. If Gauss rejected his proposal, he was already paired with someone he preferred to Riemann.

Solution 4.19: We define a weighted directed graph $G = (V, V \times V)$, where V corresponds to the set of commodities. The weight $w(e)$ of edge $e = (u, v)$ is the amount of commodity v we can buy with one unit of commodity u.

Observe that an arbitrage exists iff there is a cycle in G whose edge weights multiply out to more than 1.

Create a new graph $G' = (V, E)$ with weight function $w'(e) = -\log w(e)$. Since $\log ab = \log a + \log b$, there is a cycle in G whose edge weights multiply out to more than 1 iff there is a cycle in G' whose edge weights sum up to less than $\log 1 = 0$.

We know how to efficiently find negative weight cycles in weighted directed graphs, e.g., using the Bellman-Ford algorithm which takes $O(|V| \cdot |E|)$ time and can use this to compute the existence of an arbitrage.

Solution 4.20: First, note that the number of packets at input i is the sum of the elements in row i and the number of packets destined through output j is the sum of all the elements in column j.

Let the maximum row sum be R—then it will take at least R cycles to transfer the packets from an input corresponding to R. Similarly, if C is the maximum column sum, it will take at least C cycles to transfer the packets to an output corresponding to C, i.e., $\beta = \max(R, C)$ is a lower bound on the number of cycles.

We claim β is actually a tight bound. To do this, we first prove that we can create a matrix $A^* \geq A$ such that every row and column of A^* sums up to β.

The proof is by construction—starting with A, find a row and a column whose sums are less than β and increment that element by 1. Each successive matrix is larger than its predecessor and the process must converge to a matrix whose rows and columns all sum up to β.

Now, consider a bipartite hypergraph on vertices $\{(L, 0), \dots, (L, n - 1), (R, 0), \dots, (R, n - 1)\}$, where we have $A^*[i, j]$ edges between vertex (L, i) and (R, j). Since the row and column sums are all β, it follows that the degrees of all vertices is β.

This graph has a perfect matching—this follows from the theorem that a β-regular bipartite graph has a perfect matching which in turn follows from Birkhoff's characterization of bipartite graphs, namely a perfect matching exists iff every subset of size k has at least k neighbors.

A perfect matching is a permutation from inputs to outputs—by choosing these assignments and performing the corresponding transfer, we can reduce the number of packets to transfer from A^* by n and the resulting matrix has rows and columns summing to exactly $\beta - 1$. In this way, we can construct a schedule which transfers all the packets in $A*$ in β cycles. Since $A^* \geq A$, this schedule will also transfer all the packets in A in β cycles.

Solution 4.21: If the transmitter and receiver decide on a restricted set of pairs of symbols rather than just symbols, they can do better than 1 bit per symbol transmitted.

The insight is that a pair like (A, C) and (B, E) cannot be mistaken for each other since C and E cannot conflict.

A formal way of finding the largest set of pairs of symbols which cannot be mistaken for each other is to create a conflict graph on the 25 pairs $\{(A, A), \dots, (E, E)\}$—put an edge between (u_1, u_2) and (v_1, v_2) iff $(u_1, v_1) \in \Pi$ and $(u_2, v_2) \in \Pi$.

Now, we want to find a maximum independent set in this graph—i.e., the largest subset of vertices, not two of which are connected by an edge.

There are a number of such sets of cardinality 5—e.g.,

$$S = \{(A, A), (B, C), (C, E), (D, B), (E, D)\}.$$

Therefore we can send $\log_2 5$ bits with every two symbols which amounts to roughly 1.16 bits per symbol transmitted.

Solution 4.22: In Solution 4.10, we showed how to model the problem using a DAG, with each vertex corresponding to a player. Problem 4.22 is asking for a minimum cardinality set of vertex disjoint paths in this DAG such that each vertex appears on some path.

This problem can be reduced to a flow problem: let $G = (V, E)$ be a DAG. Construct a flow problem F as follows: define $G = (V', E')$ from $G = (V, E)$ by creating a left vertex v_l and a right vertex v_r for each vertex $v \in V$.

Add a new source vertex s, add edges from s to each left vertex, and add a sink vertex t with edges from each right vertex to t.

Add edges (v_l, v_r) for each $v \in V$. For each edge $(u, v) \in E$, add an edge (v_r, u_l).

Assign a lower bound and upper bound of 1 for each edge of the form (v_l, v_r); all other edges have a lower bound of 0 and upper bound of ∞.

By construction, the minimum feasible flow for F defines a minimum cardinality set of vertex disjoint paths.

Solution 4.23: The problem can directly be mapped into the weighted bipartite matching problem: bidders and celebrities constitute the left and right vertices; an edge exists from b to c iff b has offered money to dance with c and the weight of an edge is the amount offered for the dance. It can be solved using specialized algorithms, network flows, or linear programming.

If the requirement that bidders and celebrities be distinct is dropped, the problem becomes a weighted matching problem in a general graph which is still solvable in polynomial time.

Solution 4.24: Let ϕ be a CNF expression of n variables $x_0, \ldots, x_{n-1}$ and m clauses in which each clause contains no more than two variables.

Assume without loss of generality that each clause in ϕ contains exactly two distinct variables since singleton clauses force the value of the corresponding variable for a satisfying assignment.

Construct the directed graph G_ϕ on $2n$ vertices indexed by $x_0, \ldots, x_{n-1}, x_0', \ldots, x_{n-1}'$. For each clause $l_i + l_j$, add an edge from l_i' to l_j and l_j' to l_i, where x_i'' is interpreted as x_i.

Claim: ϕ is satisfiable iff for each i, there does not exist a path from v_{x_i} to v'_{x_i} and a path from v'_{x_i} to v_{x_i}.

Proof: If an edge exists from v_{x_i} to v_{x_j}, it means that whenever x_i

is true, then x_j must be true in a satisfying assignment for ϕ. Similar results hold for vertices corresponding to complemented variables. By the transitivity of logical implication, a path in G_ϕ from v_{l_i} to v_{l_j} implies that if l_i is true in a satisfying assignment for ϕ, then so must l_j.

Now, consider the SCCs of G_ϕ. If for some i, v_{x_i} and v'_{x_i} are both in the same SCC, there cannot exist a satisfying assignment for ϕ. Conversely, if for no i, v_{x_i} and v'_{x_i} are both in the same SCC, we will prove that a satisfying assignment for ϕ exists by constructing it as follows: observe that if some v_{x_i} or v'_{x_i} is set to true in an SCC, then all the corresponding variables in that SCC are set to true, as are all variables in the descendants of the SCC.

Start with any source SCC in the SCC DAG which contains v_{l_i} and does not have a path to v_{l_i}' (such a vertex must exist; otherwise, v_{l_i} and v_{l_i}' would be in the same SCC). Set l_i to true and update all implied assignments, including setting l_i' to false. Iteratively perform this computation until all the literals have been assigned. We can always pick a literal to assign before the assignment is complete since no v_{l_i} and v_{l_i}' are in the same SCC and we are only reducing the SCC DAG.

Each clause will be satisfied after this is completed since each clause is of the form $l_i + l_j$. Assume WLOG that we assign l_i first. If it is assigned to true, the clause is satisfied; otherwise, when l_i is assigned to false, we will set l_j to true.

Solution 4.25: Let ϕ be a set of equality and inequality constraints on variables $x_0, \ldots, x_{n-1}$. Create an undirected graph G_ϕ on vertices $x_0, \ldots, x_{n-1}$; for each equality $x_i = x_j$, add the edge (x_i, x_j).

Now examine the connected components of G_ϕ. By the transitivity of equality, we can infer that $x_i = x_j$ for all vertices x_i and x_j in a common SCC.

Therefore if for some inequality $x_p \neq x_q$, vertices x_p and x_q lie in the same SCC, the set of constraints ϕ is not satisfied.

Conversely, let there be k connected components $C_0, \ldots, C_{k-1}$. Assign the variables in C_i to the value i. This satisfies all the equality constraints and since all the inequality constraints involve variables from different SCCs, all inequality constraints are satisfied too.

Chapter 5

Algorithms on Strings

Solution 5.1: There are several interesting algorithms for substring search that run in linear-time such as Knuth-Morris-Pratt, Boyer-Moore, and Rabin-Karp algorithm. However in practice, for most applications, substring search runs faster than that. We have found Boyer-Moore algorithm to be the fastest in our experience.

The Boyer-Moore algorithm works by trying to match characters of S in T at a certain offset in the reverse order (last character of S matched first). If we can match all the characters in S, then we have found a match; otherwise, we stop at the first mismatch. The key idea behind the Boyer-Moore algorithm is to be able to skip as many offsets as possible when we are done matching characters at a given offset. We do this by building two tables—good suffix shift table and a bad character shift table.

For a given character, the bad character shift table gives us the distance of the last occurrence of that character in S to the rightmost string. If the character does not occur in S, then the entry in the table is of length S. Hence when we find a character in T that does not match for the current offset, we know how much we must move forward so that this character can match for the first time.

The good suffix shift table is a little more complex. Conceptually, for a given suffix X of S, it tells us what is the shortest suffix Y of S that is longer than X and has X as suffix. In practice, what we store is how far can we move safely, given that we have matched up to $length(X)$ characters but did not match the next character.

Solution 5.2: The most naïve way of finding whether a string S is a substring of another string T would be to test character by character at every offset in T, if we find a match for A. However this would take $O(m \cdot n)$ time, where m is the length of A and n is the length of T. We can do better than that. If at a certain offset we match a set of characters in A to that of T but they do not match all the characters in A since A has all unique characters, the characters in T that matched A will not match A at any other offset. Hence we can skip a few offsets. This essentially means that for every character in T, we compare it with a character in A at most once. This will lead to a linear-time matching algorithm that runs in $O(n + m)$ time.

Solution 5.3: This is a special case of applying a permutation with constant additional storage (cf. Problem 11.4) except that the permutation is a rotation. In the case of rotations, we get cycles of the form $(c, i{+}c, 2i{+}c, \ldots, (m{\cdot}i{+}c) \bmod n)$ for different values of c from 1 through a number of cycles. So, essentially all other cycles are a shifted version of the first cycle. For example, consider the case where $n = 6$ and $i = 2$, we get $(1, 3, 5)$ and $(2, 4, 6)$. Once we have identified the difference between the lowest and the second lowest element in any cycle, we know the number of cycles there are and their starting points.

Solution 5.4: The key idea here is that if string A is a rotation of another string B, then A must be a substring of $B \cdot B$. For example, since arc is a rotation of car, it is a substring of $carcar$. Since substring test can be done in linear-time using the Knuth-Morris-Pratt algorithm, we can test for rotation in linear-time.

Solution 5.5: We are not providing explicit solution to this problem here since there are no algorithmic ideas involved. Most times when this kind of a question is asked, you need to keep a few things in mind:
- A single pass over the string is likely going to be faster.
- You can build prefix tables to match `index.html` and `default.html` in advance to speed up the process.
- You may not know if you need to add the protocol part or not until you have reached the end of the host part. Hence it may be a good idea to leave some space for adding `http://` at the beginning of the buffer.

Solution 5.6: This problem can be reduced to finding the longest common subsequence between the input string and its reverse. We have already shown how this can be done efficiently in Problem 3.1.

Solution 5.7: This can be efficiently solved by dynamic programming. Let $C(a)$ be the minimum wasted space for arranging the last a words. If we have all the values for $C(i)$ tabulated for $i < a$, we can compute $C(a)$ by finding the number of words we can fit in the first line that minimizes $C(a)$.

Solution 5.8: This is another interesting application of dynamic programming.

Let $S(i, j)$ represent the substring of string S that contains all the characters of S from index i to $j - 1$ (inclusive). Let the edit distance between the two strings A and B be represented by $E(A, B)$. Let's say that a and b are, respectively, the length of strings A and B. We now make two claims:

- If $A[a - 1] = B[b - 1]$ (i.e., the last two characters of the strings match), then $E(A, B) = E(A(0, a-1), B(0, b-1))$. This is obviously true since any set of transformation that turns A into B can turn $A(0, a - 1)$ into $B(0, b - 1)$ and vice versa.

- If $A[a - 1] \neq B[b - 1]$ (i.e., the last two characters of the strings do not match), then

$$E(A, B) = \min \left(E(A(0, a - 1), B), E(A, B(0, b - 1)) \right) + 1.$$

We can see this to be true by observing that if there is a smaller sequence of events that leads to the transformation of A into B, there must be a step where the last character of the string becomes the same as the last character of B. This could happen either by inserting a new character at the end or deleting the last character. We can reorder the sequence such that this operation happens at the end. The length of the sequence would remain the same and we would still end up with B in the end. In case this operation was "delete", then by deleting this operation, we get a sequence of operations that turn $A(0, a - 1)$ into B. If this operation was an "insert", then by dropping this operation, we would have a set of transformations that turn A into $B(0, b-1)$. In either case, it would be a contradiction if there was a sequence of operations that turned A into B which is smaller than $\min \left(E(A(0, a-1), B), E(A, B(0, b- 1)) \right) + 1$.

We can use the above results to tabulate the values of $E(A(0, k), B(0, l))$ for all values of $k < a$ and $l < b$ in $O(a \cdot b)$ time till we get the value of $E(A, B)$.

Solution 5.9: The key to solving this problem is using recursion effectively.

If the regular expression r starts with ^, then s must match the remainder of r; otherwise, s must match r at some position.

Call the function that checks whether a string S matches r from the beginning matchHere. This function has to check several cases— (1.) length-0 regular expressions which match everything, (2.) a regular expression starting with a * match, (3.) the regular expression $, and (4.) a regular expression starting with an alphanumeric character or dot.

Of these, (1.) and (3.) are base cases, (4.) is a check followed by a call to matchHere, and (3.) requires a new matchStar function.

The `matchStar` function does a walk down the string, checking that the prefix thus far matches the alphanumeric character or dot until some suffix matches the remainder of the regular expression.

```java
public class RegExp {

  static boolean match(String r, String s) {
    if (r.charAt(0) == '^') {
      return matchHere(r.substring(1), s);
    }
    int i = 0;
    do {
      if (matchHere(r, s.substring(i))) {
        return true;
      }
    } while( i++ < s.length() );

    return false;
  }

  static boolean matchHere(String r, String s) {
    if (r.length() == 0) {
      return true;
    }
    if ((r.length() >= 2) && r.charAt(1) == '*') {
      return matchStar(r.charAt(0), r.substring(2), s);
    }
    if (r.charAt(0) == '$' && r.length() == 1) {
      return s.length() == 0;
    }
    if (s.length() > 0 && (r.charAt(0) == '.' || r.charAt(0)
        == s.charAt(0))) {
      return matchHere(r.substring(1), s.substring(1));
    }
    return false;
  }

  static boolean matchStar(char c, String r, String s) {
    int i = 0;
    do {
      if (matchHere(r, s.substring(i))) {
        return true;
      }
    } while (i < s.length() && (s.charAt(i++) == c || c == '.'));
    return false;
  }
}
```

Chapter 6

Intractability

Solution 6.1: The 0-1 knapsack problem is an NP-complete problem. However the dynamic programming solution to the problem runs in pseudopolynomial time (to be precise, its time complexity is $O(n \cdot W)$).

Let $A(w)$ be the maximum value that can be packed with weight less than or equal to w. We can use the recurrence

$$A(w) = \max\left(A(w-1), \max_i(A(w - w_i) + v_i)\right).$$

For $w \leq 0$, we set $A[w] = 0$. Computing $A[w]$ given $A[i]$, for all $i < w$, takes $O(n)$ time; therefore this DP procedure computes $A[W]$ in $O(n \cdot W)$ time.

Solution 6.2: A good way to approach this problem is to think of a related problem that can be solved exactly efficiently. The minimum spanning tree (MST) problem has an efficient algorithm and it yields a way of visiting each city exactly twice—start at any city c and perform an in-order walk in the MST with c as the root. This traversal leads to a path in which each edge is visited exactly twice.

Now consider any tour for a salesman—if we drop the final edge back to the starting city, the remaining set of edges constitute a tree. Therefore the cost of any traveling salesman problem is at least as great as the cost of the MST.

Now we make use of the fact that the distances between cities satisfies the triangle inequality to build a tour from the MST whose cost is no greater than the MST. When we perform our in-order walk, we simply skip over cities we have already visited—the direct distance from u to v cannot be more than the sum of distances on a path from u to v.

Hence we have a tour costing at most twice the cost of the MST which itself was an upper bound on the cost of the traveling salesman problem.

Solution 6.3: A natural approach to this problem is to build the assignment one warehouse at a time. We can pick the first warehouse to be the city for which the cost is minimized—this takes $\Theta(n^2)$ time since we try each city one at a time and check its distance to every other city.

Let's say we have selected the first $i-1$ warehouses $\{c_1, c_2, \ldots, c_{i-1}\}$ and are trying to choose the i-th warehouse. A reasonable choice for c_i is the one that is the farthest from the $i-1$ warehouses already chosen. This can also be computed in $O(n^2)$ time.

Let the maximum distance from any remaining cities to a warehouse be d_m. Then the cost of this assignment is d_m. Let e be a city that has this distance to the warehouses. In addition, the m warehouse cities are all at least d_m apart; otherwise, we would have chosen e and not c_m at the m-th selection.

At least two of these $m+1$ cities have to have the same closest warehouse in an optimum assignment. Let p, q be two such cities and w be the warehouse they are closest to. Since $d(p, q) \leq d(w, p) + d(w, q)$, it follows that one of $d(w, p)$ or $d(w, q)$ is not less than $d_m/2$. Hence the cost of this optimum assignment is at least $d_m/2$, so our greedy heuristic produced an assignment that is within a factor of two of the optimum cost assignment.

Note that the initial selection of a warehouse is immaterial for the argument to work but heuristically, it is better to choose a central city as a starting point.

Solution 6.4: It is natural to try and solve this problem by divide-and-conquer, e.g., determine the minimum number of multiplications for each of x^k and $x^{30/k}$, for different values of k. The problem is that the subproblems are not independent—we cannot just add the minimum number of multiplications for computing x^5 and x^6 since both may use x^3.

Instead we resort to branch-and-bound: we maintain a set of partial solutions which we try to extend to the final solution. The key to efficiency is pruning out partial solutions efficiently.

In our context, a partial solution is a list of exponents that we have already computed. Note that in a minimum solution, we will never have an element repeated in the list. In addition, it suffices to consider partial solutions in which the exponents occur in increasing order since if $k > j$ and x^k occurs before x^j in the chain, then x^k could not be used in the derivation of x^j. Hence we lose nothing by advancing the position of x^k.

Here is code that solves the problem:

```java
import java.util.LinkedList;

public class MinExp {

    public static void main( String [] args ) {
```

```
6
7        int target = new Integer(args[0]);
8
9        LinkedList<Integer> initEntry = new LinkedList<Integer >()
           ;
10       initEntry.add(1);
11
12       LinkedList<LinkedList<Integer>> partials = new LinkedList
           <LinkedList<Integer >>();
13       partials.add(initEntry);
14
15       LinkedList<Integer> shortestDerivation = null;
16
17       int shortestSoFar = Integer.MAX_VALUE;
18
19       while ( !partials.isEmpty() ) {
20         LinkedList<Integer> aPartial = partials.removeFirst();
21         for( Integer i :  aPartial ) {
22          for( Integer j :  aPartial ) {
23            Integer sum = i + j;
24            if ( sum > target ) {
25              continue;
26            } else if ( sum == target ) {
27              if ( shortestSoFar > aPartial.size() ) {
28                shortestSoFar = aPartial.size();
29                shortestDerivation = new LinkedList<Integer >(
                     aPartial );
30                shortestDerivation.add( sum );
31              }
32              continue;
33            } else {
34              if ( aPartial.indexOf(sum) == -1
35                    && (aPartial.size() < shortestSoFar )
36                    && ( sum > aPartial.getLast() ) ) {
37                LinkedList<Integer> extension = new LinkedList<
                     Integer >( aPartial );
38                extension.add(sum);
39                partials.add(extension);
40              }
41            }
42          }
43        }
44      }
45      System.out.println( "A shortest deriviation:" +
           shortestDerivation.toString() );
46    }
47 }
```

The code runs in a fraction of a second. It reports $\langle x^1, x^2, x^3, x^5, x^{10}, x^{15}, x^{30} \rangle$. In all, 7387 partial solutions are examined.

There are other potential bounding techniques: for example, from the binary representation of 30 (11110), we know that 7 multiplications suffice (computing x^2, x^4, x^8, x^{16} and then multiplying these together). In addition, we could keep out duplicate partial solutions. The code could avoid considering all pairs i, j and focus on pairs that just involve the last element since other pairs will have been considered previously. More sophisticated bounding can be applied: a chain like $\langle x, x^2, x^3, x^6, x^7 \rangle$ will require at least three more multiplications (since $\lceil \frac{30}{7} \rceil = 3$) and so this chain can be safely pruned. When selecting a partial solution to continue searching from, we could choose one that is promising, e.g., the shortest solution—this might lead to better solutions faster and therefore more bounding on other search paths.

For hand calculations, these techniques are important but they are trickier to code and our original code solves the given problem reasonably quickly.

Solution 6.5: A reasonable way to proceed is to use branch-and-bound: we choose a variable v, see if there is a satisfying assignment when $v = 0$ and if not, we try $v = 1$. If there is no satisfying assignment for $v = 0$ and for $v = 1$, the expression in not satisfiable.

Once we choose a variable and set its value, the expression simplifies—we need to remove clauses where v appears if we set $v = 1$ and remove clauses where v' appears when we set $v = 0$. In addition, if we get to a unit clause—one where a single literal appears, we know that in any satisfying assignment for the current expression, that literal must be set to true; this rule leads to additional simplification. Conversely, if all the clauses are true, we do not need to proceed further—every assignment to the remaining variables makes the expression true.

There are various choices for selecting variables. One natural choice is to pick the variable which appears the most times in clauses with two literals since it leads to the most unit clauses on simplification. Another choice is to pick the variable which is the most binate—i.e., it appears the most times in negated and nonnegated forms.

Solution 6.6: We are given a set of N unit duration lectures and M classrooms. The lectures can be held simultaneously as long as no two lectures need to happen in the same classroom at the same time and all precedence constraints are met.

The problem of scheduling these lectures so as to minimize the time taken to completion is known to be NP-complete.

This problem is naturally modeled using graphs. We model lectures as vertices, with an edge from vertex u to vertex v if u is a prerequisite for v. Clearly, the graph must be acyclic for the precedence constraints to be satisfied.

If there is just one lecture room, we can simply hold the lectures in topological order and complete the N lectures in N time (assuming each lecture is of unit duration).

We can develop heuristics by observing the following: at any time, there is a set of lectures whose precedence constraints have been satisfied. If this set is smaller than M, we can schedule all of them; otherwise, we need to select a subset to schedule.

The subset selection can be based on several metrics:
- Rank order lectures based on the length of the longest dependency chain that they are at the start of.
- Rank order lectures based on the number of lectures that they are immediate prerequisites for.
- Rank order lectures based on the total number of lectures that they are direct or indirect prerequisites for.

We can also use combinations of these criteria to order the lectures that are currently schedulable.

For example, for each vertex, we define its criticality to be the length of a longest path from it to a sink. We schedule lectures by processing vertices in topological order. At any point in our algorithm, we have a set of candidate lectures—these are the lectures whose prerequisites have already been scheduled.

If the candidate set is less than size M, we schedule all the lectures; otherwise, we choose the M most critical lectures and schedule those— the idea is that they should be scheduled sooner since they are at the start of longer dependency chains.

The criterion is heuristic and may not lead to optimum schedules— this is to be expected since the problem is NP-complete. Other heuristics may be employed, e.g., we may use the number of lectures that depend on lecture L as the criticality of lecture L or some combination of the criterion.

Solution 6.7: This problem is very similar to another very popular problem that is asked in interviews. You are given an $n \times n$ matrix in which both rows and columns are sorted in ascending order and you are supposed to find a given number in the matrix.

In this case, we are essentially looking for an implicit matrix A such that $A(i,j) = i^3 + j^3$. In our case, the matrix will have $n^{1/3}$ rows and columns. There are several algorithms for searching for a number in such a matrix that are linear in the number of rows.

One approach is to start by comparing x to $A_{n,1}$. If $x = A_{n,1}$, stop. Otherwise, there are two cases:
- $x > A_{n,1}$, in which case x is greater than all elements in Column 1.
- $x < A_{n,1}$, in which case x is less than all elements in Row n.

In either case, we have a matrix with n fewer elements to search. In each iteration, we remove a row or a column, which means we inspect $2n - 1$ elements.

```
1   bool IsSumOfcubes(int n) {
2       int m = ceil(pow(n, 1/3));
3       int i = m; int j = 0;
4       while( j < m && i >= 0) {
5           int k = i*i*i +j*j*j;
6           if (k == n) {
7               return true;
8           } else if (k < n) {
9               ++j;
10          } else {
11              --i;
12          }
13      }
14  }
```

For a tight lower bound, let x be any input. Define A to be:

$$
\begin{bmatrix}
 & & & & & x-1 \\
 & & & & & x+1 \\
 & & & & \cdots & \\
 & & & x-1 & & \\
 & & & x+1 & & \\
 & & x-1 & & & \\
 & & x+1 & & & \\
 & x-1 & & & &
\end{bmatrix}
$$

where all entries not shown are 0. We claim that any algorithm that solves the matrix search problem will have to compare x with each of the $2n - 1$ elements shown (i.e., the diagonal elements and the elements immediately below them). Call these elements the Δ elements.

Comparing x with other elements does not eliminate any of the Δ elements. Suppose an algorithm did not compare x with one of the Δ elements. Then we could make that element x (instead of $x - 1$ or $x + 1$) and the algorithm would behave exactly as before and hence return the wrong result. Therefore at least $2n - 1$ compares are necessary which means that the algorithm we designed is optimum.

Note that for this problem, if the input number is n, the size of the input is $\log n$ bits. Since the runtime is $O(n^{1/3})$, it is still an exponential algorithm in the size of the input.

Solution 6.8: Often interview questions are open-ended with no definite good solution—all you can do is provide some good heuristics and code it well. For the Collatz hypothesis, the general idea is to start with each number and iterate till you reach one. Here are some of the ideas that you can try to accelerate the check:

1. Reuse computation by storing all the numbers you have already proven to converge to 1; that way, as soon as you reach such a num-

ber, you can assume it would reach 1.

2. In order to save hash table space, you can keep only odd numbers in the hash table.

3. If you have tested every number up to k, you can stop the chain as soon as you reach a number that is less than or equal to k. Also, you do not need to store the numbers below k in the hash table, so you can keep deleting these numbers from the hash table as you progress.

4. If multiplication and division are expensive, use bit shifting and addition.

5. Since the numbers in a sequence may grow beyond 32 bits, you should use 64 bit longs and keep testing for overflow.

Solution 6.9: The brute-force solution is to consider all pairs of points: this yields an $O(n^2)$ algorithm.

A reasonable approach is to split the points into two equal-sized sets using a line $x = P$ parallel to the Y-axis. Such a line can be found by computing the median of the values for the x co-ordinates—this calculation can be performed using randomization in a manner analogous to Quicksort.

We can then compute the closest pair of points recursively on the two sets; let the closest pair of points on the left of P be d_l apart and the closest pair of points to the right of P be d_r apart. Let $d = \min(d_l, d_r)$.

Now, all we need to look at is points which are in the band $[P - d, P + d]$. In degenerate situations, all points may be within this band. So, if we compare all the pairs, the complexity becomes quadratic again. However we can sort the points in the band on their y co-ordinates and scan the sorted list, looking for points d or less distance from the point being processed.

Intuitively, there cannot be a large number of such points since otherwise, the closest pair in the left and right partitions would have to be less than d apart. This intuition can be analytically justified—Shamos and Hoey's famous 1975 paper "Closest-point problems" shows that no more than 6 points can be within d distance of any point which leads to an $O(n \log n)$ algorithm—the time is dominated by the need to sort.

The recursion can be sped up by switching to brute-force when a small number of points remain.

Solution 6.10: Here are a couple of simple heuristics that you can use to speed up primality tests:

1. It is sufficient to test for factorization up to $\lceil \sqrt{n} \rceil$.

2. You can limit yourself to prime numbers only. You may not know all the prime numbers between 2 and $\sqrt{n}$, however you can use the fact that all prime numbers other than 2 and 3 are of the form $6k + 1$ or $6k - 1$. This would speed up your computation by a factor of 3.

Chapter 7

Parallel Computing

Solution 7.1: The naïve solution would be:

```
1  public class S1 implements Servlet {
2    String wLast = null;
3    String [] closestToLastWord = null;
4
5    public void service(ServletRequest req, ServletResponse
         resp) {
6      String w = extractWordToCheckFromRequest(req);
7      if (checkWord.equals(wLast)) {
8        encodeIntoResponse(resp, closestToLastWord);
9      } else {
10       wLast = w;
11       closestToLastWord = closestInDictionary(w);
12     }
13   }
14 }
```

This solution has a race condition—Thread A might have written
wLast and then Thread B reads wLast and closestToLastWord before Thread A has a chance to update closestToLastWord. The call
to closestToLastWord could take quite long or be very fast, depending on the length of checkWord. Hence it is quite possible that between
the two write operations of Thread A, Thread B reads both wLast and
closestToLastWord.

A thread-safe solution would be to declare service to be synchronized; in this case, only one thread could be executing the method and
there is no race between write to wLast and closestToLastWord. This
leads to poor performance—only one servlet thread can be executing at
a time.

The solution is to lock just the part of the code that operates on the
cached values—specifically, the check on the cached value and the updates to the cached values:

```
1   public class S2 implements Servlet {
2     String wLast = null;
3     String [] closestToLastWord = null;
4
5     public void service(ServletRequest req, ServletResponse
          resp) {
6       String w = extractFromRequest(req);
7       String result  = null;
8       synchronized (this) {
9         if (w.equals(wLast)) {
10          result = closestToLastWord.clone();
11        }
12      }
13      if (closestToLastWord == null) {
14        result = closestInDictionary(i);
15        synchronized (this) {
16          closestInDictionary = result;
17          wLast = w;
18        }
19      }
20      encodeIntoResponse(resp, result);
21    }
22  }
```

In the above code, multiple servlets can be in their call to
`closestInDictionary` which is good because the call may take a long
time. Because we lock on `this`, the read-assignment on a hit and
write-write assignment on completion are atomic. Note that we have
to `clone` `closestToLastWord` when assigning to `result` since otherwise, `closestToLastWord` might change before we encode it into the
response.

Solution 7.2: The first attempt to solve this problem might be to have
`main` launch a new thread per request rather than process the request
itself:

```
1   class ThreadPerTaskWebServer {
2     public static void main(String [] args) throws IOException
          {
3       final ServerSocket socket = new ServerSocket(80);
4       while ( true ) {
5         final Socket connection = socket.accept();
6         Runnable task = new Runnable() {
7           public void run() {
8             handleRequest(connection);
9           }
10        }
11        new Thread(task).start();
12      }
13    }
14  }
```

The problem with this approach is that we do not control the number of threads launched. A thread consumes a nontrivial amount of resources by itself—there is the overhead of starting and ending down the thread and the resources used by the thread. For a lightly-loaded server, this may not be an issue but under load, it can result in exceptions that are challenging, if not impossible, to handle.

The right trade-off is to use a *thread pool*. As the name implies, this is a collection of threads, the size of which is bounded. Java provides thread pools through the `Executor` framework.

```
1   class TaskExecutionWebServer {
2     private static final int NTHREADS = 100;
3     private static final Executor exec
4       = Executors.newFixedThreadPool(NTHREADS);
5
6     public static void main(String[] args) throws IOException {
7       ServerSocket socket = new ServerSocket(80);
8       while (true) {
9         final Socket connection = socket.accept();
10        Runnable task = new Runnable() {
11          public void run() {
12            handleRequest(connection);
13          }
14        };
15        exec.execute(task);
16      }
17    }
18  }
```

Solution 7.3: Our strategy is to launch a thread T per `Requestor` object. Thread T in turn launches another thread, S, which calls `execute` and `ProcessResponse`. The call to `execute` in S is wrapped in a try-catch `InterruptedException` loop; if `execute` completes successfully, `ProcessResponse` is called on the result.

After launching S, T sleeps for the timeout interval—when it wakes up, it interrupts S. If S has completed, nothing happens; otherwise, the try-catch `InterruptedException` calls `error`.

Code for this is given below:

```
1   class Requestor {
2     public String execute(String req) {
3       return "response:" + req;
4     }
5     public String error(String req) {
6       return "response:" + req + ":" + "TIMEDOUT";
7     }
8     public String execute(String req, long delay) {
9       try {
10        Thread.sleep(delay);
11      } catch (InterruptedException e) {
```

```
12          return error(req);
13        }
14        return execute(req);
15      }
16      public void ProcessResponse(String response) {
17        System.out.println("ProcessResponse:" + response);
18        return;
19      }
20    }
21
22    public class AsyncThread {
23      public static final long TIMEOUT = 500L;
24      public static void main(String [] args) {
25        Dispatch(new Requestor(), "t1", 1000L);
26        Dispatch(new Requestor(), "t2", 100L);
27        Dispatch(new Requestor(), "t3", 10L);
28        Dispatch(new Requestor(), "t4", 1L);
29        Dispatch(new Requestor(), "t5", 200L);
30      }
31      public static void Dispatch(
32          final Requestor r, final String request,
33          final long delay) {
34        Runnable task = new Runnable() {
35          public void run() {
36            Runnable actualTask = new Runnable() {
37              public void run() {
38                String response = r.execute(request, delay);
39                r.ProcessResponse(response);
40              }
41            };
42            Thread innerThread = new Thread(actualTask);
43            innerThread.start();
44            try {
45              Thread.sleep(TIMEOUT);
46              innerThread.interrupt();
47            } catch (InterruptedException e) {
48              e.printStackTrace();
49            }
50          }
51        };
52        new Thread(task).start();
53      }
54    }
```

Solution 7.4: There are two aspects to the design—first, the data-structures and second, the locking mechanism.

One solution is to use two data-structures. The first is a heap in which we insert key-value pairs: the keys are runtimes and the values are the thread to run at that time. A dispatch thread runs these threads; it sleeps from call to call and may be woken up if a thread is added to or deleted from the pool. If woken up, it advances or retards its remaining sleep time based on the top of the heap. On waking up, it looks for the thread at the top of the heap—if its launch time is the current time, the dispatch thread deletes it from the heap and executes it. It then sleeps till the launch time for the next thread in the heap. (Because of deletions, it may happen that the dispatch thread wakes up and finds nothing to do.)

The second data-structure is a hash table with thread ids as keys and entries in the heap as values. If we need to cancel a thread, we go to the heap and delete it. Each time a thread is added, we insert it into the heap; if the insertion is to the top of the heap, we interrupt the dispatch thread so that it can adjust its wake up time.

Since the heap is shared by the update methods and the dispatch thread, we need to lock it. The simplest solution is to have a single lock that is used for all read and writes into the heap and the hash table.

Solution 7.5: We want to be able to indicate whether the string is being read as well as whether the string is being written to. We achieve this with a pair of locks—LR and LW and a read counter locked by LR.

A reader proceeds as follows: it locks LR, increments the counter, and releases LR. After it performs its reads, it locks LR, decrements the counter, and releases LR. A writer locks LW, then iteratively performs the following: it locks LR, checks to see if the read counter is 0; if so, it performs its write, releases LW, and then releases LR. In code:

```
1   import java.util.Date;
2   import java.util.Random;
3
4   class Reader extends Thread {
5
6       public void run() {
7          while ( true ) {
8             synchronized (RW.LR) {
9               RW.readCount++;
10            }
11            System.out.println( RW.data );
12            synchronized (RW.LR) {
13              RW.readCount--;
14            }
15            doSomeThingElse();
16         }
17      }
18  }
19
20  class Writer extends Thread {
21
22      public void run() {
23         while ( true ) {
24            synchronized (RW.LW) {
25               synchronized (RW.LR ) {
26                  if (RW.readCount == 0) {
27                    RW.data = new Date().toString();
28                  }
29               }
```

```
30              }
31              doSomeThingElse () ;}
32          }
33      }
34  }
35
36  public class RW {
37
38      static String data = new Date().toString();
39      static Random random = new Random();
40
41      static Object LR = new Object();
42      static int readCount = 0;
43      static Object LW = new Object();
44
45      public static void main( String [] args ) {
46          Thread r0 = new Reader(); Thread r1 = new Reader();
47          Thread w0 = new Writer(); Thread w1 = new Writer();
48          r0.start(); r1.start();
49          w0.start(); w1.start();
50          while ( true );
51      }
52  }
```

Solution 7.6: We want to give writers the preference. We achieve this by modifying the solution above to have a reader start by locking LW and then immediately releasing LW. In this way, a writer who acquires the LW lock is guaranteed to be ahead of the subsequent readers.

Solution 7.7: We can achieve fairness between readers and writers by having a bit which indicates whether a read or a write was the last operation performed. If the last operation performed was a read, a reader on acquiring a lock must release the lock and retry—this gives writers priority in acquiring the lock; a similar operation is performed by writers.

Solution 7.8: This problem can be solved for a single producer and a single consumer with a pair of semaphores—*fillCount* is incremented and *emptyCount* is decremented whenever an item is added to the buffer. If the producer wants to decrement *emptyCount* when its count is 0, the producer sleeps. The next time an item is consumed, *emptyCount* is incremented and the producer is woken up. The consumer operates analogously. The Java methods, `wait` and `notify`, can be used to implement the desired functionality.

  If there are multiple producers and consumers, the solution above has two races—two producers can try writing to the same slot and two consumers can read from the same slot. These races can be removed by adding mutexes around the *putItemIntoBuffer* and *removeItemFromBuffer* calls.

Solution 7.9: A casual implementation is susceptible to races. For example, a new customer sees the barber cutting hair and goes to the waiting room; before he gets to the chair, the barber completes the haircut, checks the waiting room, and goes back to his chair to sleep. This is a form of livelock—the barber and the customer are both idle, waiting for each other. As another example, in the absence of appropriate locking, two customers may arrive simultaneously, see the barber cutting hair, and a single vacant seat in the waiting room, and go to the waiting room to occupy the single chair.

One way to achieve correct operation is to have a single mutex which allows only one person to change state at a time. The barber must acquire the mutex before checking for customers; he must release it when he either begins to sleep or begins to cut hair. A customer must acquire the mutex before entering the shop; he must release it when he sits in either a waiting room chair or the barber chair.

For a complete solution, in addition to the mutex, we need event semaphores to record the number of customers in the waiting room and the number of people getting their hair cut. The event semaphore recording the number of customers in the waiting room is used to wake up the barber when a customer enters; the event semaphore recording the number of customers getting a haircut is used to wake up waiting customers.

Solution 7.10: The natural solution is for each resource to have a lock. The problem arises when each thread i requests lock i and then $i+1$ mod n. Since all locks have already been acquired, the thread deadlocks.

One approach is to have a central controller, which knows exactly which resources are in use and arbitrates conflicting requests. If resources are not available for a thread, the controller can reject his request.

Another solution is to order the resources and require that resources be acquired in increasing order and released in decreasing order. For example, if all threads request simultaneously, resource $n-1$ will be left unrequested (since Thread $n-1$ will request 0 first, and then $n-1$). Thread $n-2$ will then succeed at acquiring resource $n-1$ since Thread $n-1$ will block on Resource 0.

This solution is not starvation-free, e.g., T2 can wait forever while T1 and T3 alternate. To guarantee that no thread starves, one could keep track of the number of times a thread cannot execute when his neighbors release their locks. If this number exceeds some limit, the state of the thread could change to `starving` and the decision procedure to enter the critical section could be supplemented to require that none of the neighbors are starving. A philosopher that cannot pick up locks because a neighbor is starving is effectively waiting for the neighbor's neighbor to finish eating. This additional dependency reduces concurrency—raising the threshold for transition to the `starving` state reduces this effect.

Chapter 8

Design Problems

Many of the problems in this chapter can be the basis for PhD-level research. A comprehensive discussion on the solutions available for such problems is outside the scope of this book. In an interview setting when someone asks such a question, you should have a discussion in which you demonstrate an ability to think creatively, understand design trade-offs, and attack unfamiliar problems. The answers in this chapter are presented in this context—they are meant to be examples of good responses in an interview and are not definitive state-of-the-art solutions.

Solution 8.1: As mentioned in the prologue to this book, one approach is to do a coarse pixelization of the tiles and for each potential tile position, find the tile in the image that is closest to it in terms of a norm defined over each pixel color. If the image collection is limited, you would often end up with significant errors. Since the human eye perceives the average color of a region, it has been observed that if you adjust the average target color of a tile based on errors made by its neighboring tiles, it improves the overall quality.

Often the target image may have very similar color for a large number of tiles in the background. If we pick the same image over and over for a contiguous region, it stands out in the mosaic and does not create very good aesthetics. Hence the mosaic tools would usually allow the users to specify constraints on how often a tile can be repeated or a minimum separation between the two copies of an image.

Given a rectangle in the target image, finding the best image that can approximate it essentially boils down to searching for the nearest neighbor in some k-dimensional space (where k is the number of color pixels used to approximate the image). Since we can do some preprocessing on the library of images, it makes sense to do some spatial indexing. A very simple indexing scheme for relatively low value of k would be to just form a k-dimensional grid and place the images to the closest point on the grid. A more sophisticated approach would be to use R-trees for indexing.

Finding the overall best fit under the constraints of how often an image can be repeated is NP-hard. However greedy approaches work reasonably well.

Solution 8.2: The predominant way of doing this is to build inverted indices. In an inverted index, for each word, we store a list of locations where the word occurs. Here location is defined to be the pair of document id and the offset in the document. The list is stored in sorted order of locations (first ordered by document id, then by offset). When we are looking for the documents that contain a set of words, what we need to do is find the intersection of lists for each word. Since the lists are already sorted, the intersection can be done in linear-time (linear in the total size of the lists). There are various optimizations that can be done to this basic infrastructure. We list a few thoughts below.

- Compression—compressing the inverted index helps both with the ability to index more documents as well as memory locality (fewer cache misses). Since we are storing sorted lists, one way of compressing is to use delta compression where we only store the difference between the successive entries. The deltas can be represented in fewer bits.
- Caching—the distribution queries is often fairly skewed and it helps a great deal to cache the results of some of the most frequent queries.
- Frequency-based optimization—since search results often do not need to return every document that matches (only top ten or so), only a fraction of highest quality documents can be used to answer most of the queries. This means that we can make two inverted indices, one with the high quality documents that stays in the memory and one with the remaining documents that stays on the disk. This way if we can keep the number of queries that require the secondary index to a small enough number, then we can still maintain a reasonable throughput and latency.
- Intersection order—since the total intersection time depends on the total size of lists, it would make sense to intersect the words with smaller sets first. For example, if we are looking for "USA GDP 2009", it would make sense to intersect the lists for GDP and 2009 before trying to intersect the list for USA.

We could also build a multilevel index to improve accuracy on documents. For high priority web pages, we can recursively from "document" abstraction introduce a notion of "paragraph" and then "sentence" to index further down. That way the intersections for the words might be within the same context. We can pick results with closer index values from these lists.

Solution 8.3: This is a well studied problem because of its implications for building a high speed Internet backbone. There are a number of approaches that have been proposed and used in IP routers. One simple approach is to build a trie data-structure such that we can traverse the trie for an IP address till we hit a node that has a label. This essentially requires one pointer indirection per bit of input. The lookup speed can be improved a little at the cost of memory by making fatter nodes in the trie that consume multiple bits at a time.

There are a number of approaches that have been tried in software and hardware to speed the lookup process:

- Binary search on hash tables—we can have one hash table for each possible length of prefix and then do a search for the longest matching prefix by looking through all the hash tables. However this could take 32 hash table lookups. One way of reducing this is to do a binary search for the longest matching prefix. In order for binary search to work, we would have to insert additional prefixes in the hash tables to ensure that if a longer prefix exists, binary search does not terminate early. This can be done by performing a binary search for each prefix and insert additional dummy entries wherever the binary search terminates early. This could inflate the size of hash tables by at most $\log_2 32$ (in practice, it is much smaller).

- Ternary Content Addressable Memory (TCAM)—a TCAM is a special piece of hardware, where instead of storing 0s and 1s, a single unit of memory can also store a third state called the "don't care" state. Also, the contents of memory can be addressed by partial contents of the memory. TCAMs with 32 address bits are used to store prefixes. Each prefix is padded with "don't care" bits to make it 32 bits. This way, when we use an IP address to address the TCAM, we get all the matching prefixes. A priority logic gate then selects the longest matching prefix.

Solution 8.4: The basic idea behind most spelling correction systems is that the misspelled word's edit distance from the intended word tends to be very small (one or two edits). Hence if we keep a hash table for all the words in the dictionary and look for all the words that are within two edit distances of the text, most likely, the intended word will be found in this set. If the alphabet has m characters and the search text has n characters, we would need to perform roughly $n \cdot m^2$ hash table lookups. When we intersect all the strings within two edit distance with the dictionary words, sometimes we can land up with a fairly large set of words and it is important to provide a ranked list of suggestions to the users such that the most likely candidates are at the top. This is often done by various probabilistic models. There are various interesting ideas that can be used to improve the spelling correction system:

- Typing errors model—often spelling mistakes are a result of typing errors. Typing errors are easy to model based on keyboard layouts.
- Phonetic modeling—a big class of spelling errors happen when the person spelling it knows how the words sounds but does not know the exact spelling. In such cases, it helps to map the text to phonemes and then find all the words that map to the same phonetic sequence.
- History of refinements—often users themselves provide a great amount of data about the most likely misspellings by first entering a misspelled word and then correcting it. This kind of historic data is often immensely valuable for spelling correction.
- Stemming—often the size of dictionary can be reduced by only keeping the stemmed version of the words in it and stemming the query text as well.

Solution 8.5: Stemming is a fairly large topic and different systems have adopted different approaches. Porter stemmer developed by Martin Porter is considered one of the most authoritative algorithms for stemming in the English language. Here we mention some basic ideas related to stemming, however this is in no way a comprehensive discussion on stemming approaches.

The basic idea in most stemming systems works based on some simple rewrite rules, such as, if the word ends with "es" or "s" or "ation", then we remove them. Sometimes, a simple termination may not work, for example, wolves ↦ wolf. In order to cover this case, we may have a rule to replace a suffix "ves" to "f". In the end, most rules amount to matching a set of suffixes and depending upon which one we end up with, we may apply a certain transformation to the string. One way of efficiently doing this could be to build a finite state machine based on all the rules.

A more sophisticated system might have several exceptions to the broad rule based on the stem matching some patterns. For example, the Porter stemmer defines several rules based on a pattern of vowels and consonants.

Other approaches include use of stochastic method to learn rewrite rules and N-gram based approaches where we look at the surrounding words to determine the correct stemming for a word.

Solution 8.6: This problem as posed, has some ambiguity:

- Since we usually download one file in one request, if a file is greater than b bytes, there is no way we can meet the constraint of serving fewer than b bytes every minute, unless we can work with the lower layers of networking stack such as the transport layer or the network layer. Often the system designer could look at the distribution of file sizes and conclude that this problem happens so infrequently that we do not care. Alternately, we may choose to serve no more than the first b bytes of any file.

  — Given that the host's bandwidth is a resource for which there could be contention, one important design choice to be made is how to resolve a contention. Do we let requests get served in first-come first-served order or is there a notion of priority? Often crawlers have a built-in notion of priority based on how important the document is to the users or how fresh the current copy is.

One way of doing this could be to maintain a server with which each crawler checks to see if it is okay to hit a particular host. The server can keep an account of how many bytes have been downloaded from the server in the last minute and not permit any crawler to hit the server if we are already close to the quota. If we do not care about priority, then we can keep the interface synchronous where a server requests for permission to download a file and it immediately gets approved or denied. If we care about priorities, then the server may enqueue the request and inform the crawler when it is alright to download the file. The queues at the permission server may be based on priorities.

In case the single permission server becomes a bottleneck for the system, we can use multiple servers such that the responsibility of a given host is decided by hashing the host name and assigning it to a particular server based on the hash range.

Solution 8.7: Since the web graph can have billions of nodes and it is mostly a sparse graph, it is best to represent the graph as an adjacency list. Building the adjacency list representation of the graph itself may require significant amount of computation, depending upon how the information is collected. Usually, the graph is constructed by downloading the pages on the web and extracting the hyperlink information from the pages. Since the URL of a page can be arbitrarily long and varies a lot in size, it is often a good idea to represent the URL by a hash value.

The most expensive part of PageRank algorithm is the repeated matrix multiplication. Usually, it is not possible to keep the entire graph information in a single machine's RAM. There are usually two approaches to solving this problem:

  — Disk-based sorting—in this approach, we keep the column vector X in memory and load each row at a time. For a given row A_i, we write out pairs of numbers $\langle j, A_{ij} \cdot X_j \rangle$ to disk. Then we sort the pairs by their first component on disk and then add up the second component to get the result vector. The advantage of this approach is that as long as we can hold the column vector in the RAM, we can do the entire computation on a single machine. However this approach can be fairly slow because disk-based sorting is usually slow.

- Partitioned graph—in this approach, we use n machines and partition the vertices (web pages) into n sets. Usually, the partitioning is done by partitioning the hash space such that it is easy to determine which vertex maps to which machine. Given this partitioning, each machine loads its vertices and their outgoing edges into RAM. Each machine also loads the parts of the PageRank vector that corresponds to its vertices. Then each machine does a local matrix multiplication. Since some of the edges on each machine would correspond to the nodes that are owned by other machines, the result vector is going to contain nonzero entries for vertices that are not owned by the local machine. So, at the end of local multiplication, we need to send updates to other hosts so that these values can be correctly added up. The advantage of this approach is that we can process arbitrarily large graphs as long as we have sufficient number of machines.

Solution 8.8: If we have sufficient RAM on a single machine, the most simple solution would be to maintain a min-heap where we maintain all the events by their priority. Since we are interested in a scalable solution to this problem, we need to partition the problem across multiple machines.

One way of doing this could be to hash the events and partition them into ranges so that one hash range corresponds to one machine. This way, the insert and delete operations can be done by just communicating with one of the servers. However in order to do the extract-min operation, we need to send a find-min message to all the machines, infer the min from all their responses, and then try to delete it.

Since at a given time, all the clients would be interested in the same event (the highest priority event), it is hard to distribute this problem well. If a large number of clients are trying to do this operation at the same time, we may run into a situation where most clients will find that the absolute min event they were trying to extract has already been deleted. If the throughput of this service can be handled by a single machine, we can keep one server that is responsible for responding to all the machines. This server can prefetch top hundred or so events from each of the machines and keep them in a heap.

In many applications, we do not need strong consistency guarantees. What we need is that overall, we spend most of our resources taking care of the highest priority jobs. In such cases, a client can pick one of the hash ranges randomly and just request the highest priority job from the corresponding machine. This would work great for distributed crawler application but it would be a bad idea for event driven simulation.

Solution 8.9 : Often clients of a service care more about the 99-th or the 95-th percentile latency for the server rather than the mean latency since they want most of the requests to be serviced in a reasonable amount of time even if an occasional request takes very long. If our architecture is such that at a time only a fixed number of requests can get served and other pending requests must wait for a slot to open up before getting served, it is important to design our queuing system in such a way that the requests that take a very long time to serve do not block many small jobs behind them.

Consider the case where the time it takes for the server to process a request is a function of the request. Given the distribution of requests, the service time follows a Pareto distribution. In such cases, it greatly helps to have two queues and pick a good threshold such that the requests that take longer than the threshold time, go to one queue and the requests that take less than or equal to the threshold time, go to the other queue. We pick the threshold such that the majority of jobs go to the faster queue and the jobs in this queue are never blocked behind a big job. The larger jobs do have to wait more behind the larger jobs but overall this strategy can greatly reduce the 99-th percentile latency.

Often the system designer does not know how long a given request is going to take in advance in order to make the right queuing decision. It has been shown that even in such cases, it is advantageous to keep two queues. When a request comes in, it is put in the fast queue, however when it takes longer than a certain threshold time, we cancel the request and put it at the back of the slow queue.

Solution 8.10 : Reasonable goals for such a system could include:
  – providing users with the most relevant ads
  – provide advertisers with the best possible return on their investment
  – minimizing the cost of running such an operation

There are two key components to building such a system: (1.) the front-facing component, by which advertisers can add their advertisements, control when their ads get displayed, how much and how they want to spend their advertising money, and review the performance of their ads and (2.) the ad-serving system which selects which ads to show on the searches.

The front-facing system can be a fairly conventional website design. Users interact with the system using a browser and opening a connection to the website. You will need to build a number of features:
  – User authentication—a way for users to create accounts and authenticate themselves.

— User state—a set of forms to let advertisers specify things like their advertising materials, their advertising budget etc. Also a way to store this information persistently.

— Performance reports—a way to generate reports on how and where the advertiser's money is being spent.

— Human interactions—even the best of automated systems require occasional human interaction and a way to interfere with the algorithms. This may require an interface for advertisers to be able to contact customer service representatives and an interface for those representatives to interact with the system.

The whole front-end system can be built using, for example, HTML and JavaScript, with a LAMP stack (Linux as the operating system, Apache as the HTTP server, MySQL as the database software, and PHP for the application logic) responding to the user input.

The ad-serving system would probably be a less conventional web service. It needs to choose ads based on their "relevance" to the search, perhaps some knowledge of the user's search history, and how much the advertiser is willing to pay. A number of strategies could be envisioned here for estimating relevance, such as, using information retrieval or machine learning techniques that learn from past user interactions.

The ads can be added to the search results by embedding JavaScript in the results that pulls in the ads from the ad-serving system directly. This helps isolate the latency of serving search results from the latency of serving ad results.

Solution 8.11: The key technical challenge in this problem is to come up with the list of articles—the HTML code for adding these to a sidebar is trivial.

One suggestion might be to add articles that have proven to be popular recently. Another is to have links to recent news articles. A human reader at Jingle could tag articles which he believes to be significant. He could also add tags such as finance, politics, etc. to the articles. These tags could also come from the HTML meta-tags or the page title.

We could also sometimes provide articles at random and see how popular they prove to be; the popular articles can then be shown more frequently.

On a more sophisticated level, Jingle could use automatic textual analysis, where a similarity is defined between pairs of articles—this similarity is a real number and measures how many words are common to the two. Several issues come up, such as the fact that frequently occurring words such as "for" and "the" should be ignored and that having rare words such as "arbitrage" and "induction" in common is more important than having say, "America" and "international".

Textual analysis has problems, such as the fact that two words may have the same spelling but completely different meanings (anti-virus means different things in the context of articles on AIDS and computer security).

One way to augment textual analysis is to use collaborative filtering—using information gleaned from many users. For example, by examining cookies and time-stamps in the web server's log files, we can tell what articles individual users have read. If we see many users have read both A and B in a single session, we might want to recommend B to anyone reading A. For collaborative filtering to work, we need to have a substantial number of users.

Solution 8.12:   An online poker playing service would have a front-end system which users interact with and a back-end system which runs the games, manages money, looks for fraud, etc.

The front-end system would entail a UI for account management—this would cover first-time registration, logging-in, managing online persona, and sending or receiving money. In addition, there would be the game playing UI—this could be as simple as some HTML rendering of the state of the game (cards in hand, cards on the table, bets) and a form to enter a bet. A more sophisticated UI might use JavaScript to animate cards being dealt, change the expression on player's images, status messages or smileys from players, etc.

The back-end needs to be able to form tables of players, shuffle in a truly random manner, deal correctly, check if the player's moves are legal, and update player's finances. It can be implemented using, for example, a Java servlet engine which receives HTTP requests, sends appropriate responses, and updates the database appropriately.

One of the big challenges in such a system is fault-tolerance. On the server side, there are standard techniques for this, such as replication.

On the client side, there is the possibility that a player may realize he is in a poor situation and claim that his Internet connection went down. This can be resolved by having a rule that the server will bid on the player's behalf if the player does not respond quickly enough. Another possibility is having the server treat the player who is disconnected as being in the game but not requiring any more betting of him. This clearly can be abused by the player, so the server needs to record how often a player's connection hangs in a way that is favorable to him.

Collusion between players is another serious problem. Again, the server logs can be mined for examples of players working together to share knowledge of their cards or squeeze other players out. In addition, players can themselves flag suspicious play and customer service representatives can investigate further.

Random number generation is an intensely studied problem but is still easy to get wrong. A fairly frequent problem is using process id as a seed for a random number generator, which means that there are only roughly 20,000 possible sequences of random numbers. This means that, on an average, knowing the first 4 cards is enough to predict the order of the rest of the cards since $\log_2 \binom{52}{4} \approx 18.04 > \log_2 20000 = \approx 14.28$.

Solution 8.13: At its core, a driving directions service needs to store the map as a Graph, where each intersection and street address is a vertex and the roads connecting them are edges. When a user enters a starting address and an ending address, it finds the corresponding vertices and finds the shortest path connecting the two vertices (for some definition of shortest). There are several issues that come up:

- Address normalization—a given address may be expressed by the user in different ways, for example, "street" may be shortened to "st", there may not be a city and state, just zip code or vice versa. We need a way to normalize the addresses to a standard format. Sometimes an underspecified address may need to be mapped to some concrete address, for example, a city name to the city center.
- Definition of shortest—different users may have different preferences for routing, for example, shortest distance or fastest path (considering average speed on the road), avoiding use of freeways, etc. Each of these preferences can be captured by some notion of edge length.
- Approximate shortest distance—given the enormity of a graph representing all the roads in a large country, it would be fairly difficult for a single server to compute the shortest path using standard shortest path algorithms and return in a reasonable amount of time. However using the knowledge that most long paths go through a standard system of highways and the fact that the nodes and edges in the graph represent points in euclidean space, we can devise some clever approximation algorithms that run much faster.

Solution 8.14: To quickly lookup an ISBN number, we would want a hash table data-structure. However it would take $O(n)$ time to find the least-recently-used item in a hash table to discard. One way to improve the performance would be to be lazy about garbage collection such that the cost of removal of least-recently-used ISBNs can be amortized over several lookups. To be concrete, let's say we want the cache to be of size n, then we do not delete any entries from the hash table till it grows to the size of $2n$. At this point, we go over the entire hash table, looking at the number of times this item was used, find the median number of times a value in the hash table was used, and then discard everything below the median. This way, the cost of delete operations is $O(n)$ but it will happen at least at the interval of n lookups, hence the amortized cost of deletion is $O(1)$ at the cost of doubling the memory consumption.

Solution 8.15: Assume that the bandwidth from the lab machine is a limiting factor. It is reasonable to first perform trivial optimizations, such as combining the articles into a single file and compressing this file.

Opening 1000 connections each five minutes from the lab server to the 1000 machines in the datacenter and transferring the latest news articles is not feasible since the total data transferred will be approximately 5 terabytes (without compression) every five minutes.

Since the bandwidth between machines in a datacenter is very high, we can copy the file from the lab machine to a single machine in the datacenter and have the machines in the datacenter complete the copy. Instead of having just one machine serve the file to the remaining 999 machines, we can have each machine that has received the file initiate copies to the machines that have not yet received the file. In theory, this leads to an exponential reduction in the time taken to perform the copy.

There are several issues which have to be dealt with: should a machine initiate further copies before it has received the entire file? (This is tricky because of link or server failures.) How should the knowledge of machines which do not yet have copies of the file be shared? (There can be a central repository or servers can simply check others by random selection.) If the bandwidth between machines in a datacenter is not a constant, how should the selections be made? (Servers close to each other, e.g., in the same rack, should prefer communicating with each other.)

Finally, it should be mentioned that there are open source solutions to this problem, e.g., Unison, which would be a good place to start.

Solution 8.16: Think of the hosts as being vertices in a directed graph with an edge from A to B, if A initially know B's IP address.

We will study variants of this problem—synchronized or unsynchronized hosts and known or unknown bounds on the network; compare them with respect to convergence time, message size, and the number of messages. We assume the graph is strongly connected (otherwise, the problem is unsolvable).

First, assume that the hosts are all synchronized to a common clock (there are standard protocols which can allow computers to synchronize within a few tens of milliseconds; alternately, GPS signals can be used to achieve even tighter synchronization).

We will consider the case where the number of hosts N and the diameter D of the network is known to all the hosts. Our algorithm will elect the host with the highest IP address as the leader. The simplest algorithm for leader election is flooding—each host keeps track of the highest IP address it knows about; the highest IP address is initialized to its own IP address.

Since hosts are synchronized, we can proceed in rounds. In each round, host propagates the highest IP address it knows of to each of its (initial) neighbors. After D rounds, if the highest IP address a host knows of is its own, it declares itself the leader.

There is a small improvement to this algorithm which reduces the number of messages sent—a host sends out an update only when the highest IP address it knows about changes.

It takes D rounds to converge and $|E| \cdot D$ messages are communicated. The number of iterations to convergence can be reduced to $\log_2 D$ by having each host send the set of hosts it has discovered in each iteration to each host it knows about. This leads to faster convergence since the distance to the frontier of undiscovered hosts doubles in each iteration. However it requires much more communication—the final round involves N hosts sending N messages and each message has the ids of N hosts. Furthermore, unlike the original algorithm, this variant requires messages to potentially traverse longer routes (in the original algorithm, a host communicated only with the hosts it knew about initially). The algorithm works correctly even if D is just an upper bound on the true diameter.

When N and D are completely unknown, leader election can be performed through a distributed BFS. Each host starts by sending out a search message to all of its outgoing neighbors. In any round, if a host receives a search message, it chooses one of the hosts from which it received a search as its parent and informs its parent about its selection. (Since we are assuming an IP network, a child can directly communicate its selection back to its parent.)

This procedure constructs a BFS tree for each host. Completion can be detected by having hosts respond to search messages with both a parent or nonparent message as well as a notification of completion from its children. When BFS completes, each host has complete knowledge of the graph and can determine the leader.

Now, we consider the asynchronous case. The flooding algorithms we considered earlier cannot be directly generalized to asynchronous hosts because there is no notion of a round. However we can simulate rounds by having hosts tag their messages with the round number. A host waits to receive all round r messages from all its neighbors before performing its round r update.

Note that this algorithm cannot avoid sending messages if the highest IP it knows about does not change in round r since the neighbors depend on receiving all their round r messages before they can advance.

Solution 8.17: Discovery and leader election are identical, so the solution to Problem 8.16 works here too.

Chapter 9

Discrete Mathematics

Solution 9.1: It is tempting to try and pair up terms in the numerator and denominator for the expression for $\binom{n}{k}$ that have common factors and try to somehow cancel them out. This approach is unsatisfactory because of the need to have factorizations.

The binomial coefficients satisfy several identities, the most basic of which is the *addition formula*:

$$\binom{n}{k} = \binom{n-1}{k} + \binom{n-1}{k-1}.$$

There are various proofs of this identity, ranging from the combinatorial interpretation to induction and finally, direct manipulation of the expressions.

This identity yields a straightforward recursion for $\binom{n}{k}$. The base cases are $\binom{r}{r}$ and $\binom{r}{0}$, both of which are 1. The individual results from the subcalls are integers and if $\binom{n}{k}$ can be represented by an int, they can too; so, overflow is not a concern.

The recursion can lead to repeated subcalls and consequently exponential runtimes. There is an easy fix—cache intermediate results as in dynamic programming. There are $O(n^2)$ subproblems and the results can be combined in $O(1)$ time, yielding an $O(n^2)$ complexity bound.

Solution 9.2: Let $F(n)$ be the number of ways of climbing n stairs through a combination of one or two steps. We note that $F(1) = 1$ and $F(0) = 1$. Now, all paths that lead us to cross n steps either start with a single step or a double step. In case of a single step, there are $F(n-1)$ ways of completing the path. In case of a double step, there are $F(n-2)$

ways of completing the path. Hence

$$F(n) = F(n-1) + F(n-2).$$

This leads to a simple dynamic programming algorithm that can compute $F(n)$ in $O(n)$ time. An interesting thing to note here is that $F(n)$ has the same recurrence relationship as the Fibonacci numbers and $F(n)$ is actually the $(n+1)$-th Fibonacci number.

Solution 9.3: This problem can be modeled using undirected graphs where vertices correspond to guests. There is a pair of edges between every pair of guests. Color an edge between a pair of guest "blue" if they are friends, otherwise, color it "red".

Then the theorem is equivalent to the claim that in any clique on six vertices, where the edges are either blue or red, there is a subset of three vertices, all connected by edges of the same color.

Choose any vertex v. Examine the five edges with an endpoint in V_0. There must be at least three edges which are of the same color c (this follows from the pigeon-hole principle). Let $(v, \alpha), (v, \beta), (v, \gamma)$ be three such edges. Now, either there is an edge colored c between one of α, β and γ, in which case v and the vertices in α, β and γ are connected by edges colored c or there is no such edge, in which case α, β and γ are themselves connected by edges that are of the same color.

Solution 9.4: Number the doors from 1 to 500. Let's start with some examples—door 12 is toggled on days 1, 2, 3, 4, 6, 12; door 3 is toggled on days 1 and 3; door 1 is toggled on day 1; door 500 is toggled on days $1, 2, 4, 5, 10, 20, 25, 50, 100, 125, 250, 500$.

The pattern that emerges is the following: a door is toggled as many times as its id has divisors. Divisors come in pairs: $12 = 1 \times 12 = 2 \times 6 = 3 \times 4$. So, the total number of divisors is even, except when the number is a perfect square. For the perfect square case, the total number of divisors is odd. Therefore the doors that are open at the end of the process are those with ids $1, 4, 9, 16, 25, 36, 49, 64, 81, 100, 121, 144, 169, 196, 225, 256, 289, 324, 361, 400, 441, 484$—these are 22 doors altogether. In the general case, it would be $\lfloor \sqrt{n} \rfloor$, where n is the number of doors.

Solution 9.5: Let $F(k, l)$ be the maximum number of floors that can be tested by k identical balls and at most l drops. We know that $F(1, l) = l$. If we are given an additional ball to drop, we can drop the first ball at $F(k, l-1)$ floor. If it breaks, then we can use the remaining balls and $l-1$ drops to determine the floor exactly; if it does not break, then we could drop the first ball at $F(k, l-1) + F(k, l-2)$ floor. If it breaks, we can use the remaining k balls and $l-2$ drops to narrow down the exact floor between $F(k, l-1) + 1$ and $F(k, l-1) + F(k-1, l-2)$. Continuing this argument till $k-1$ drops of the first ball, we can test up to $\sum_{i=1}^{l-1} F(k, l-i)$ floors. Hence

$$F(k+1, l) = \sum_{i=0}^{l-1} F(k, l-i).$$

Given the above recurrence relationship it is straightforward to observe that $F(k+1, l) = \binom{k+l-1}{k}$ since it follows exactly the same recurrence relationship. (One easy way to notice this is to tabulate some concrete values for $F(k, l)$.) Now, since $F(k, l)$ monotonically increases in k and l, we can easily invert it to determine the number of drops needed, given the number of balls and the number of drops.

Solution 9.6: A good way to begin this problem is to come up with some strategy that guarantees a positive return. It is possible to guarantee a $2\times$ return by waiting till the last card and betting the entire amount on the last card whose color is uniquely determined by the the 51 cards that have already been seen.

To do better than a $2\times$ return, consider the case of a deck of 4 cards with 2 red cards and 2 black cards. If we do not bet on the first card, there will be three remaining cards. Assume, without loss of generality, that two cards are black and one is red. If we bet $\$\frac{1}{3}$ on the next card being black and are successful, then we have $\$\frac{4}{3}$ which we can double on the last card for a $\frac{8}{3} > 2$ return. If we lose, then the two remaining cards are black, in which case we can double our remaining money twice, i.e., achieve a $\frac{2}{3} \times 2 \times 2 = \frac{8}{3} > 2$ return. Note that this analysis assumes we can bet arbitrary fractions of the money we possess.

Now, we consider the case where we can only bet in penny increments. Let $Q(c, r, t)$ be the most we can guarantee, when we have c cents to gamble with and there are r red cards remaining out of a total of t cards. We can bet b cents, $0 \le b \le c$ on the next card. Since we have to design a strategy that maximizes the worst-case payoff, the maximum amount we can make on betting on red cards is given by

$$Q_R(c, r, t) \quad = \quad \max_{b \in \{0,1,2,...,c\}} \min\left(Q(c+b, r-1, t-1), Q(c-b, r, t)\right).$$

The maximum we can make by betting on black cards is

$$Q_B(c, r, t) \quad = \quad \max_{b \in \{0,1,2,...,c\}} \min\left(Q(c+b, r, t-1), Q(c-b, r-1, t)\right).$$

Hence $Q(c, r, t) = \max\left(Q_R(c, r.t), Q_B(c, r, t)\right)$ which yields a dynamic programming algorithm for computing the maximum payoff—base cases are of the form $Q(c, 0, t)$ and $Q(c, t, t)$, both of which are $c \times 2^t$.

However if we directly try and compute $Q(100, 26, 52)$, the algorithm runs for an unacceptably long time. This is because we will be exploring paths for which c grows very large. Since we are given the maximum payoff on a dollar when fractional amounts can be bet is less than 9.09, we can prune computations for $Q(c, r, t)$ when $c \geq 909$. The following code implements the dynamic programming algorithm with this pruning; it computes the maximum payoff, 808, in two minutes.

```java
1   import java.lang.Math;
2   import java.util.HashMap;
3
4   public class CardSelect {
5
6     private static int numCards = 52;
7     private static int numRed = 26;
8     private static int upperBound = 909;
9     private static HashMap<Integer, double[][]> cache;
10
11    public static void main( String [] args ) {
12      cache = new HashMap<Integer, double [][]>();
13      computeBestPayoff(100);
14    }
15
16    private static double cacheLookup(int c, int r, int t) {
17      return cache.containsKey(c) ? cache.get(c)[r][t] : -1.0;
18    }
19
20    private static void computeBestPayoff(int cash) {
21      System.out.println("Optimum_payoff_is_" +
22          computeBestPayoff(cash, numRed, numCards));
23    }
24
25    public static double computeBestPayoff(
26        int c, int r, int t) {
27      if (c >= upperBound)
28        return c;
29
30      if ((r == t) || (r==0))
31        return c * Math.pow(2, t);
32
33      double best;
34      if ((best = cacheLookup(c, r, t)) != -1.0) {
35        return best;
36      } else {
37        for (int b = 0 ; b <= c; b++) {
38          double redLowerBound = Math.min(
39              computeBestPayoff(c + b, r - 1, t - 1),
40              computeBestPayoff(c - b, r, t - 1) );
41
42          double blackLowerBound = Math.min(
43              computeBestPayoff(c - b, r - 1, t - 1),
44              computeBestPayoff(c + b, r, t - 1) );
45
46          double betterMove =
```

```
47                    Math.max(blackLowerBound, redLowerBound);
48                 best = Math.max(best, betterMove);
49              }
50          }
51          double [][] tmp;
52          if (!cache.containsKey(c)) {
53             tmp = new double[numRed+1][numCards+1];
54             for (int i = 0 ; i <= numRed; i++ )
55                for (int j = 0 ; j <= numCards; j++ )
56                   tmp[i][j] = -1.0;
57             cache.put(c, tmp);
58          }
59          cache.get(c)[r][t] = best;
60          return best;
61      }
62  }
```

Solution 9.7: The process will converge since at each step, we reduce the number of integers in A by one. The number of odd integers removed in each step is even since we either remove two odd integers or none. Therefore if there were an even number of odd integers to begin with, the last integer must be even; if there were an odd number of odd numbers to begin with, it must be odd.

Solution 9.8: Consider the thought experiment of starting at an arbitrary city with sufficiently large amount of gas so that we can complete the loop. In this experiment, we note the amount of gas in the tank as the vehicle goes through the loop at each city before loading the gas kept in that city for the vehicle. If we start at a different city with a different amount of gas, the amount of gas in the tank at each city should still vary in the same fashion with a constant offset. If we pick the city where the amount of gas in the tank is minimum as the starting point, clearly we will never run out of gas. This computation can be easily done in linear-time with a single pass over all the cities.

Solution 9.9: Consider the case where exactly one person has green eyes. The statement from the explorer would make it clear to the person with green eyes that he has green eyes since nobody else that he sees has green eyes.

Now, suppose there are two inhabitants with green eyes. The first day, each of these two inhabitants would see exactly one other person with green eyes. Each would see the other person on the second day too, from which they could infer that there must be two inhabitants with green eyes, the second one being themselves. Hence both of them would leave the second day.

Using induction, we can demonstrate that if there are k inhabitants with green eyes, all the green-eyed inhabitants would leave after the k-th assembly. We already saw the base case, $k = 1$. Suppose the induction hypothesis holds for $k - 1$. If there are k inhabitants with green eyes, each inhabitant with green eyes would see $k - 1$ other inhabitants with green eyes. If at the k-th assembly, they see that nobody has departed, it would indicate that they themselves have green eyes and hence all the green-eyed inhabitants would leave on the k-th day.

As for the second part of the question, for $k = 1$, it is fairly obvious that the explorer gave new knowledge to the person with green eyes. For other cases, the new information is a bit subtle. For $k = 2$, the green-eyed inhabitants would be able to infer the color of their eyes on the second day based on the information that everyone on the island knows that there are green-eyed inhabitants and yet no one left. For $k = 3$, they are able to infer because everyone knows that everyone knows that there are green-eyed inhabitants and yet on the second day no one left.

Suppose x is some fact and $E(x)$ represents the fact that everyone knows x to be true. In this case, let g represent the fact that there are some green-eyed inhabitants on the island. Then on the k-th day, all the green-eyed inhabitants would use the fact $E^K(g)$ to infer that they have green-eyes. Essentially, what the explorer did by announcing the fact in the assembly is that it became "common knowledge", i.e., $E^\infty(g)$ became true.

Solution 9.10: If the assumption is that once you have broken the bar into two pieces, they become separate problems, then it does not matter what order you do it—you will require 15 total breaks in any scenario.

If, on the other hand, the assumption is that the whole bar stays together (as it would if you were breaking it inside its wrapper, for instance), then you can do a little better. You could simply break it along all axes (say, first the vertical and then the horizontal) for a total of 6 breaks.

Solution 9.11: Player 1 can always win. The key observation in this game is that we want to force the play to be symmetrical around the diagonal, i.e., $(0, 0), (1, 1), \dots, (n, n)$ with our opponent forced to move first in terms of breaking the symmetry. If that is the case, we can follow each of his moves by a matching move reflected in this diagonal which will eventually force him to select the $(0, 0)$ space.

The way to force this type of play is to be the first person to select $(1, 1)$—this causes the play area to be just the column $(0, [0 - n])$ and the row $([0 - n], 0)$ (i.e., an "L" shape). At that point, we can successfully mirror any move that Player 2 makes, forcing him to eventually choose (0,0).

```
1   WinChomp () :
2       Choose (1 ,1)
```

```
3  |    Until you win:
4  |        Wait for Player 2 to choose square (i,j)
5  |        Choose square (j,i)
```

Solution 9.12: Suppose the set of remaining squares are of the form of a rectangle and one additional square (which must be on the lower row) and Player 2 is to move. The remaining set of squares will be of the form of a rectangle (if Player 2 plays the lower row) or a rectangle with a set of additional squares on the lower row. In either case, Player 1 can recreate the state to be a rectangle and one additional square, i.e., Player 1 can force a win. By playing $(1, n - 1)$ as his initial move, Player 1 can create this situation and therefore force a move.

Solution 9.13: Suppose Player 2 has a winning strategy. Suppose Player 1 chose $(n - 1, m - 1)$ as his initial choice and Player 2 countered with position (i, j), leaving the set S of squares. Now, it is Player 1's turn and from this set, by hypothesis, Player 2 can force a win. However Player 1 could have chosen (i, j) as his initial move and the set of remaining squares would be S (since the square $(n - 1, m - 1)$ is above and to the right of all other squares) with Player 2's turn.

This contradicts the hypothesis that Player 2 has a winning strategy; therefore Player 1 must have a winning strategy.

Note that this does not give an explicit strategy as we did for Problem 9.11 and Problem 9.12.

Solution 9.14: Number the coins from 1–50. Player F can choose all the even-numbered coins by first picking Coin 50 and then always picking the odd number coin at one of the two ends. For example, if Player G chooses Coin 1, then in the next turn, Player F chooses Coin 2. If Player G chooses Coin 49, then F chooses Coin 48 in the next turn. In this fashion, F can always leave an arrangement where G can only choose from odd-numbered coins.

If the value of the coins at even indices is larger that of the coins at odd indices, F can win by selecting the even indices and vice versa. If the values are the same, he can simply choose either and in each case, he cannot lose.

Solution 9.15: The problem can be solved using dynamic programming.

Let $P(m, n)$ be the largest margin of victory that a player can achieve when the coins remaining are indexed by m to n, inclusive.

The function P satisfies the following:

$$P(m, n) = \max \Big(C[n] - P(n + 1, m), C[m] - P(n, m - 1) \Big) \text{ if } n > m$$
$$P(m, m) = C[m] \text{ if } n = m.$$

In the general case, we can compute P for n coins by dynamic programming—there are $n(n + 1)/2$ possible arguments for P and the work required to compute P from previously computed values is constant. Hence P can be computed in $O(n^2)$ time.

Solution 9.16: The easiest way to prove this is to imagine another man (call him Bob) descending the mountain on Saturday, in exactly the same fashion as Adam did on Sunday. When ascending on Saturday, Adam will pass Bob at some time and place—this is the time and place which Adam will be at on Sunday.

Chapter 10

Probability

Solution 10.1: It is easy to solve this problem when $k = 1$—we simply make one call to the random number generator, take the returned r value mod n. We can swap $A[n-1]$ with $A[r]$.

For $k > 1$, we start by choosing one element at random as above and we now repeat the same process with the $n - 1$ element subarray $A[0 : n-2]$. Eventually, the random subset occupies the slots $A[n-1-k : n-1]$ and the remaining elements are in the first $n - k$ slots.

The algorithm clearly is in-place. To show that all the subsets are equally likely, we prove something stronger, namely that all permutations of size k are equally likely.

Formally, an m-permutation of a set S of cardinality n is a sequence of m elements of S with no repetitions. Note that there are $\frac{n!}{(n-m)!}$ k-permutations.

The induction hypothesis now is that after iteration m, the subarray $A[n-m-k : n-1]$ contains each possible m-permutation with probability $\frac{(n-m)!}{n!}$.

For $m = 1$, any element is equally likely to be selected, so the base case holds.

Suppose the inductive hypothesis holds for $m = l$. Consider $m = l + 1$. Consider a particular $(l+1)$-permutation, say $\langle \alpha_1, \ldots, \alpha_{l+1} \rangle$. This consists of a single element α_1 followed by the l-permutation $\langle \alpha_2, \ldots, \alpha_{l+1} \rangle$. Let E_1 be the event that α_1 is selected in iteration $l + 1$ and E_2 be the event that the first l iterations produced $\langle \alpha_2, \ldots, \alpha_{l+1} \rangle$. The probability of $\langle \alpha_1, \ldots, \alpha_{l+1} \rangle$ resulting after iteration $l + 1$ is simply $Pr(E_1 \cap E_2) = Pr(E_1|E_2) \cdot Pr(E_2)$. By the inductive hypothesis, the probability of permutation $\langle \alpha_2, \ldots, \alpha_{l+1} \rangle$ is $\frac{(n-m)!}{n!}$. The probability $Pr(E_1|E_2) = \frac{1}{n-l}$ since the algorithm selects from elements in $0 : n-l-1$ with equal probability. Therefore:

$$Pr(E_1 \cap E_2) = Pr(E_2|E_1) \cdot Pr(E_1) = \frac{1}{n-l} \cdot \frac{(n-l)!}{n!} = \frac{1}{\frac{(n-l-1)!}{n!}}.$$

The algorithm generates all random k-permutations with equal probability, from which it follows that all subsets of size k are equally likely.

We make k calls to the random number generator. When k is bigger than $\frac{n}{2}$, we can optimize by computing a subset of $n - k$ elements to remove from the set. When $k = n - 1$, this replaces $n - 2$ calls to the random number generator with a single call.

Solution 10.2: We store the first k packets. Consequently, we select the n-th packet to add to our subset with probability $\frac{k}{n}$. If we do choose it, we select an element uniformly at random to eject from the subset.

To prove correctness, we use induction on the number of packets that have been read. Specifically, the inductive hypothesis is that all k-sized subsets are equally likely after $n \geq k$.

The number of k-size subset is $\binom{n}{k}$, so the probability of any k-size subset is $\frac{1}{\binom{n}{k}}$.

For the base case $n = k$, there is exactly one subset of size k which is what the algorithm has computed.

Assume the inductive hypothesis holds for $n > k$. Suppose we have processed the $n+1$-th packet. The probability of a k-size subset that does not include the $n + 1$-th packet is the probability that we had selected that subset after reading the n-th iteration and did not select the $n + 1$-th packet which is

$$\frac{1}{\binom{n}{k}} \cdot \left(1 - \frac{k}{n+1}\right) = \frac{k!(n-k)!}{n!} \cdot \left(\frac{n-k+1}{n+1}\right) = \frac{k! \cdot (n-k)! \cdot (n-k+1)}{n! \cdot (n+1)}.$$

This equals $\frac{1}{\binom{n+1}{k}}$. So, the inductive hypothesis holds for subsets excluding the $n + 1$ element.

The probability of a k-size subset H that includes the $n + 1$-th packet p_{n+1} can be computed as follows: let G be a k-size subset of the first n packets. The only way we can get from G to H is if G contains $H - \{p_{n+1}\}$. Let G^* be such a subset; let $\{q\} = H - \{p_{n+1}\}$.

The probability of going from G to H is the probability of selecting p_{n+1} and dropping q that is equal to $\frac{k}{n+1} \cdot \frac{1}{k}$. There are $n+1-k$ candidate subsets for G^*, each with probability $\frac{1}{\binom{n}{k}}$ (by the inductive hypothesis) which means that the probability of H is given by

$$\frac{k}{n+1} \cdot \frac{1}{k} \cdot (n+1-k) \cdot \frac{1}{\binom{n}{k}} = \frac{(n+1-k)(n-k)!k!}{(n+1)n!} = \binom{n+1}{k},$$

so induction goes through for subsets including the $n+1$-th element.

Solution 10.3: We can make use of the algorithm for problem 10.1 with the array A initialized by $A[i] = i$. We do not actually need to store the elements in A, all we need to do is store the elements as we select them, so the storage requirement is met.

Solution 10.4: The process does not yield all permutations with equal probability. One way to see this is to consider the case $n = 3$. There are $3! = 6$ permutations possible. There are a total of $3^3 = 27$ ways in which we can choose the elements to swap and they are all equally likely. Since 27 is not divisible by 6, some permutations correspond to more ways than others, ergo not all permutations are equally likely.

The process can be fixed by selecting elements at random and moving them to the end, similar to how we proceeded in Problems 10.1 and 10.3.

Solution 10.5: Our solution to Problem 10.1 can be used with $k = n$. Although the subset that is returned is unique (it will be $\{0, 1, \dots, n-1\}$), all $n!$ possible orderings of the elements in the set occur with equal probability. (Note that we cannot use the trick to reduce the number of calls to the random number generator at the end of Solution 10.1.)

Solution 10.6: The first thing to note is that three segments can make a triangle iff no one segment is longer than the sum of the other two: the "only if" follows from the triangle inequality and the "if" follows from a construction—take a segment and draw circles at the endpoints with radius equal to the lengths of the other circles.

Since the three segment lengths add up to 1, there is a segment that is longer than the sum of the other two iff there is a segment that is longer than $\frac{1}{2}$.

Let $l = \min(u1, u2)$, $m = \max(u1, u2) - \min(u1, u2)$, and $u = 1 - \max(u1, u2)$; these are the lengths of the first, second, and third segments, from left to right. If one segment is longer than 0.5, then none of the others can be longer than 0.5; so, the events $l > 0.5$, $m > 0.5$, and $u > 0.5$ are disjoint.

Observe that $l > 0.5$ iff both $u1$ and $u2$ are greater than 0.5; the probability of this event is $\frac{1}{2} \times \frac{1}{2}$ because $u1$ and $u2$ are chosen independently. Similarly $m > 0.5$ iff both $u1$ and $u2$ are less than 0.5, which is $\frac{1}{2} \times \frac{1}{2}$.

To compute the probability of $m > 0.5$, first we consider the case that $u1 < u2$. For $m > 0.5$, we need $u1$ to be between 0 and 1 and $u2$ to be between $0.5 + u1$ and 1. This probability can be expressed by the integral

$$\int_{u1=0}^{0.5} \int_{u2=u1+0.5}^{1} 1 \cdot du1 \cdot du2$$

which evaluates to $\frac{1}{8}$.

By symmetry, the probability of $m > 0.5$ when $u1 > u2$ is also $\frac{1}{8}$. Hence the probability of a segment being longer than $\frac{1}{2}$ is $\frac{1}{4} + \frac{1}{4} + \frac{1}{4} = \frac{3}{4}$. So, the probability of being able to make a triangle out of the segments is $1 - \frac{3}{4} = \frac{1}{4}$.

For the second case, we fail to be able to make a triangle in case $u1 > 0.5$, $u2 - u1 > 0.5$, or $1 - u2 > 0.5$. The first probability is simply $\frac{1}{2}$.

The second probability is given by the integral

$$\int_{u1=0}^{0.5} \int_{u2=u1+0.5}^{1} \frac{1}{(1 - u1)} \cdot du2 \cdot du1.$$

Note that the probability density function for $u2$ is different from the previous case since $u2$ is uniform in $[u1, 1]$, not $[0, 1]$. This integral evaluates to $\frac{1 + \log_e \frac{1}{2}}{2}$. The third probability can also be computed using an integral but by symmetry, it must be the same as the second probability. Hence the final probability is $\frac{1}{2} + 2 \cdot \frac{1 + \log_e \frac{1}{2}}{2} \approx 0.807$.

Intuitively, the second formulation leads to a higher probability of a long line segment because there is less diversity in the points. For the first case, the points are spread randomly; for the second, there is a 0.5 chance that the first point itself precludes us from building the triangle. Another way to think of it is that if we put down a lot of points, the first method will lead to short segments with little variation in lengths but the second method will give us a skewed distribution and the first few segments will be considerably longer.

These computations can be verified by a numerical simulation. Here is an example code to perform this:

```
1
2   public class triangle {
3      static final int numTrials = 1000000;
4      public static void main( String [] args ) {
5         uniform ();
6         inOrder ();
7      }
8
9      public static void uniform () {
10        int overHalf = 0;
11        for (int i = 0 ; i < numTrials; i++) {
12           double u1 = Math.random ();
13           double u2 = Math.random ();
14           double min = Math.min(u1, u2);
```

```
15        double max = Math.max(u1, u2);
16        if (min > 0.5 || max < 0.5 || max - min > 0.5) {
17          overHalf++;
18          }
19      }
20      System.out.println("uniform_-_overHalf:numTrials_=_"
21          + overHalf + ":" + numTrials );
22    }
23
24    public static void inOrder() {
25      int overHalf = 0;
26      for (int i = 0 ; i < numTrials; i++) {
27        double x, y, z;
28        if ((x = Math.random()) > 0.5) {
29          overHalf++;
30        } else {
31          if ((y = (Math.random()*(1.0 - x))) > 0.5) {
32            overHalf++;
33          } else {
34            if ((z = (1.0 - (x + y))) > 0.5) {
35              overHalf++;
36            }
37          }
38        }
39      }
40      System.out.println("inOrder_-_overHalf:numTrials_=_"
41          + overHalf + ":" + numTrials );
42    }
43 }
```

Solution 10.7: The probability that a given ball does not land up in a given bin is $(n-1)/n$. The probability that none of the balls land up in the bin is $\left(\frac{n-1}{n}\right)^m$. Hence the expected number of empty bins can be given as $n\left(\frac{n-1}{n}\right)^m$. Note that this can be closely approximated by $n \cdot e^{m/n}$. Hence as long as on an average, each server is handling significantly more than one client, there should be very few idle servers.

Solution 10.8: Let X_i be the random variable, which is 1 if $\sigma(i) = i$ and 0 otherwise. (Such a random variable is often referred to as an "indicator random variable".) The number of fixed points is equal to $X_1 + X_2 + \cdots + X_n$. Expectation is linear, i.e., the expected value of a sum of random variables is equal to the sum of the expected values of the individual random variables. The expected value of X_i is $0 \cdot \frac{n-1}{n} + 1 \cdot \frac{1}{n}$ (since an element is equally likely to be mapped to any other element). Therefore the expected number of fixed points is $n \cdot \frac{1}{n} = 1$.

We can compute the expected length of μ by defining indicator random variables $Y_1, \ldots Y_n$, where $Y_i = 1$ iff $\forall j < i \ (\sigma(j) < \sigma(i))$. Observe that the length of μ is simply the sum of the Y_is. The expected value of Y_i is $\frac{1}{i}$, since $\forall j < i \ (\sigma(j) < \sigma(i))$ iff the largest of the first i elements is at position i, which has probability $\frac{1}{i}$ since all the permutations are equally likely. Therefore the expected value for the length of μ is $1+\frac{1}{2}+\frac{1}{3}+\cdots+\frac{1}{n}$, which tends to $\log_e n$.

Note that for both parts of the problem, we used the linearity of expectation which does not require the individual random variables to be independent. This is crucial since the X_is and Y_js are not independent—for example, if the first $n-1$ elements get mapped to themselves, then the n-th element must also map to itself.

Solution 10.9: Basically, we want to produce a random number between 0 and $b-a$, inclusive.

We can produce a random number from 0 to $l-1$ as follows: let j be the least integer such that $l \le 2^j$.

If l is a power of 2, say $l = 2^j$, then all we need are j calls to the 0-1 valued random number generator—the j bits from the calls encode a j bit integer from 0 to $l-1$, inclusive and all such numbers are equally likely; so, we can use this integer.

If l is not a power of 2, the j calls may or may not encode an integer in the range 0 to $l-1$. If the number is in the range, we return it; since all the numbers are equally likely, the result is correct.

If the number is not in the range, we try again. The probability of having to try again is less than $\frac{1}{2}$ since $l > 2^{j-1}$. The probability that we take exactly k steps before succeeding is at least $(1-\frac{1}{2})^{k-1}\cdot\frac{1}{2} = \frac{1}{2}^k$. The expected number of trials before we converge to a solution is bounded by $1\cdot\frac{1}{2} + 2\cdot(\frac{1}{2})^2 + (\frac{1}{2})^3 + \cdots$ whose limit is 2.

Solution 10.10: Let $F_X(x)$ be the cumulative distribution function for X, i.e., $F_X(x) = $ probability that $X \le x$.

To generate X, we perform the following operation: we select a number r uniformly at random in the unit interval. We then project back from F_X to obtain a value for X, i.e., we return $s = F_X^{-1}(r)$.

By construction, the probability that the value we return is less than or equal to α is $F_X(\alpha)$, so the cumulative distribution function of the random variable we created is exactly that of X.

Solution 10.11: First we prove that if $\langle X_1, X_2, \ldots \rangle$ is a sequence of Bernoulli IID random variables, with $p(X_i = 1) = p)$, then the expected time to see the first 1 is $\frac{1}{p}$. The reasoning is as follows: define F_i to be the event that the first 1 comes on the i-th trial. Then $Pr(F_i) = (1-p)^{i-1}\cdot p$. Hence the expected time is $S = \sum_{i=1}^{\infty} i\cdot(1-p)^{i-1}\cdot p$. This sum simplifies to $\frac{1}{p}$ (multiply both sides by p, subtract, and sum the infinite geometric series on the right).

Now, we consider the problem of dice rolls. The key is to determine the expected time to see the k-th new value. Clearly, the expected time to see the first new value is just 1. The time to see the second new value from the first new value is $\frac{1}{5/6}$ since the probability of seeing a new value, given that one value has already been seen, is $5/6$. In this way, the time taken to see the third new value, given that two values have already been seen, is $\frac{1}{4/6}$. Generalizing this idea, the time taken to see the k-th new value, given that $k-1$ values have already been seen, is $\frac{1}{(6-(k-1))/6}$.

Hence the expected time to see the sixth new value is $\frac{6}{6} + \frac{6}{5} + \frac{6}{4} + \frac{6}{3} + \frac{6}{2} + \frac{6}{1} \approx 14.7$.

Solution 10.12: Let f be the price for the option. A fair price is determined by the no-arbitrage requirement. Suppose we start with a portfolio of x shares and y options in S—x and y may be negative (which indicates that we sell stocks or sell options).

The initial value of our portfolio is $x \cdot 100 + y \cdot f$. On Day 100, two things may have happened:
- The stock went up and the portfolio is worth $x \cdot 120 + y \cdot 20$.
- The stock went down and the portfolio is worth $x \cdot 70$.

If we could choose x and y in such a way that our initial portfolio has a negative value—which means that we are paid to take it on—and regardless of the movement in the stock, our portfolio takes a nonnegative value, then we will have created an arbitrage.

Therefore the conditions for an arbitrage to exist are:

$$
\begin{aligned}
x \cdot 120 + y \cdot 20 &\geq 0 \\
x \cdot 70 &\geq 0 \\
x \cdot 100 + y \cdot f &< 0
\end{aligned}
$$

A fair price for the option is one in which no arbitrage exists.

If f is less than 0, an arbitrage exists—we are paid to buy options, lose nothing if the price goes down, and make \$20 per option if the price goes up. Therefore $f \geq 0$, so we can write the third inequality as $y \leq -\frac{100}{f}x$. The first equation can be rewritten as $y \geq -6 \cdot x$.

Combining these two inequalities, we see that an arbitrage does not exist if $-\frac{100}{f} \geq -6$, i.e., $f \leq \frac{100}{6}$. Outside of the interval $[0, \frac{100}{6}]$, we do have an arbitrage.

For example, if $f = 19 > \frac{100}{6}$, then the option is overpriced and we should sell ("write") options. If we write b options and buy one share, we will start with a portfolio that is worth $100 + 19 \cdot b$. If the stock goes down, the options are worthless; so, our portfolio is worth \$70. If the stock goes up, we lose \$20 on each option we wrote but see a gain on the stock we bought. We want the net gain to be nonnegative and the initial portfolio to have a negative value, i.e.,

$$120 + 20 \cdot b \ \geq \ 0$$
$$100 + 19 \cdot b \ < \ 0$$

Combining the two inequalities, we see that any value of b in $[-6, -\frac{100}{19})$ leads to an arbitrage.

Solution 10.13: Suppose our initial portfolio consists of x_0 stocks, x_1 options, and x_2 bonds.

Proceeding as above, we see the condition for an arbitrage to exist is:

$$100 \cdot x_0 + f \cdot x_1 + x_2 \ < \ 0$$
$$120 \cdot x_0 + 20 \cdot x_1 + 1.02 \cdot x_2 \geq 0$$
$$70 \cdot x_0 + 1.02 \cdot x_2 \geq 0$$

Writing the linear terms as Ax, we see that if $det(A) \neq 0$, then we can always find an arbitrage since we can solve $Ax = b$. We will denote row i of A by A_i.

The determinant of A equals $70(1.02f - 20) + 1.02(100 \cdot 20 - 120f)$. This equals 0 when $f = 640/51 \approx 12.549 = f^*$, so an arbitrage definitely exists if the option price is not equal to f^*.

Conversely, if the option is priced at f^*, $det(A) = 0$ and in particular $A_0 = 0.6275 \cdot A_1 + 0.3583 \cdot A_2$. Since A_0 is a linear combination of A_1 and A_2 with positive weights, then if $A_1 x \geq 0$ and $A_2 x \geq 0$, $A_0 x$ must also be ≥ 0, so no arbitrage can exist.

Solution 10.14: Let x be the price of the stock on day 100. The option is worthless if $x < 300$. If the price is $x \geq 300$, the option is worth $x - 300$ dollars. The expected value of x is given by the integral

$$\int_{300}^{\infty} (x - 300) \cdot \frac{e^{-\frac{(x-300)^2}{2 \cdot (20)^2}}}{\sqrt{2\pi (20)^2}} dx.$$

The integral can be evaluated in closed form—let $y = x - 300$ and let's write σ instead of 20. The expression above simplifies to

$$\int_{0}^{\infty} y \cdot \frac{e^{-\frac{y^2}{2 \cdot \sigma^2}}}{\sqrt{2\pi \sigma^2}} dy.$$

The indefinite integral $\int w \cdot e^{-w^2} dw$ has the closed form solution $-\frac{e^{-w^2}}{2}$, so the definite integral equals $\sigma \sqrt{\frac{1}{2\pi}} \approx 0.39\sigma$. Therefore the expected payoff on the option on day 100 is $0.39 \cdot 20 = \$7.8$.

Solution 10.15: The first thing to ask is what are you trying to optimize? There are various objectives, all of which are reasonable—maximize expected profit, minimize loss, maximize ratio of expected profit to variance, etc.

Let's say we want to maximize profit. The expected profit is $\int_{X=B}^{X=400}(1.8X - B) \cdot \frac{1}{400}dB$. This simplifies to $\frac{0.9 \cdot 400^2 - 400B + 0.1B^2}{400}$. The derivative is $0.2B - 400$.

The expected profit has a negative derivative in the range of interest—$B \in [0, 400]$. This means that as we increase B, we get less and less profit, so we should keep $B = 0$.

In retrospect, this result makes sense since if we win the auction, we are paying twice of X in expectation and getting only $1.8X$ in return.

Solution 10.16: If the probability of winning is p, then the expected gain is $-1 + p \cdot w$. Hence for a fair game, $w = 1/p$.

The face value of the card can be any number between 1 and 13. For the dealer, all values are equally likely. Hence if the player's card has a face value i, then the probability of winning for the player is $(i - 1)/13$. If the player always takes only one random card, his probability of winning is $(1/13) \sum_{i=1}^{13} (i - 1)/13 = 6/13$. Hence it makes sense to ask for the next card only if the first card yields a probability less than $6/13$, i.e., the face value of the first card is 7. If we are given that the face value of the first card is 7 or more, then the chances of winning are $(1/7) \sum_{i=7}^{13} (i - 1)/13 = 9/13$; otherwise, it is $6/13$. Hence the overall probability of winning is $\frac{7}{13} \cdot \frac{9}{13} + \frac{6}{13} \cdot \frac{6}{13} = 99/169$. Thus the fair value would be $169/99 \approx 1.707$.

Solution 10.17: We can trivially achieve a probability of success of $\frac{1}{2}$ by always choosing the first card.

A natural way to proceed is to consider the probability $p_k(f)$ of winning for the optimum strategy after k cards remain, of which f are red cards. Then $p_k(f) = \max\left(\frac{f}{k}, \frac{f}{k} \cdot p_{k-1}(f - 1) + (1 - \frac{f}{k}) \cdot p_{k-1}(f)\right)$.

The base cases for the recurrence are $p_1(1) = 1$ and $p_1(0) = 0$. Applying the recurrence, we obtain $p_2(2) = 1, p_2(1) = \frac{1}{2}, p_2(0) = 0$, and $p_3(3) = 1, p_3(2) = \frac{2}{3}, p_3(1) = \frac{1}{3}, p_3(0) = 0$. This suggests that $p_k(f) = \frac{f}{k}$, which can directly be verified from the recurrence. Therefore the best we can do, $p_{52}(26) = \frac{26}{52} = \frac{1}{2}$, is no better than simply selecting the first card.

An alternate view of this is that since the cards in the deck are randomly ordered, the odds of the top card we select being red is the same as the card at the bottom of the deck being red, which has a $\frac{f}{k}$ chance of being red when there are f red cards and k cards in total.

Solution 10.18: If we always select the first secretary, we have a $\frac{1}{n}$ chance of selecting the best secretary.

One way to do better is to skip the first $\frac{n}{2}$ secretaries and then choose the first one in the remaining set that is superior to the best secretary interviewed in the first $\frac{n}{2}$ secretaries. This has a probability of succeeding of at least $\frac{1}{4}$ since the probability that the second best secretary lies in the first half and the best secretary is in the second half is at least $\frac{1}{4}$. Note that the probability of this is actually more than $\frac{1}{4}$ since the second best secretary is in the first half, there is a higher than 0.5 probability that the best secretary is in the second half.

It is known that if we follow a strategy of skipping the first s secretaries and selecting the first secretary who is superior to all others so far, the probability is maximized for s closest to n/e and the maximum probability tends to $1/e$.

Solution 10.19: Let L be the event that the selected coin is tail-biased, U be the event that the selected coin is head-biased, and $3H5$ be the event that a coin chosen at random from the bag comes up heads 3 times out of 5 tosses.

We want to compute $Pr(L|3H5)$. By Bayes' rule, this is $\frac{Pr(L\cap 3H5)}{Pr(3H5)}$. Applying Bayes' rule again, this probability equals

$$
\frac{Pr(3H5|L) \cdot Pr(L)}{Pr\big(3H5 \cap (L\cup U)\big)}
$$

$$
= \frac{Pr(3H5|L) \cdot Pr(L)}{Pr(3H5 \cap L) + Pr(3H5 \cap U)}
$$

$$
= \frac{Pr(3H5|L) \cdot Pr(L)}{Pr(3H5|L) \cdot Pr(L) + Pr(3H5|H) \cdot Pr(H)}
$$

$$
= \frac{\binom{5}{3} \cdot 0.4^3 \cdot 0.6^2 \cdot 0.5}{\binom{5}{3} \cdot 0.4^3 \cdot 0.6^2 \cdot 0.5 + \binom{5}{3} \cdot 0.4^2 \cdot 0.6^3 \cdot 0.5}
$$

$$
= 0.4
$$

For the second part, we can use the Chebyshev inequality to compute the number of trials we need for a majority of n tosses of the tail-biased coin to be heads with probability $\frac{1}{100}$. Let L_i be the event that the i-th toss of the tail-biased coin comes up heads. It will be convenient to use a Bernoulli random variable X_i to encode this event, with a 1 indicating heads and 0 indicating tails.

The mean μ of the sum X of n Bernoulli random variables which are IID with probability p is $n \cdot p$; the standard deviation σ is $\sqrt{np(1-p)}$. In our context, $\mu = 0.4n$ and $\sigma = \sqrt{6n/25}$.

The Chebyshev inequality gives us a bound on the probability of a random variable being far from its mean. Specifically, $Pr\big(|X - \mu| \geq k\sigma\big) \leq \frac{1}{k^2}$.

For the majority of n tosses to not be tails, it is necessary that the sum of the n coin tosses is greater than or equal to $0.5n$. We want to bound this probability by $\frac{1}{100}$, so we take $k = 10$. We want to solve for n such that $0.5n - 0.4n \geq 10 \cdot \sqrt{6n/25}$, i.e., $0.1n \geq 4.9\sqrt{n}$ which is satisfied for $n \geq 2400$. Note that the analysis is not tight—the Chebyshev inequality refers to the probability of $|X - \mu| \geq k\sigma$ but we are only looking at $X - \mu \geq \sigma$.

The Chebyshev inequality holds for all random variables if they have a variance. We can obtain a tighter bound by applying a Chernoff bound, which is specific to the sums of Bernoulli random variables. Specifically, Chernoff bounds tell us that $Pr\big(X \geq (1 + \delta)\mu\big) \leq e^{\frac{-\mu\delta^2}{3}}$. We want to bound $Pr\big(X \geq 0.5n = (1 + 0.25)(0.4n)\big)$, so $\delta = 0.25$. Thus we want $e^{\frac{-0.4n(0.25)^2}{3}} < 0.01$; taking natural logs we obtain $-\frac{0.4n(0.25)^2}{3} < \ln 100 = -4.6$, which holds for $n > 552$.

The Chernoff bound is also pessimistic—through simulation code attached below, we determined that when $n = 553$, only 17 times in 10^7 trials did we see a majority of tails; when $n = 148$, tails was not a majority in 0.88% of the trials.

```java
1    import java.util.Random;
2
3    public class TailCoin {
4      public static void main( String [] args ) {
5        int numFails = 0;
6        int numTrials = new Integer( args[0] );
7        double bias = 0.4;
8        int N = new Integer( args[1] );
9        Random r = new Random();
10       for ( int i = 0 ; i < numTrials; i++ ) {
11         int sum = 0;
12         for ( int j = 0 ; j < N; j++ ) {
13           sum += ( r.nextDouble() < bias ) ? 1 : 0;
14         }
15         if (sum >= N/2) numFails++;
16       }
17       System.out.println("fails:trials\t=\t"
18           + numFails
19           + ":" + numTrials
20           + "\n\tratio\t=\t"
21           + ( (double) numFails/(double) numTrials) );
22     }
23   }
```

Solution 10.20: First, we show that any deterministic algorithm must examine all Boolean variables. The idea is that an adversary can force the value of any subexpression to be unknown till all the variables in the subexpression have been read. For example, suppose variable X is ANDed with variable Y. If the algorithm reads the value of X before Y, we return true; when Y is queried, we return false. In this way, the value of $X \wedge Y$ is determined only after both the variables are read.

This generalizes with induction: the inductive hypothesis is that an L_k expression requires all the variables to have been read before its value is determined and its final value is the value of the last variable read. For a subexpression of the form $\phi \wedge \psi$, where ϕ and ψ are L_k expressions, if all the variables from ϕ are read before all the variables from ψ are read, the adversary chooses the last variable read from ϕ to be true, forcing the algorithm to evaluate ψ. A similar argument can be used for subexpressions of the form $\phi \vee \psi$.

Suppose we evaluate an expression by choosing one of its two subexpressions at random to evaluate first; we evaluate the other subexpression only if the expression's value is not forced by the subexpression that we evaluated first.

For example, if we are to evaluate an L_{k+1} expression of the form $((\phi_0 \wedge \phi_1) \vee (\psi_0 \wedge \psi_1))$, where the subexpressions $\phi_0, \phi_1, \psi_0, \psi_1$ are L_k expressions, we randomly choose one of $(\phi_0 \wedge \phi_1)$ and $(\psi_0 \wedge \psi_1)$ to evaluate first. If the first expression evaluated is true, we can ignore the second; otherwise, we evaluate the second. If the first expression is true, we reduced the number of variables queried by at least half. If the first expression is false, at least one of the two subexpressions is false and we have a probability of 0.5 of selecting that subexpression and avoiding evaluating the other subexpression. So, in the worst-case, we can expect to avoid one of the four subexpressions $\phi_0, \phi_1, \psi_0, \psi_1$. Therefore the expected number of variables queried to evaluate an L_{k+1} expression, $Q(k+1)$ satisfies

$$Q(k+1) \leq 3 \cdot Q(k).$$

From this, $Q(k) = 3^k$. It is straightforward to use induction to show that there are a total of $n = 4^k$ variables in an L_k expression, so $Q(k) = n^{\log_4 3} = n^{0.793}$.

Chapter 11

Programming

Solution 11.1: The fastest algorithm for manipulating bits can vary based on the underlying hardware.

The time taken to directly compute the parity of a single number is proportional to the number of bits:

```
1  short parity(long a) {
2    short result = 0;
3    for (; a != 0; a = a >> 1) {
4      result = result ^ (a & 1);
5    }
6    return result;
7  }
```

A neat trick that erases the least significant bit of a number in a single operation can be used to improve performance in the best and average cases:

```
1  short parity2(long a) {
2    short result = 0;
3    while (a) {
4      result ^= 1;
5      a = a & (a - 1);
6    }
7    return result;
8  }
```

But when you have to perform a large number of parity operations and more generally, any kind of bit fiddling operation, the best way to do this is to precompute the answer and store it in an array. Depending upon how much memory is at your disposal (and how much fits efficiently in cache), you can vary the size of the lookup table. Below is an example implementation where you build a lookup table "precomputed_parity" that stores the parity of any 16-bit number i as

206

precomputed_parity[*i*]. This array can either be constructed during static initialization or dynamically—a flag bit can be used to indicate if the entry at a location is uninitialized. Once you have this array, you can implement the parity function as follows:

```
1  short parity3(long a) {
2    short result = precomputed_parity[a >>16];
3    result ^= precomputed_parity[a & 0xFFFF];
4    return result;
5  }
```

Solution 11.2: Similar to computing parity (cf. Problem 11.1), the fastest way to reverse bits would be to build a precomputed array `precomputed_reverse` such that for every 16-bit number i, `precomputed_reverse[i]` holds the bit-reversed i. Then you can do something like this:

```
1  long reverse_bits(long l) {
2    return (precomputed_reverse[l & 0xFFFF] << 16) |
3      precomputed_reverse[l >> 16] ;
4  }
```

Solution 11.3: Again, here precomputed arrays can speed things significantly. For all possible 256 values of a byte, we can store the corresponding run-length encoded values. One tricky thing here is that a particular sequence of identical consecutive bits may cross the byte boundary and you may need to combine the results across the byte boundaries. This just requires some additional logic to see if the last bit of the previous byte matches the first bit of the current byte or not and accordingly either simply concatenate the encoded sequence or add the first number for the current byte to the last number for the previous byte.

Solution 11.4: We can use the fact that every permutation can be expressed as a composition of disjoint cycles, with the decomposition being unique up to ordering.

For example, the permutation $(3, 1, 2, 4)$ can be represented as $(1, 3, 2)(4)$, i.e., we can achieve the permutation $(3, 1, 2, 4)$ by these two moves: $1 \mapsto 3, 3 \mapsto 2, 2 \mapsto 1$ and $4 \mapsto 4$.

If the permutation was given to us as a set of disjoint cycles, we could easily apply the permutation in constant amount of additional storage since we just need to perform rotation by one element. So, what remains is a way to identify the disjoint cycles that constitute the permutation.

Again, it is fairly easy to identify the set of cycles if you have an additional N bits: you start from any position and keep going forward (from i to $A[i]$) till you hit the initial index, at which point you have found one of the cycles. Then you can go to another position that is not already a part of any cycle. Finding a position that is not already a part of a cycle is easy if you have a bit-vector that could indicate whether we have already included a given position in a cycle or not.

One way to do this without using additional $O(N)$ storage could be to use the sign bit in the integers that constitute the permutation:

```
 1   void ApplyPermutation(int * permutation, int* A, int n) {
 2     for (int i = 0; i < n; ++i) {
 3       if (permutation[i] > 0) {
 4         // Start searching for a cycle from i.
 5         int j = i;
 6         int tmp = A[i];
 7         do {
 8           int k = permutation[j];
 9           int swap_var = A[k];
10           A[k] = tmp;
11           tmp = swap_var;
12           // Mark j as visited.
13           permutation[j] *= -1; // sets the sign bit
14           j = k;
15         } while(j != i);
16       }
17     }
18     // Restore the sign for permutation.
19     for (int i = 0; i < n; ++i) {
20       permutation[i] *= -1;
21     }
22   }
```

The above code will apply the permutation in $O(N)$ time but implicitly we are using additional $O(N)$ storage (even if we are borrowing it from the sign bit of permutation matrix). We need $O(N)$ storage to remember all the visited cycles.

We can avoid this by just going from left to right and applying the cycle only if the current position is the leftmost position in the cycle. In order to test whether the current position is the leftmost position or not, you will have to traverse the cycle once more. This boosts the runtime to $\Theta(N^2)$.

```
 1   void ApplyPermutation2(int * permutation, int* A, int n) {
 2     for (int i = 0; i < n; ++i) {
 3       // Traverse the cycle to see if i is the min element
 4       bool min_element = true;
 5       int j = permutation[i];
 6       while( j != i) {
 7         if (j < i) {
 8           min_element = false;
 9           break;
10         }
11         j = permutation[j];
12       }
13       if (min_element) {
```

```
14        int j = i;
15        int tmp = A[i];
16        do {
17           int k = permutation[j];
18           int swap_var = A[k];
19           A[k] = tmp;
20           tmp = swap_var;
21           j = k;
22        } while(j != i);
23     }
24   }
25 }
```

Solution 11.5: The solution is very similar to the previous problem. All you need to do is decompose the permutation into a set of cycles and invert each cycle one step back. For example, the permutation $3, 1, 2, 4$ can be represented as $(1, 3, 2)(4)$. Hence the inverse can be represented as $(2, 3, 1)(4)$ which amounts to $2, 3, 1, 4$.

In order to save additional space, we can use exactly the same set of tricks as in the above problem.

Solution 11.6: If you try to figure out the position for each character in a single pass, it becomes fairly complex. If you do this in two stages, it becomes fairly easy. In the first step, invert the entire string and in the second step, invert each word. For example, *ram is costly* $\mapsto$ *yltsoc si mar* $\mapsto$ *costly is ram*. Here is an example code that achieves this:

```
1  void InvertString(char* input, size_t length) {
2    for (int i = 0; i < length /2; ++i) {
3      swap(input + i, input + length − i − 1);
4    }
5  }
6
7  void ReverseWords(char* input) {
8    size_t length = strlen(input);
9    InvertString(input, length);
10   int start = 0;
11   while(start < length) {
12     int end = start;
13     while(end < length && input[end] != '␣') {
14       end++;
15     }
16     InvertString(input+start, end−start);
17     start = end + 1;
18   }
19 }
```

Solution 11.7: Here is an example code that reverses a linked list and returns the head pointer for the reversed list. The only important thing here is that you save the pointer to the next node before overwriting it.

```
1   Node* ReverseLinkedList(Node* head) {
2     Node* prev = NULL;
3     Node* current = head;
4     while(current != NULL) {
5       Node* tmp = current->next;
6       current->next = prev;
7       prev = current;
8       current = tmp;
9     }
10    return prev;
11  }
```

Solution 11.8: There are two elegant solutions to this problem. One solution is that you try to reverse the linked list and one of the two things can happen:

1. You reach the null pointer at the end of the list—this indicates that this was a correctly constructed linked list.
2. You reach the head pointer of the list which indicates that the linked list has a loop.

Of course this operation is destructive, i.e., you modify your input but you can restore the input by reversing it again.

Another interesting approach is to have two pointers traverse the linked list and in every step, you advance the pointers. The first pointer is advanced by one position and the second one is advanced by two positions. If you have a correctly constructed linked list, then both the pointers will end up at the tail of the list. However if you have a circular linked list then you would be in an infinite loop. Since the second pointer is traversing the loop twice as fast as the first, it will often intersect with the first pointer in the loop. If you find the two pointers intersect, this would indicate the list is circular.

Solution 11.9: This is more of a trick question than a conceptual one. Given the pointer to a node, it is impossible to delete it from the list without modifying its predecessor's next pointer and the only way to get to the predecessor is to traverse the list from head. However it is easy to delete the next node since it just requires modifying the next pointer of the current node. Now if we copy the value part of the next node to the current node, this would be equivalent to deleting the current node.

(This question used to be commonly asked but it would be poor practice to use this solution in real life—for example, a reference to the successor of the node that was just deleted is now corrupted.)

Solution 11.10: At first glance, it would appear that the search function does a constant amount of work and then recurses on a subarray that is less than half as big as the array passed in—a classic $O(\log n)$ algorithm.

However the array slicing—the construction of the subarray—is potentially expensive, depending on how it is implemented. Different languages implement array slicing in different ways: the elements may be aliased to elements in the original array or they may be copied. If a copy is being made, this copy takes $\Theta(l)$ time to compute, where l is the length of the array slide. Therefore the recurrence is $T(n) = \Theta(n) + T(\frac{n}{2})$, which solves to $T(n) = \Theta(n)$.

The right way to perform binary search, which avoids the copy, passes integer indexes denoting the range to perform search on (alternately, a while loop can be used to avoid recursion). See Problem 1.2 for more details.

Index of Problems

Made in the USA
Lexington, KY
06 December 2010